REINHOLD MESSNER

FREE SPIRIT

A CLIMBER'S LIFE

REINHOLD MESSNER

FREE SPIRIT

A CLIMBER'S LIFE

TRANSLATED BY JILL NEATE

THE
MOUNTAINEERS

Published by
The Mountaineers
1001 SW Klickitat Way, Suite 201
Seattle, WA 98134

2 1 0 9 8
5 4 3 2 1

Manufactured in the United States of America

Cover photograph: *Reinhold Messner* by Nigel Parry/CPi
Frontispiece: *The South-West Face of the Marmoladi di Penia on which Messner pioneered the Südtiroler Weg with Konrad Renzler* by Jürgen Winkler

Book design and cover design: Helen Cherullo
Book layout: Brian Metz/Green Rhino Graphics

Cataloging-in-Publication Data available from the Library of Congress

Everything tests man, say the gods,
So that he, robustly nurtured, learns to give thanks for all,
And understands the freedom,
To set out to where he will.

—Friedrich Hölderlin

CONTENTS

PHOTOGRAPHIC ACKNOWLEDGEMENTS

All photographs were supplied by Reinhold Messner, except for the following which are reproduced by permission of the photographers or suppliers:

Chris Bonington: yak pasture, p 255
Alison Chadwick/Mount Everest Foundation: p 187 (both photos)
Diadem Archives: pp 38, 43, 146, 156, 183
Leo Dickinson: p 142, above; p 206
Oswald Oelz: p 220, above right
John Pollock: p 191
Jürgen Winkler: frontispiece, pp 35, 124

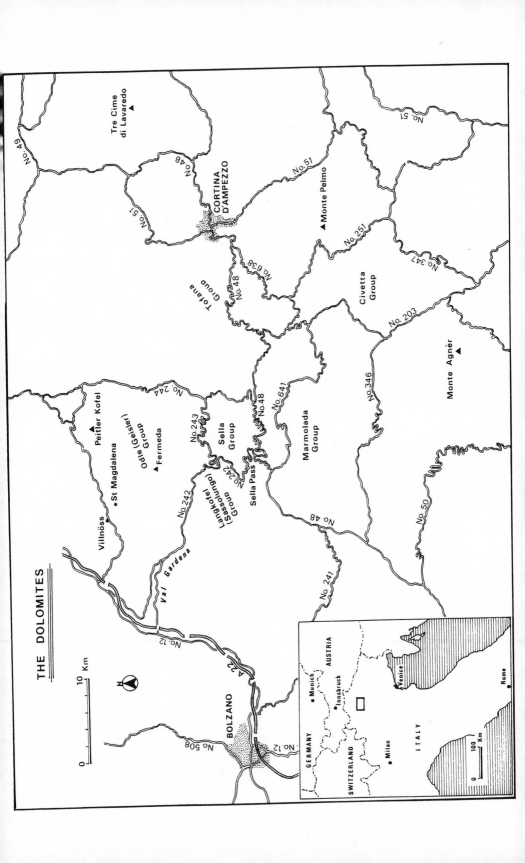

THE DOLOMITES

10 Km

N

Bolzano
Villnöss
St Magdalena
Peitler Kofel
Odle (Geisler) Group
Fermeda
Val Gardena
Langkofel (Sassolungo) Group
Sella Group
Sella Pass
No. 242
No. 243
No. 244
No. 241
No. 48
No. 12
No. 508
A22
No. 641
Marmolada Group
Tofana Group
CORTINA D'AMPEZZO
No. 48
No. 51
No. 49
Tre Cime di Lavaredo
Monte Pelmo
No. 51
No. 638
No. 251
No. 347
Civetta Group
No. 203
No. 346
No. 50
Monte Agnèr

GERMANY
SWITZERLAND
AUSTRIA
Munich
Innsbruck
Milan
Venice
ITALY
Rome
100 Km

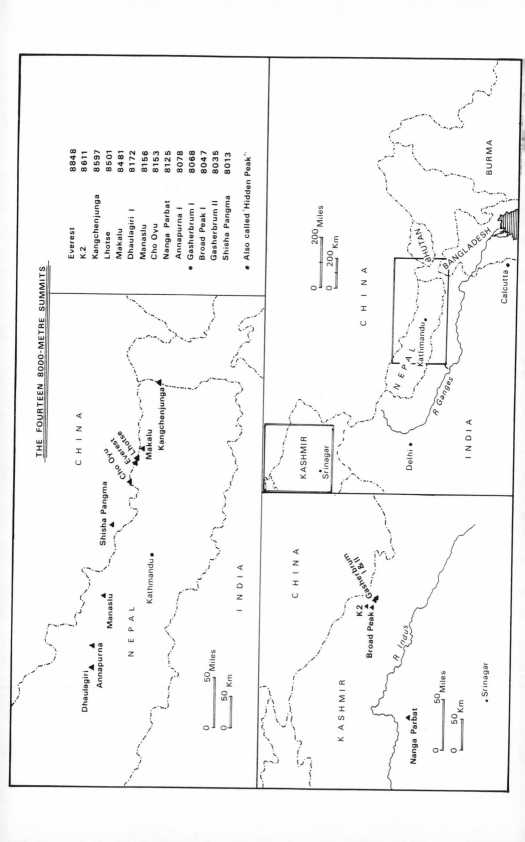

THE FOURTEEN 8000-METRE SUMMITS

Everest	8848
K.2	8611
Kangchenjunga	8597
Lhotse	8501
Makalu	8481
Dhaulagiri I	8172
Manaslu	8156
Cho Oyu	8153
Nanga Parbat	8125
Annapurna I	8078
* Gasherbrum I	8068
Broad Peak I	8047
Gasherbrum II	8035
Shisha Pangma	8013

* Also called 'Hidden Peak'.

1

A CHILDHOOD PARADISE

1949–60

OUR HOUSE WAS A HOUSE like many others on the village street, with red tiles on the roof, a chimney, a staircase of square-cut porphyry and a wild grapevine, which in summer grew completely over the east side of the building. The stone wall underneath the stairway was scarcely four metres high and yet Father always made a fuss if we clambered about on it, which was why we went to play in the barns of the neighbouring farms, hid in treetops or climbed up to the belfry, if the church tower door was left open. From there we could see St Magdalena, the last village in the valley, where our grandparents lived and with whom we spent the summer months. If anywhere was a childhood paradise, this was it.

For the summer months Father rented a hut on the alpine pasture of the Gschmagenhartalm, and each year for a number of weeks worked up there with Mother. In the autumn they brought back with them a great sack of pine kernels, and told stories about our local mountains, the Geislerspitze and the Mittagsscharte, and the chamois in the Puezkar.

Often I sat amongst our hen-houses and rabbit hutches, and gazed at the clouds as they passed over the narrow strips of sky which were visible between high wooded ridges and gloomy mountains. They came and went, their play often lasting only a few minutes, so steep and confined is this place called Pitzack where I grew up.

All year long Villnöss was my whole world. There was no nursery school and so we village kids played in gangs from dawn to dusk. When I was four or five years old, I became curious and wanted to know where the clouds disappeared to. What lay behind these mountains which stood around my valley like an impassable barrier? The peasants had no time for such inquisitiveness.

11

Their farms lay in the valley and they only seldom took the local bus to market. In the village everyone went on foot for there were only a few motor vehicles in 1949. They did not understand the townspeople who came to Villnöss for walking and climbing. Tourism scarcely existed.

The farmers in the valley were industrious folk, tough and dependent for work in the fields on two horses and their children. There were no big, stately houses. On the sunny side of the valley were the small and medium-sized farms, in the valley bottom some cottages. The fields stretched upward, the soil predominantly dry and bare, with pasture land above the tree-line. Immediately above that the Dolomites began, giving the head of the valley a wild and at the same time harmonious conclusion.

Father was the schoolmaster in St Peter. In his youth, shortly before the Second World War, he had climbed the Geislerspitze. Now that his climbing partner had emigrated, he wanted to take us lads with him on the Grosse Fermeda and the Furchetta to show us the world of his youthful memories.

I still had not started school when my parents first took me with them to the Gschmagenhartalm. My elder brother Helmut and I plodded along behind Father. There, where the roadway ceased and a steep, narrow path began, we halted for the first time. While Father picked raspberries, I asked Mother how far it still was, I was so tired already. In zigzags the path then led through a big clearing; further up we crossed other paths and climbed over roots and boulders. Isolated spruces stood amongst the pines and far above bloomed the alpine roses.

Once we got to the open alpine meadow, the Geislerspitze stood so directly over us that it was like looking through binoculars; out of the pale-coloured cirque they soared aloft, frighteningly big and oppressive. Never before had I seen anything so enormous.

The hut stood among rocks near a group of pines. Father opened up the shutters and then went off to fetch water. Strictly speaking, Helmut and I should have gone back that same day to our grandparents. However when it turned out that the petrol lamp had been forgotten at the first rest stop, the moment came for us to earn ourselves a few days' holiday on the Gschmagenhart.

'You may stay if you fetch the lamp,' said Father, and then on the door-step: 'Take care, there are four paths to cross, and hurry now, it will soon be dark!' Already we were running down across the meadow. All exertion was forgotten, all tiredness gone.

Beginning to acquire a head for heights with Father, four of my seven brothers and my sister Waltraud, at home in Villnöss, 1951.

In the wood it was slippery and often the path could not be recognised. The simple, clearly marked path which we had ascended behind Father was now mysterious. The previous certainty was a trap which, now that we were alone, opened up at each junction. An experienced mountaineer or hunter always finds his way through a wood. We, however suspected a deer behind every noise. At each turning we stood puzzled.

From break to break, from tree to tree, we groped our way downwards. When we actually found the lamp, we were filled with childish pride. We would be allowed to spend a few days on the Gschmagenhartalm!

Soon we knew the names of the Geislerspitze: the Kleine Fermeda on the far right, the Grosse Fermeda, the Villnösser Turm (Tower), the Odla . . . they are the lesser Geisler, separated from the main group by the col called the Mittagsscharte. There stands the broad Sass Rigais, more than 3000 metres high, and left of that the beautiful and slender Furchetta, which is almost the same height. Then come the Wasserkofel, the Valdussa-Odla, the Wasserstuhl and the Kampiller Turm. I remembered the stories we had heard from Father, who had stood on all the summits which we could see. Perhaps it was then that my desire to climb all these spires was born.

At last the day came when we were allowed to go too. At five o'clock in the morning we were wakened up. I crawled out of the warm hay, pushed back the heavy barn door, saw the stars still in the sky, and with teeth chattering pulled on my clothes. I was not excited but I was full of expectation.

Half an hour later we set off up the meadow to the edge of the forest. Hoar-frost hung on the yellowed grass, and the pine trees rose up like black monsters against the bright cirque. A red splash indicated the beginning of the path which led down to the Munkelweg at the northern foot of the Geislerspitze, along from Bogles to St Zenon. Now the sun had risen and was caressing the North Face of the Furchetta. This gave the impression that up above was a touch of warmth in that unreachable world—as if the Geislerspitze were a gigantic curtain, a wall separating two worlds. The air was clear, coldly transparent. It carried every sound far and wide, so that we whispered instinctively,

At Weissbrunn Father filled the water-bottle. The path led through a wood of dwarf pines, then in zigzags through the last patches of grass and past weather-beaten pines. The ascent of the cirque to the Mittagsscharte seemed endless to me. In the morning light the Geislerspitze seemed to surpass all concept of height. And beyond I sensed innumerable and still undisturbed secrets.

At the last tree, a crooked pine, which had grown to scarcely the height of two men, we rested. Father stuck his cigarette tin in a hollow stump, laid a flat stone on top and said it was time to get going.

The climbing in the cirque was more strenuous than I had pictured to myself from my parents' stories. The higher we went the finer became the scree, the more I slipped backwards at each step. Thus I soon learned that in climbing one uses the whole boot sole and preferably uses large boulders as footholds. 'You must climb slowly and steadily if you want to reach your goal,' said Father wisely.

The first snow lay on the Mittagsscharte. And beyond a sea of peaks! On the other side we ran down the cirque as far as the mouth of the third ravine. We always picked the gullies with the finest scree and leaped downhill effortlessly, digging in our heels, so that the stones spurted.

'That's the beginning of the climb,' cried Father. We stopped. A delicate splashing penetrated the silence: now and then a stone fell. 'The sun is melting the ice which has formed during the night,' said Father, pulling the hemp rope out of his rucksack. My heart began to pound: the climbing was about to start!

We were standing at the beginning of a steep rock couloir. The walls to left and right were yellow, in places overhanging. My self-confidence failed me as I gazed upwards. Jammed blocks the size of a house barred the couloir above me, and all the shadowy places glistened with ice.

Mother led, with Father close behind Helmut and me. Yet he did not rope us up. The climbing was far simpler than I had expected. There always was a ledge, a way to slip through. We were able to do without the rope until just below the top. No single pitch was anything like as difficult to overcome as the stone wall at home. Besides, a wire cable was fixed on the steepest bits.

I was tired and after each rise of rock my eyes searched for the summit. I was looking out for the ridge or a big cairn. To this day I don't know what gave the climb so much suspense that I, a five-year-old, kept going. I could have sat down but I didn't.

Then suddenly we saw it: 'Yes, that's the top,' confirmed Father. An airy ridge still separated us from it. To the right the face fell steeply to the Wassertal, to the left it was so exposed that I had not the confidence to look down. There was a man descending. 'Very exposed,' he said, giving me a hand. I heard that word for the first time, understood it too. On the summit sat several climbers who had come up the East Ridge. They shook us by the hand as if it were a proper party and we joined in the high spirits. I was infinitely tired. Around us only sun and wind, and beneath us, 1000 metres below, the Gschmagenhartalm, to which we must return that same day.

The Sass Rigais was a day out for the grown-ups; for me it was the beginning of a lifelong passion.

MY PARENTS GAVE US CHILDREN, nine in all, our enthusiasm for rambling. When I was a child, the Villnöss valley meant the world as far as I was concerned; amongst tree roots, the crumbling churchyard wall and empty hay sheds we lived in a realm of adventure, which we ruled as robbers and conquerors.

When I was bigger the valley seemed small and narrow to me; there were no more mysteries there, so I looked for them in the wide world: with the Indians I travelled through the Andes of South America, for weeks I forced my way through the jungle in New Guinea, overcame with my brother the highest mountain face on earth. Yet the more I saw, the further I travelled, the more clearly did I recognise that nowhere was I at home except in the Dolomites.

When I was a little boy the East Face of the Kleine Fermeda seemed to me to be the hardest thing there was in the way of a rock face. It looked so steep and unfriendly that my eyes could not see holds anywhere. A mysterious route ran up its deep chimney, which dripped with moisture. I wanted to climb it although I was only twelve years old. My imagination was so taken up by it that I dreamed of it.

So a wall, just a rock wall, transformed every stone in the village into a climbing nursery. I had already known for a long time that one must always have three firm holds when climbing, either two handholds and a foothold or two footholds and a handhold. Diligently I held to this three-point rule and practised at home on the stairway, on the wall of the churchyard, on a scrap of rock in the stream-bed.

The experience I have amassed since then has robbed this wall of its enchantment. Today it is a constant source of wonder to me that this 300-metre-high flight of rock could once have been the most important thing that there was, the moist chimney with the two jammed blocks the essence of difficulty; in a word, a big mystery.

When I stood under the East Face for the first time I was a schoolboy. With a simple granny knot I tied myself to the rope, placed it round my shoulders so that the end which was tied to my father came under my right arm, with the other over my left shoulder. This was the shoulder belay.

My father hung two pitons from his chest harness and climbed away. I stood below, followed all his movements and endeavoured to pay out the rope. After thirty metres my father stopped, took in the rest of the rope and wedged himself in the chimney in such a way that I would not be able to pull him out.

'Come on!' he shouted down and the echo of his words reverberated from wall to wall. 'Climbing!' To start with the rock was broken. Carefully I tested each hold before putting weight on it, tapped at doubtful holds with my boot end and endeavoured to press down on the holds as far as possible.

After the first few pitches it became more difficult. The two walls of the chimney were about a metre apart and stretched vertically upwards. They seemed to me like endless columns. Far above, a block wedged in the chimney barred any further view. Above that the mystery must lie, of that I was firmly convinced.

Father was always the first to spot the right direction. In his capacity as leader of our rope he weighed up the difficulties of the successive pitches and pointed out especially hard places to me. To begin with I was amazed at his experience. He could spot each stance from below and anticipate the forthcoming difficulties.

The East Face of the Kleine Fermeda is of Grade III difficulty. By then I already knew that Grade III meant 'difficult'. Altogether there were at that time six grades of difficulty. Grade I was the lowest, for routes which were easy, where the hands were used only now and then to keep in balance. The sixth grade signified difficulties which, by definition, could be achieved only by the best climbers in the world. Would I ever be able to reach the sixth grade?

Today I know that the sixth grade was somewhat exaggerated. There were at that time already a thousand climbers who had mastered the sixth grade. Sixty years earlier less than twenty had been able to climb to such extremes. Nowadays, at an estimate, there are more than one hundred thousand—in America, in Great Britain, in Japan and above all in central Europe, where extreme rock-climbing originated.

Although I was inexperienced and the exposure of the route impressed me, I was not scared when my father offered me the lead below the second overhang in the chimney. I was to be allowed to go first on the rope!

'Take plenty of care and climb slowly,' he emphasised. 'And when you're up, hang your belay sling on a firm rock spike.'

A fall by the leader is always extremely dangerous. For example, on a pitch of thirty metres he can fall up to twice that distance. For the second it is extraordinarily difficult to control such a fall. If he is not fastened to several pitons or spikes of rock, he will be torn from the face. I have made it a principle always to have a model belay at each stance. As leader my main maxim was, however, never to fall; and so it has remained to this day.

I looked once more at Father who was standing in the chimney and who had belayed himself to a piton. He had the rope secure in his hand and showed no signs of concern. On the contrary, from the calmness of his movements I realised to my relief that he believed me to be capable of the coming pitch.

For five years I had only been allowed to climb as the second on the rope. Now I was thrilled to see the rope no longer running up from my chest, but down between my legs. On one occasion Father wanted to warn me about friable holds but, before he had finished speaking, I had already got round the dangerous spot.

On the subsequent pitches we shared the lead alternately. Happily, and as carefully as possible, I climbed on when it was my turn. When we reached the summit I thought that I must seem a bit more grown-up.

WE LADS AT THAT TIME were so young, so inexperienced. We wore wide cord breeches, faded anoraks and had a hemp rope. We couldn't dance, bought the girls no flowers and blushed if by chance we tied one of them on the rope. Nevertheless we were hungry for adventures.

The North Face of the Sass Rigais was forgotten after Emil Solleder and Fritz Wiessner climbed the neighbouring North Face of the Furchetta in 1925, thereby ushering in a new epoch in the development of the Dolomites. A hundred years before, climbers had been concerned solely with reaching summits, but around the turn of the century, leading mountaineers began to climb individual faces, edges and ridges. No longer was the summit the sole criterion, but the importance attached to the routes of greater or lesser difficulty by which one could reach it. So climbers tried to find still harder, more direct routes near those already available, and later this had an effect on mountaineering in the Andes, Himalaya and Karakoram.

The route up the North Face of the Sass Rigais was a puzzle for us lads at that time: a maze of cracks, ledges and chimneys, which were engraved on this 800-metre-high limestone wall. No other wall looked so dark and spectral—like the legs of a giant spider. The route was so little known to us that I stuck a photograph of Sass Rigais in my pocket so as not to lose the way up above.

On a July afternoon my younger brother Günther and I pitched our tent near the tree-line. Firstly we fetched water and firewood and Günther collected dry pine needles. Then we dug a ditch around the tent. Before night fell we cushioned the floor of the tent with the pine needles because at that time we did not possess any lilos. During the night we shivered with the cold.

In the morning the cold was at its worst. Secretly we both thought of giving up but, because neither of us was prepared to admit this, we shouldered our rucksacks and struggled up the cirque to the start of the climb. We were rather subdued.

A few weeks before Father had brought us a helmet from town as protection against stonefall. It was one of the early models, made of white plastic and with a peak in front. It was more suitable for mining than falling. At the foot of the climb we stuffed gloves, a cap and newspaper in it for padding.

As we had only one helmet we took it in turns to wear it when we were second. In the middle of the face, where a gully subject to stonefall had to be crossed, we considered we should both wear it. For that we would have had to pull it across the ravine on the rope, and the rope was too short for this manoeuvre, so I climbed without it and consequently faster, in order not to be killed by the stonefall.

On the big, sloping ramp in the middle of the face we lost the route. We climbed much too high. Only when we could go no higher did we discover the correct line. Far below us an area of grey slabs led up to a crack in the headwall.

As we stood under the wall we understood how our father had tried this face in vain in his youth. Steep and wet it stood before us. When I considered that in bygone days people had climbed without pitons, equipped solely with hemp rope and *scarpetti* (rope-soled slippers), my respect for the pioneers grew. From this point Father had abseiled off. Now even his retreat seemed to us a pioneering effort.

We had two pitons with us, two iron pins which the village blacksmith had made to our design. Together they weighed a pound and the eyes were so stout that it was only with difficulty that we could snap in the two karabiners, which the head of the village fire brigade had lent us.

Also the rope, a laid nylon rope, was stiff and obstinate. We could have attempted the Indian rope-trick with it. I say this now, thirty years later, when we have such good equipment available that our mental attitude to these faces has altered completely. At that time we knew nothing of all that and, with a helmet, the two pitons and our first nylon rope, fancied ourselves in training for the Eiger North Face.

At small stances I banged in one of the pitons and made myself fast, so as to be able to belay Günther. Doggedly he laboured to knock them out again, as we still had need of them. In the exit cracks, which were completely iced up, for the first time I banged in a piton for a running belay. It was the first one I had ever put in and, as Günther was unable to remove it, I was not a little proud that it was so firm. At the same time, however, I was a bit sad because we now had only a single piton.

In the summit book we recorded, alongside our names, the North Face route up which we had climbed.

With that ascent of the North Face of the Sass Rigais our childhood ended. We had accumulated our experience. I had learned to take on the responsibility of great difficulties, and to remain true to myself at all times. Then and there I became what I am today.

The middle part of the Sass Rigais North Face. Günther and I were inexperienced and modestly equipped, but had already developed the instinct to survive.

2

THE FUTURE WAS A STRAIGHT LINE

1961–65

AS FAR AS THE START OF the really steep face, we had climbed as a pair, belaying each other alternately. My father knew this part of the route well, possibly in his youth he had been the first to do it; no one knew for sure. At all events, he had brought me up this open couloir before, which leads out of the cirque under the Fermeda towers in a V-shaped notch between the Kleine Fermeda and the Seceda-Kamm. From below, from the valley, this ravine looked like a half-open book, and until late summer patches of snow lay amongst its grey rocks.

Now, up above, everything looked quite different. It was gloomy and cold. Only in the sky, far above the soaring vertical rock walls to left and right of us, was there a bright gleam. After a few easy pitches we squeezed ourselves through a narrow fissure and then climbed together over less steep rocks. The mountain now lay before us as a shapeless and enormous mass of rock, so complex that on my own I would not have been able to find the way.

This is always the case. What appears logical and rectilinear from below is a maze up on the mountain. The dimensions are misplaced but the steepness does not seem alarming. It scares you only when you look down. Orientation becomes a serious problem. But my father knew the way and I climbed behind him, without any qualms, trusting in him completely.

Where the steep rock of the Kleine Fermeda forms a shallow recess, we stopped. A series of hands-breadth cracks threaded straight as an arrow up the grey limestone of this Dolomite face. It was vertical and higher than several church towers one on top of the other.

21

Was there really a route up that? We didn't know exactly. However, I wanted to find out and begged my father to let me climb up a bit further. At first he hesitated then let me carry on. There were good holds but the rock wasn't completely firm. Father warned me to be careful, while he—following all my movements—attended to the rope and belayed as best he could.

I was at that time a schoolboy. After many easy mountain trips I was footsure and persevering but no extreme climber. Neither my father nor I knew really whether, on such a steep face, one would have been able to hold the other in the event of a fall. The rope between us, this forty metres of stiff nylon rope, was more a psychological aid than a practical one.

I got up the first part well. Of course my fingers were numb on the cold rock but my hands and feet continually found firm holds, so that I was able to climb higher without fear. Swiftly, handhold by handhold, foothold by foothold, I pushed and hoisted myself upwards. In front of me, the field of view had shrunk to a few square metres of passing rock. I had forgotten all about the scenery behind me. The wind whispered now and then on the ridges above me, and out of the valley came the sound of rushing water. Still the glittering grey flight of rock rose immeasurably high when I gazed upwards, steeper still now than at the start. Somewhere above that, clouds went sailing by.

My father kept on paying out rope. He looked a bit anxious. After forty metres the rope ran out and I found a tiny stance. Father now had to follow but he hesitated. I could not stand properly and hung awkwardly from the rock. I was scarcely in a position to look after the rope and to belay. Father was of the opinion I should come down. 'Abseil!' On a single rope that was out of the question. Abseiling would only have been possible if I had been able to anchor the rope twenty metres lower down. I didn't fancy climbing down, so climbing on seemed to me the safest way out.

What to do? I looked down at Father, who continued to hesitate, and then upwards to where overhanging rock, with black streaks of water, barred the view. Instinctively I took firmer hold on the rock. 'I'll climb solo to the top,' I called down to Father. 'Then I'll come back down the easy ordinary route.' My father didn't agree, but he said nothing. So I untied myself from the rope, let it fall and stood 'free as a bird' on the face. I was now completely on my own. To overcome anxiety and not to lose strength I climbed on smoothly, for with the first jerky movement I might have lost my grip. I must be very attentive now and not make mistakes. Soon I was climbing calmly. I avoided all the dangerous, loose holds. I must manage without them.

Anxiously my father followed my every movement until he could no longer see me. Then he took the rope and climbed up to the gap under the normal route. There he waited, sitting still in the sun.

As the angle of the face relented I raced up the rock. I encouraged myself. Now that I was past the overhangs nothing more could hold me up. I had done it. As far as I could see no great difficulties were to be expected further up. Nevertheless I looked ahead intently. Beyond each edge of rock I expected the unexpected.

Nobody in the valley had known anything about this route, which Castiglioni had first climbed, as I found out later. No piton or cairn showed me the way. I climbed upwards, following nothing but my instincts. Over a last rock step and a shallow crack I reached the summit ridge and a few minutes later the summit itself. With that, tension was gone. I knew the way down.

My father had been more anxious than I had feared. Seeing the face again across the Panascharte on the way back, he shook his head again and again. Also I had too much respect for such height and steepness to become over-confident. However, it was then that I began to understand that we should leave no traces behind on these rock walls, otherwise the mystery was taken away from them, that incomprehensible something that made me shiver on the way down.

IN THE SUMMER OF 1963 I climbed my first 'sixer'—the Tissi Route on the first Sella Tower—and my first ice face, the North Face of Similaun in the Ötztal Alps. I was eighteen years old. However my biggest trip this summer, if not the hardest, was the traverse of the Ortler, Zebru and Königspitze—a row of ridges and faces of mixed terrain, which had filled me with enthusiasm. All my capacity for enthusiasm was now directed towards mountaineering. When I went running in the gym period I was training for the ice faces; when I was on the nursery crags I was practising for the Dolomite walls.

Meanwhile I was a student, learning to be a surveyor in Bolzano and only home in the summertime, when I had to help with my father's growing poultry farm. Each weekend, however, Günther and I went off on a trip. We two, I the second oldest and Günther the third oldest of the St Peter in Villnöss schoolboys, had not got on especially well together as children. Now for the first time, with our growing passion for climbing, we became an inseparable pair.

Already in spring 1964 we had achieved a string of hard rock and ice routes. On the North Face of the Königspitze, Heindl Messner, a young farmer and distant relation from Villnöss, was my partner, but then, with

Günther, I climbed the North Face of the Vertain, the North Face of the Hochfeiler and the North Face of the Ortler, where we climbed directly up the vertical hanging glacier. Finally in July, with Paul Kantioler, also from Villnöss, and Heindl Messner, I managed an ascent of the North Face of the Furchetta. We started too far left, towards the East Face, and opened up, without planning it, a variation of the famous Solleder Route, which for years had been my biggest pipe-dream.

Günther and I were now a co-ordinated team, with experience on rock and ice at the highest grade of difficulty and we dreamed of going a step further. In the summer of 1965 we wanted to put our dreams into practice: first ascents in the Dolomites, a visit to the western Alps and all the ice faces in South Tyrol were on our programme. In April we attempted the North Face of the Hochferner. In thick driving snow we gave up at a height of 3100 metres.

A FEW WEEKS AFTER our adventurous retreat from the North Face of the Hochferner, Günther and I were sitting once more in front of the small hut on the alpine pasture high above the Pfitschtal, which had already sheltered us after our first attempt. The North Face was again in mist. To the west, however, the last, weak evening sunbeams broke through the flying cloud cover. The bare scenery acquired a tinge of cheerfulness and warmth. Two trembling anemones turned their faces to the sun. We too.

Then the icy wind blew through our sweat-soaked shirts and we crept into the hut and straight into the pungent hay. We were not tired but we wanted to rest for the following day, for the North Face of the Griessferner. Soon we began to doze, no more. Günther dreamed of good weather and at the same time saw the shreds of mist whisking by. Half asleep, he talked of firm ice full of holds and yet in his dream his eyes were caught by deep crevasses. Still the morning did not come.

The first rope-lengths were easy. In spite of the mist, we climbed together over dirty, riven ice, avoiding some ice towers tall as houses. Everything looked rather sinister. Suddenly there was blue sky above us, all the contours were clear and our goal firmly outlined. Beneath us was a sea of mist. We paused and gazed as if we were standing on a shore. Above us the wall was an open face: in fantastic sequence ice balconies, mouldings, clefts and séracs towered up over one another. Blue and near fabulous, this gigantic world of ice shimmered. The impression was terrific—liberating and oppressive at the same time.

The first vertical obstacle, a chimney, was overcome by bridging. Short walls and steep gullies alternated with narrow ledges and flat areas. Each pitch had its special charm. We had gone quite a long way before I dared go no deeper into this fabulous labyrinth. A huge crevasse gaped in the centre of the North Face of the Griessferner! Insurmountable. Shocked by so many séracs, I shouted down, 'Günther, we must go back', then I thought of the abseiling, the dangers, the drop. There had to be a way somewhere. Günther came on anyway.

Above us stood an ice wall some twenty metres high. The crux! We didn't puzzle over it for long and looked for a weak spot. No, here there was no way forward. At best, technical climbing and we had only ten ice screws with us. I tried it and soon hung far above Günther. It seemed fierce, slightly overhanging, almost like extreme rock. Then the ground above, the summit upswing, was no longer steep, but good firm snow and magnificent to climb on. Without having to belay any more, together we reached the summit of the Griessferner.

We started down the direct Vanis Route on the North Face of the Hochferner. Thus we made up for our failure a few weeks previously. Tiredly we reached our stone hut. It was noon. We lay in the sunshine and blinked now and then at the Griessferner's hanging glacier, whose secret we had shared.

GÜNTHER AND I SOUGHT out new and harder routes for ourselves; each of us was hurt at least once by falling stones. But a week later we would be back again. Together we made many excursions and accumulated experiences, but always we dreamed of the really big adventures.

We read books by Heinrich Harrer, Hermann Buhl and Walter Bonatti. We listened to alpine lectures and the reminiscences of the 'extremers' in unheated huts. Only much later on, when I had already journeyed to all the continents, did I sense that adventure is not made up of distant lands and mountain tops, rather it lies in one's readiness to exchange the domestic hearth for an uncertain resting-place.

At that time, each spring, I ticked off the possible new starting points on the faces and observed the state of the ice gullies in the northern gorges. Until I was twenty I asked my father for permission each time I wanted to go further afield or needed his Lambretta motor-scooter. After that I still announced my departure. 'Tomorrow we're going to the North Face of the Grosse Fermeda,' I called into the kitchen. I began to pack my rucksack, filled Günther with enthusiasm for the undertaking and did not wait for Father to forbid it. He was generous when it came to giving us our freedom in the mountains.

Today I am amazed that my father did not forbid us to make such first ascents. At that time I had a confused picture of freedom: today the name is the only thing people know about freedom. They want to be free of laws, free of everyday cares, free of hate, free of ambition. Who knows what freedom is? No one. I often think we mountaineers get nearest to it, this paradise on earth. Or, to put it another way: the truly free climber is one who obeys no rules. He is no high flyer, keeping up with the Joneses; no slave of others or of the summit fall line, like the direttissima men. I am sorry for them all, but especially for those who do not realise at all that rules force their way between them and the mountains.

The plan stood firm. With Heindl and Paul, Günther and I would go straight up the cirque to the Fermeda North Face. Heavily laden we went through the village. The passers-by grinned or shook their heads. Just above the forest it became steep and dwarf pines stood everywhere; also isolated, bushy Arolla pines.

Günther was smaller than I, dark. We had no beards then and our hair was short-cropped, just like the sheep on the spring drive up to the alpine pastures. We wore corduroy breeches, mountain boots with moulded rubber soles and faded anoraks. In the rucksack were some pitons, piton hammer, a pullover and other odds and ends.

The sun rose and the bright light changed the black and white into a colourful world. All night terrors, all morning anxieties were banished. We four gazed upwards at this long, grey face and noted that there were stances there from which it must be possible to find a way of climbing on. From our perspective the face had contracted to the possible.

It was St Peter and St Paul Day, a church festival in Villnöss. We wanted to celebrate it on the Fermeda towers. We started up a steep gully between the Grosse Fermeda and the Villnösser Turm. The traverse above that was exposed, and we climbed directly up to a big platform. From there a crack led upwards to the right for twenty-five metres to a stance. Now it continued up a twenty-metre-high, shallow dièdre and then left up an overhanging crack dièdre to a chimney. We climbed into this and balanced over to the left-hand wall. There was a foothold there just the size of a boot. From this we let ourselves fall back again on the other wall and pulled ourselves two metres up the overhanging wall. There followed a smooth dièdre and, after two further pitches, we climbed like acrobats over slabs to the summit. Almost throughout, the rock had been poor.

Not until years later was this first ascent mentioned in the climbing journals. 'The 600-metre-high North Face of the Grosse Fermeda (V+) was ascended for the first time during summer 1965 by the Villnöss climbers Paul Kantioler, Heindl Messner, Günther Messner and Reinhold Messner. The route runs directly up the well-rounded north corner of the Grosse Fermeda.'

In 1965 I WENT TO THE western Alps for the first time. Together with my brother Günther I wanted to get to know new dimensions, bigger mountains. We managed a repeat of the North Face Direct of Les Courtes and the fifth ascent of the North Face Direct on the Triolet. There we descended by a new route on the north-west side, the route which Renato Casarotto and Giancarlo Grassi repeated in ascent fifteen years later. We had trained ourselves specially for these undertakings by long-distance running. Also we had practised ice climbing during the winter on frozen waterfalls.

That same summer I was lucky enough to do some classic routes in the Bernina group and more first ascents in the Dolomites: the South Face Direct of the Neunerspitze (Sasso Nove) in the Fanis region and the North-West Pillar of the Villnösser-Odla (500 metres; Grade V+). To this day the route has never been repeated.

That summer I was happy, from June to September, from morning to night. What I enjoyed was the feeling of immortality, the haze in the air when I had not had enough sleep and went unresistingly to the start of the climb, or in the evening sat grazed and weightless from tiredness on the summit. The future was a straight line. With fingers wedged in cracks, forced marches day after day, cheese and bread in the rucksack, I led—often hard on the limit of the possible—a carefree existence.

What I had learned in my early school years and at home would have sufficed for my life. Later on I wasted my time on the school bench. I was destined by my family to become a technical engineer. No one knows why. There is for me no subject more boring than engineering and nothing that lies further from me. A decade was to pass before I was able to free myself of a society which classifies people into professional groups. By nature people have no profession. Perhaps a calling. For myself I had become addicted to the intense experiences I enjoyed in the mountains. In freedom there is sacrifice but no frontiers.

COMING FROM THE SFULMINI RANGE, I rambled with my client towards the Tosa Hut. At that period I did a lot of guiding so as to earn money and to get to know new climbing areas. Along the Sentiero delle Bocchette we passed under the Campanile Basso. There I noticed two lads starting the ascent of the East Face of the Campanile, also known as Guglia di Brenta. It was already late afternoon. They'll have to hurry, I thought, if they don't want to bivouac. My 'Herr' was in his late fifties, a school chaplain by profession and a capable mountaineer. In the Brenta group we had repeated many classic routes together, on the Cima Margarita, on the Cima Tosa, on the Torre di Brenta. We had also been on the Guglia di Brenta. His enthusiasm was still great. Solely about the Steger Route on the Cima Alta had the pastor nothing good to say. It had demanded his utmost.

He liked hard routes and bore cold and wet without complaining. But this West Face had been too much for him. The blame lay with this Herr

In the summer of 1965, fingers wedged in cracks, cheese and bread in the rucksack, we ranged the Dolomites, here, left, on the South Face of the Torre Grande and, right, on the Dilona route.

Steger; he had wrongly classified the route at the time of the first ascent in 1928. Perhaps it was the fault of the rain which we encountered on the last third of the face. Of that he did not speak, only of an overhang and vertical cracks, which were far undergraded. 'This is not Grade III, it's Grade V.' Also, he had known all the time about the keyhole through which he had had to crawl. Of course Hans Steger, who made the first ascent, had been a great climber, perhaps one of the best in the 1920s. But the grading of his route was wrong and, even if heaven had long ago forgiven the error, my pastor was never going to pardon it. It was the medium difficulty which had decided us to choose this route: III–IV. At that time Grade VI was the highest grade of difficulty and my client climbed to Grade IV maximum. We went well together. I matched myself to his pace and he did not mind if now and then I climbed a harder variation, as a proof of my diligence, so to speak. He was even happy if, on free afternoons, I climbed some route or other by myself.

At the Tosa Hut we were welcome guests. The daughter of the hut guardian made a fuss of me and on rainy days I often sat for hours in the kitchen. It went no further. Spiritual supervision did not disturb us, for I was then bashful and inexperienced in love. The Herr Pastor read Mass on Sunday and I had the task of translating the sermon into Italian. Sentence by sentence. That none of those present broke into loud laughter at my inadequate Italian was largely because Italians are for the most part tolerant people, and because I was the spiritual gentleman's mountain guide.

Every time we returned there was a big hello. They were all pleased about our trips. People wished the Herr Pastor luck: 'At his age . . . and such routes!' 'Hats off to the pastor!' Dino, the hut guardian, insisted upon serving us personally when his daughter was needed in the kitchen—a lot of salad and fruit, as he knew from previous years. Often he sat down by us, enquired about our plans and always wanted to know when there would be another Mass. Like the other Sundays: at eight o'clock.

He told us then of his days as a mountain guide, of his own first ascents. He knew a lot about the history of the opening up of the Brenta. The talk was often of Paul Preuss and naturally of the East Face of the Guglia. Dino himself had climbed it at that time, when as yet there were no pitons sticking in it. 'It's as steep as a church tower, but with holds. Only one can't have a rest anywhere. Vertical rock from top to bottom.' '*Un capolavoro*, a masterpiece,' he often said. At that, the lads on the East Face came to mind again. Were they all right?

I excused myself, ran to my room and fetched the rope. Outside I tied it on my back and sped off. Up into the Bocca di Brenta. A fresh wind blew in my face. I raced round under the western side. Across scree and hard snow I ran towards the valley until I was under the South Face. A few people stopped aghast. 'He's crazy,' I heard one of them say. Yes, I was crazy. I wanted the Guglia this evening and alone.

The whole south-west diédre was in sunshine. As my eyes fixed on the Fehrmann Route, the first shadows of the evening met me. Soon the sun would be going down. There was no doubt, the way up was clearly defined by the natural features. Always straight up. Three hundred metres of firm, vertical rock.

I swung myself from crack to crack, bridged up an overhanging diédre on the outside, heaved myself over a small ledge to the right. I climbed on and on, dynamically, rhythmically, all concentration. My body was tensed. I could not stop, I was no longer myself, the climbing had taken me over.

Even for a Grade VI climber, this fourth and fifth grade climbing was beautiful. Everything about me was movement. The rhythm increased and my skills grew with this increase. I gazed ahead, all the time seeking out the best route, and could not stop. I was quite alone and needed no one to safe-guard me. High above I quitted the diédre and climbed to the right. There the sun still shone and everything on the wall fell into place. I did not know how far or how high I had climbed. Time and space are only two dimensions.

Some minutes later I was standing below the East Face of the Guglia, having run around the north side of the summit tower on a broad ledge. From somewhere came the strumming sound of pitons being knocked in. That must be the pair from this afternoon, I thought. Now they will be abseiling.

I paused to reflect, then I started climbing. It was already late and the East Face had been without sun for hours. That's why I hesitated. Now all was forgotten: the cold rock, the descent, the night.

After twenty metres I found the first piton, paid no attention to it. The first overhang I avoided on the right. Already the difficulties were decreasing. I climbed out on the summit. It was not the first time I had been on top of the Guglia—and I was not alone. The other two were still there. They had also reached the top and wanted likewise to begin the descent. Would I like to abseil with them? Yes, please. And was I going to the Tosa Hut? I nodded. Then we set off together.

On Sundays Günther and I were allowed to borrow Father's motor-scooter. The Helicopter, as we called it, was also our transport to remoter places like the western Alps.

It was already dark when we got to the hut. As I was introducing my companions to the Herr Pastor, the guardian asked me to make an announcement in the common room: 'Mass will be said at eight o'clock tomorrow and the sermon will also be given in Italian.'

OUR 'HELICOPTER' ROARED NOISILY up the pass to Falzarego. We called Father's motor-cycle the 'Helicopter' when he wasn't around. He placed the motor-scooter, a clapped-out Lambretta, at our disposal on Sundays and Günther and I would travel as far as possible up into some valley on it, force ourselves up through forest and scree to the start of this or that face, climb it or turn round halfway up, look for the fastest way back to the valley, and, tired out, ride home.

By then we already knew the Dolomites thoroughly and were only out to climb the big walls by their classic routes. We dreamed of the Solleder Route on the Civetta North-West Face, of the south face routes on the

Marmolada, of the North Face of the Grosse Zinne (Cima Grande di Lavaredo). We knew our alpine history better than that of the Italian War of Independence. We were especially bewitched by the daring of Hans Vinatzer, Emil Solleder, Emilio Comici, Gino Soldà, Riccardo Cassin, Anderl Heckmaier and Hias Rebitsch.

At that time my hero was Emil Solleder. He it was who had come to the Dolomites just fifty years before and had solved all the great problems on which the best climbers of the pre-First World War period had failed. Above all his style impressed me. In one day only he climbed the 1100-metre-high North-West Face of the Civetta, and solved the problem of the Furchetta North Face even faster. A year later, in 1926, he climbed the East Face of the Sass Maor. He made necessary the introduction of the sixth grade, and his three great routes along with the North Face of Pelmo rated for a long time as the hardest in the Dolomites, even in the whole of the Alps.

We were riding past below the face of the Civetta and Günther shouted in my ear: 'That's next on the list!' We did not know then what was in store for us on the North Face of Pelmo.

We were already saddle-sore. Nine months of squatting on the school bench had failed to harden us. 'Going to college isn't even useful for that,' laughed my brother, who had joined me in Bolzano to study commerce.

We had often seen Monte Pelmo on picture postcards and still more often admired its striking form from the Mittagsscharte in the Geisler group. At last we could observe its broad North Face at close quarters. We turned off the road, stopped our machine and gazed up at the wall. It looked damned wet. Beneath patches of snow could be seen long black streaks—melt-water.

On the way to the Rifugio di Fiume the 'Helicopter' once more lived up to its name but it did its duty. Another look at the face and the weather promised to hold. At the hut entrance, the guardian's wife barred our way. Inspecting us from head to toe, she made a face, as if she had never come across people in our get-up. In her mind baby faces obviously did not go with extreme climbing breeches.

We wondered if we were at the wrong hut and asked somewhat confusedly whether this was the starting point for the Pelmo North Face. '*Sapete che la parete nord è molto difficile?*' she replied. Yes, certainly we knew it was especially difficult, that was precisely why we were here. We sought out difficulties, we were even proud of our first great climbs which we had mastered under our own steam. Of course we knew that one could climb Monte Pelmo more easily from the south than via its smooth, vertical North Face.

However, we didn't want to reach the summit, we wanted to climb the North Face, even though the guardian's wife was scowling.

We made up the bed, got the rucksacks ready, asked the guardian to leave the key in the front door and went into the common room. The guardian made a fire in the open hearth and soon the room was like a smoke-curing kitchen. Like smoked-out foxes we quitted the room and went to bed. That smoke—I thought as I fell asleep—is a sign of bad weather and, if the weather is not good tomorrow, we don't want to climb.

We awoke early. The outlines of the face were clearly recognisable. The sky was full of stars. In stocking-feet we crept down the stairs to the living room. We wanted to get outside straight away. What a disappointment! The door was locked, the key missing: we were caged.

Using his understanding of household affairs, my brother found the key in a drawer in the kitchen. Our first climbing problem was overcome. It was three o'clock in the morning. The way to the face was clear.

We stumbled up through the forest, crossed a plantation of dwarf pines, and in the first dawn ascended the cirque to the beginning of the climb. With the daylight our self-confidence increased. The tension between familiarity and pleasure made us especially alert.

We were standing at the start of the route as the first rays of the sun touched the summit. Although from our worm's-eye view the highest point seemed to be within easy reach we knew that 850 metres separated us from it.

We jumped the enormous crevasse between rock and glacier at its weakest spot and started up the first rock buttress. However, after the first few metres we could not get any higher. The terrain looked easy and the guidebook spoke of no difficulty; but we had to admit that we had deceived ourselves: the rock was smooth, washed out, damp and in part broken. We roped up. I led off while Günther belayed. My first moves were stiff, awkward, without the proper rhythm. Four pitons were sticking in this pitch; we did not find as many anywhere later on.

Soon we were accustomed to the rock and the moves became more fluent. The extreme climbing began. We traversed higher on friable slabs, turned a steep step by means of a narrow crack, followed a steep gully and reached a wide ledge. On this we traversed left, bridged up a dièdre, worked our way across the smooth wall to the right into a chimney, surmounted an overhang in this by bridging and reached a small ledge, which led us to the first big stance on the face.

Completely absorbed in the climbing, we had overlooked the fact that the weather had deteriorated. We could no longer see the next steep step. Mist veiled the face. Nevertheless we found the correct crack, worked our way up it and above traversed right between two overhangs.

In spite of the rain which had now set in, the joy of the climbing kept us cheerful. The route was clearly indicated. We had reached the lower edge of the second platform when the rain suddenly degenerated into a cloudburst. Without protection we stood there, in the storm, in the middle of the North Face of Pelmo. Like mad things we stormed up a gully down which a waterfall was already gushing. We had to find shelter as fast as possible! We both felt that it was a matter of survival, with 500 metres of wall beneath us and the summit far away. A steep little step barred the gully. I looked at each hand- and foothold, considered each move in advance and sprang into the waterfall. The cold water nearly took my breath away. It ran up my sleeves, down my collar, in my boots and soaked me to the skin. That not only made up for missing our morning wash, it was an icy shower-bath. Up above I found a cave. Puffing and blowing, I threw myself inside and had a breather. The first stones were already rumbling down the waterfall into the depths.

Günther could no longer hear my climbing commands. The storm howled, the water roared, the stones crashed. From time to time thunder sounded above this hellish noise. I tugged three times on the rope, to tell him to start climbing. Being no longer able to make use of the gully, Günther climbed up hard rock to the right of it and crept, safe but dripping, to join me in the cave.

We stared aghast into the grey of the mist: through the darkness projectiles whizzed past. Stonefall. Soon the rain turned to snow, a cold wind shook us. Continually drops of moisture fell from the protecting overhang. We were dripping wet. It was just after ten o'clock in the morning. We had two-thirds of the face behind us and no idea how the rest of it would go. We put on everything we had, and stuck the bivouac sack over the lot. For the time being we wanted to wait it out. The dream of a fast ascent of the Pelmo North Face was over. We just wanted to be off this wall.

Nothing alarms me more in the mountains than stonefall, avalanches or a sudden change-round in the weather. Difficulties one can overcome, whether quickly or slowly is immaterial. Or one can turn back. But one is at the mercy

Günther and I found ourselves at the mercy of storm and stonefall on the formidable North Face of Monte Pelmo. (photo: Jürgen Winkler)

of changes in the weather. Sometimes one can wait, often time alone decides.

We knew we were alone, dependent on ourselves. At that time there was no helicopter rescue from the face, so no one would be able to come to fetch us. The thick mist made that still more obvious to us. Yet we were lucky. After two hours it cleared up. The bad weather passed over, the stonefall fell silent, the mist lifted. Only now and then were stones still exploding on the ledges below. In the west stood a bank of dark clouds.

We crept out of the cave, sorted everything out and looked at the way ahead. The fact that the route, which now ran up a rounded edge, was fairly safe from stonefall decided us to continue the ascent. Water ran down the gullies and cracks, for the snow had not frozen. It lay heavy and wet on the ledges and clung to the rope. Quickly we were back in the swing of it, all going smoothly. Only the fierce storm out of the north-west, which was now hitting the face, made the waiting on the stances almost unbearable. It ate its way into our wet clothes, it threw the water that dripped from the overhangs right in our faces. It shook us—like the cold, which pervaded our entire bodies. We were hypothermic and in this condition would not have survived a bivouac.

Everywhere the rock was streaming, I shuddered at the thought of it. Just to the right of the almost vertical rock I climbed stiff and trembling up a smooth wall—a big straddle brought me to an extremely loose chimney, which led to an overhanging crack. This crack made me work, so that I got warmed up and the old certainty returned. I reached the stance, a deep crack with ice in its depths. Günther followed. Via a concealed chimney we came to easier ground. We exchanged the lead, yet made only slow progress. Meanwhile the shadows of the rising shreds of mist were creeping across the face. There was a ghostly atmosphere about us, as if we were in another, reversed world. Suddenly the sun broke through. Full of confidence we climbed out on the edge, out into warm sunlight. Although it was harder there than in the gully, we made better progress. Pitch after pitch we put behind us. But the face did not want to come to an end. After each pitch we hoped to reach the summit stone-shoot but still it did not materialise. Only a fresh, gloomy bank of clouds thrust itself nearer and nearer. Soon they swallowed up the sun again.

Already the storm-borne cloud bank was nearly upon us, driving snow-flakes before it. Get a move on, I thought, get going, off this face before it's too late. A second storm discharged itself over us: hail, snow, storm, thunder. The mountain quaked. Like madmen we climbed on. Without using intermediate pitons, always upwards. There was no more talk of waiting; it would have been the end.

Then a red rope hanging over the next steep step, caught my eye. I started . . . was there another rope party on the wall? No, the rope hung from some pitons between two huge overhangs. A piton, tied to it, clinked against the rock as it swung in the wind. Suddenly a sentence came into my head: 'They got to an area of overhangs and could go neither forwards nor backwards.' We were climbing into a trap. Last summer the radio had carried a report of a rescue from this face. Two climbers had lost their way on the North Face of Pelmo and had had to be rescued by the Bergwacht.

'They got to an area of overhangs and could go neither forwards nor backwards.' That had been the announcer's commentary. We were in the same place. We peered to the right, scouted to the left, around the edge—impossible! Therefore it had to be straight up.

Once more I summoned up all my reserves of energy. A small overhang, a steep, smooth wall and then an overhanging crack—a stance. I drew a deep breath. Günther led the pitch up to the summit couloir and I climbed past him to take it on. What a deception! Here the rock was iced up and rotten. Rills ran everywhere. After several attempts I gave up and tried my luck on the left edge of the gully. Eight hundred metres above the cirque I was climbing on vertical rocks. Once I had done it, I felt a lot better.

A bent piton showed us that we were not the first people who had had to come up this way. After three further pitches we were standing on the summit, happily once more on level ground. At last. Our fingers were raw, bloody. Our clothes hung heavy and wet about us. It was raining. Like monsters, shreds of mist darted past us; they obscured our view totally.

No time for a rest. We must get down—back to the hut. Cairns marked the way. We found the ordinary route. In mist we ran along ledges and soon reached the bottom of the climb. Now came an endless march around the west side of Pelmo. In darkness and mist we reached the road to the Straulanza Pass. A further cloudburst poured down on us; blinded by the lightning, we continued as in a trance.

We didn't look for another place to shelter. Dripping wet we reached the hut where, after lots of banging, the guardian opened the door to us. He had given us up for good. From him we learned that the day's three storms had caused severe devastation throughout the country.

It took us two days to get back home after our adventure on the North

Face of Pelmo, because roads were blocked with mud slides and some bridges collapsed. Father's confidence in our climbing skill had, however, increased.

My brother Günther. We were a co-ordinated team on rock and ice, until I began to pursue what Günther called my 'crazy solos'.

3

THE WALL OF WALLS

1965–66

MY SISTER HAD GOT TO KNOW HIM. He had enquired after her on his way to the North Face of the Furchetta and now he sat in our kitchen-cum-living room. Sepp Mayerl was known at that time as one of the climbers who got on in all fields. He was no specialist. Not so experienced on ice as on rock, he was at the forefront of alpine climbing. And this same Sepp Mayerl invited me to climb with him. With him I climbed the Tissi Route on the Tofana di Rozes and the Via Italia on the Piz-de-Ciavàces. A new world opened up to me.

With his extraordinary aptitude and admiration for Toni Egger it was no wonder that before long he was climbing in the Lienz Dolomites. He repeated the classic routes on the Hochstadel and, often alone, found new routes on the Laserwand. He became a member of the climbing group 'Alpenraute Lienz'.

Sepp was a self-employed steeplejack and moved from place to place restoring church towers without using scaffolding. He would re-clad a tower here, clean the faces of the church tower clock there or gild the balls on the spire. Through his work he expanded his mountaineering, travelling to the Wilder Kaiser, the Julian Alps, the Karwendel and the Dolomites. Thus he came to us. News of his ability quickly spread through South Tyrol and soon he was in great demand as a climbing partner. On weekdays mostly he hung high above the villages, on Sundays he climbed the hardest faces in the Dolomites.

I didn't know how to belay. What use was the traditional shoulder belay to the second man if the leader's stance was not perfect? Sepp Mayerl explained to me how one set up a one hundred per cent belay, and from him I learned how to manage the rope neatly. Artificial climbing with étriers hung from pitons I got from him too. On the Via Italia, an almost exclusively technical climb, my strength ran out, so clumsy was I to begin with on this overhanging terrain.

During the winter months Sepp had more free time than in summer and he utilised it skiing through his home mountains or in making winter ascents, such as the Hochstadel North Face in the Lienz Dolomites. Year by year his powers grew and with them his experience. Already this winter we had both climbed the North-West Face of the Sass Pordoi. It was the second winter ascent of the Fedele Route. Subsequently we went off through the Val di Mesdi, then still a seldom frequented ski tour.

The wintry Tofana Pillar was to be the last preparation for our biggest 1965/66 winter project: the first repeat of the Bonatti Route on the Matterhorn North Face. We got only as far as the middle of the face. After the Angel Traverse it began to snow and the descent wasn't easy. Time and again snow slides poured over us and we reached the foot of the face on our last piton.

Back at college I was in hot water. I had always been a good pupil, but now I was getting bad reports, even in my favourite subjects, German and history; later on it was the same with Herr Wackernell, who instructed us on the building of bridges, roads and houses.

There were only a few months to go to the final examinations—a trade test which confers the title of surveyor to be sure, but which concludes a very superficial training. I felt sure of passing the exam, even though all the instructors were against me. I was not prepared to be a model student just to keep in their good books. By then I was grown up and was making my own decisions. I had learned to survive on the hardest faces. The other part of my life could not consist of being submissive, of repeating the teachers' aphorisms and otherwise shutting up!

In an old sawmill in Villnöss I studied for the final examination. Between-times I climbed on the stone walls round about. Each weekend I was in the mountains: Drei Zinnen, Mugonispitze, Marmolada. In June I flunked the exam.

THE CIVETTA WAS ONE of my favourites and I knew it well. In 1966 I was there once more: this time Heini Holzer was my partner. Heini and I were good friends. Both twenty years old, both hard up, but full of curiosity. Heini was a romantic who wanted recognition but he was reliable, no matter how much he idealised reality. We pursued the same aims and climbed happily together. We spent two weeks in the Civetta range and although between climbs we were able to afford only spaghetti at best, we were in high spirits. Free as the motto 'what price the world', we lived in a tent by the lake called

Coldaisee and climbed every day. In only two weeks we were to succeed on the hardest and biggest routes. An early repeat of the Philipp-Flamm Route, the East Face of the Cima Bancon, several first ascents. Twelve of the big Civetta and Pelmo routes we put behind us without incident. These were the most successful weeks of my mountaineering career. The disgrace of scholastic failure was already almost forgotten. Besides, there was the chance to resit in the autumn.

The Civetta is rich in rock forms. It is a gigantic wall several kilometres wide, the 'Wall of Walls', as it is called. To the left of the principal flight are portly towers and on the right buttresses reaching for the sky.

In the Valozzer chain stands the broad mass of the Busazza and right in front the 'Tower of Towers', the finely drawn Torre Trieste. On the left the Torre Venezia stands out imposingly, in between the Cima Bancon pushes itself forward like a ship's prow. Hidden in the Pelsakamm lie the Campanile Brabante, the top of which is broader than the bottom, and the Guglia di Rudatis, which stands there like a needle. It's a wonder they haven't fallen down. Everything blends together in harmony—each summit by itself would not be exciting. However, as a whole the massif of the Civetta is a unique mountain—a perfect mountain.

Like a huge organ the North-West Face of the Civetta overshadows the Alleghe valley. Seldom does it receive any sunshine. No birds nest up there, think those who wander past beneath this mighty flight of rock. But it is not so. Rare birds do roost up there from time to time. 'We must roost' was the jargon at that time of extreme climbers when it was necessary to bivouac. At that time a bivouac was as much a part of a big rock climb as his stout boots are to the walker. One had always to be prepared for it and to look for a suitable place in time. Often I found a protected spot, sometimes only a narrow ledge, on rare occasions a cave.

Those who did not want to have to bivouac in ètriers on overhanging faces had to take a hammock with them. It is no pleasure to sleep in these soft swings, and getting into one is awkward. Without hammocks and without a sleeping-bag, however, sleeping was unthinkable.

In the Dolomites in summer a simple Zdarsky sack sufficed for us as protection against weather and cold. On the big mixed routes in the western Alps I took a down jacket with me as a precaution, so as not to freeze if there was a sudden fall in temperature. Such falls can turn summer into winter. Even in good weather a night in the open required stamina. A bivouac is always unpleasant, even if one remembers it with pleasure.

For many hours Heini and I had been climbing the hardest cracks on the Punta Civetta. We were fairly late starting the Aste Route. And it was raining. Frequently we had to wait because waterfalls made further progress on the face impossible. Heini Holzer was a small, restless chap. In cracks he climbed well, but on the open face he sometimes lost control. On this particular day he had insisted on leading all the way. Around five o'clock in the afternoon we began our preparations for the night. Protected from the rain by a mighty overhang, we could work undisturbed. At first we lay down on a narrow ledge and tried to sleep. It was hard and cold. For a while we dozed alongside each other. However, suddenly our nest pleased us no more. And when Heini wanted something different, something different it had to be. Even if the difference proved only to be in his imagination. Heini was a reliable climbing partner with that superficial cheerfulness which injured people frequently exhibit. He had had a hard childhood. Later, before he became a professional mountaineer, he earned his living as a chimney-sweep. But not only did he have to live a spartan life, he also wanted one. His romantic and at the same time élitist picture of the world prescribed it. Why do things the hard way when you don't have to? I thought to myself. Why be cold when we could have been warm? In no time we were wide awake. Again we began nest building.

At the end of the dièdre we spun ropes between the face and the top of a pillar. We plaited our eighty-metre-long rope into a net. The home-made hammock was ready. It needed only two secure handrails—who wants to tumble out of bed 700 metres above the floor?—and we laid ourselves down in the soft nest.

We clapped the bivi sack over us and warmed each other up. Now we slept up there like two eagles in an eyrie. The hard free climbing of the past day lay in our arms and legs. Our route had led up a system of cracks, dièdres and chimneys, and had been continuously extremely hard. Immediately after the broken rocks at the start the climbing had become exposed: the face was vertical and no pitons would go in for many pitches. On the Aste Route climbing slings are superfluous.

The Wall of Walls, the North-West Face of the Civetta rises like a huge set of organ pipes over the Alleghe valley. In the sixties it offered some of the hardest climbing in the Alps.

When we awoke next morning our glance went first to the gigantic over-hang which arched over us. That was a hard nut for breakfast. I looked down through the mesh of the hammock: for hundreds of metres the view downwards was uninterrupted, as far as the cirque.

We were able to turn the overhang on the right. Up an extremely hard crack we climbed the summit couloir and above this, after several hours, the Punta Civetta. It was a bright morning. The weather had finally turned good. Up out of the hollow of the alpine meadow tinkled scattered cow bells. We stretched out in the sun and frittered away our time—as people always like to call this pleasure in the useless.

WE HAD SAVED THE GRANDEST climb on the Civetta at that time till last. The slender sickle of the waning moon stood above Monte Pelmo as we left our tent by the Coldaisee. It was still night-time. Silently we stumbled up the cirque under the face of the Civetta, time and again having to use the torch. From the Tissi Hut, too, a point of light approached the northern face.

Once arrived at the foot of the face, we looked for the start of the climb, shining our torches up the wall. How ridiculous that seemed to me. The beam from our torch on this 1000-metre-high wall was like trying to illuminate a cathedral with one match.

The centre of the Civetta face offered at that time some of the hardest climbs in the whole arc of the Alps. Back in 1925 Emil Solleder, from Munich, and Gustl Lettenbauer, who had already failed in an attempt, found a direct route to the summit—a route which for several years counted as the hardest in the world. There were waterfalls to climb up, dark, overhanging mossy chimneys, and inevitable stonefall to look out for. The Solleder Route became compulsory. The best climbers attempted it: Toni Schmid, who later with his brother was the first to climb the North Face of the Matterhorn; Leo Rittler, the daredevil from the Kaisergebirge; Walter Stösser with his friends Hall and Schutt; the Eiger North Face man, Anderl Heckmaier, naturally; Hans Steger and Paula Wiesinger; Fritz Kasparek, Attilio Tissi and all the rest: the climbing heroes of the inter-war period. In 1932 Leo Maduschka, a romantic dreamer and the poet of the 'Bergvagabunden', perished in the waterfalls of the Civetta during a sudden change in the weather. The face became a legend.

Between 1930 and 1940 still harder ascents were put up: the Andrich-Fae on the Punta Civetta, the Ratti on the Cima Su Alto and the Comici on the main peak. After the Second World War, between 1950 and 1960, the Livanos Dièdre was opened up and then the Philipp-Flamm. This last, climbed for the first time in September 1957 by Walter Philipp and Dieter Flamm in three days, is a huge system of dièdres to the left of the Solleder. It leads up the Punta Tissi, a 2992-metre-high pinnacle on the ridge of the Civetta. Thus there is no summit—it's all about the route. This Philipp-Flamm was notorious and feared; it rated as the largest scale free climb in the eastern Alps. The chroniclers totted up—as with the Solleder thirty years before— the number of times it had been repeated. The best climbers from Germany, Britain, France, Austria and Switzerland came to attempt this route. The Belgian Claudio Barbier, who had made the second ascent with Ernst Steger from the South Tyrol, expressed himself to be more than respectful of this route: 'Rather the Andrich-Fae solo than the Philipp-Flamm roped,' was his verdict.

Frightful rumours circulated about it and Sepp Mayerl, the steeplejack from the eastern Tyrol, whom Heini and I esteemed above all others, had described the Philipp-Flamm as his hardest climb. He had fallen a few metres below the Schuppendach (the Garage Roof), and plunged thirty metres. One rope had broken and he was left hanging on the other, bleeding, injured and shocked.

Now Heini and I were sitting under this wall which would take no more than forty pitons throughout its 900 metres of climbing. We felt crushed by the dark heaviness above us, by this vertical wall so difficult to inspect, as we looked for a possible start at the upper edge of the scree slope. What if it rains? If we don't make it? If one of us falls? It was still dark. We sat down again under an overhanging block of rock. During this waiting, this period of inaction, uneasiness condensed into anxiety. Yet with the daylight the doubts fell away. With visibility tranquillity returned to the scenery and to us. Far below, the lights of Alleghe faded. The slowly reddening horizon in the east was serrated, the stars now scarcely visible.

Stones fell continually from above. A few stone salvos burst near us in the cirque. Instinctively we ducked. In spite of all the dangers we wanted to be up there. We were ambitious and we wanted to experience new frontiers. Yesterday we had lain all day in the sun by the Coldaisee, preparing ourselves psychologically for this moment.

Both of us had read a great deal about the Philipp-Flamm Route on the Punta Tissi. Both of us were anticipating the climb of a lifetime. We were not trying to prove anything. We just wanted to come through and do justice to ourselves. This climb was not about proving which of us, man or mountain, was the stronger—neither victory nor defeat was the alternative, rather the conquest of self.

It had got light. We hurried up a stonefall-prone gully to the beginning of the vertical wall above. We roped up quickly and began climbing the vertical rock. Yes, they were right, few pitons went in on this Philipp-Flamm. However, the holds were firm and we felt strong. We climbed safely. Unexpectedly quickly we reached the beginning of the big yellow dièdre—the key to the wall. Three hundred metres high, smooth and overhanging, it rose obliquely up to the left.

Slowly I worked myself up the smoothly polished left-hand wall of the dièdre, step by step. Sometimes only by centimetres. Time and again I believed myself to be at the end of my capabilities, yet always I found another hold, a finger's breadth on which I could stand. Heini led the next pitch. Up a tortuous crack in the back of the dièdre he forced himself higher. Cracks were his speciality. After fifteen minutes he was standing forty metres above me, like a fly on the wall.

Belayed from above, I followed, handed over the rucksack which, with us, was customarily carried by the second, and continued climbing. For my peace of mind Heini assured me that he had secured himself to three pitons. If you want to survive in climbing you secure yourself impeccably at stances, that we had learned from Sepp Mayerl.

The crack dièdre now in front of me was the crux pitch—with one place where neither feet nor hands could find hold. The rock was completely smooth. In earlier days a piton had been placed there. Now, however, the flake of rock behind which the safety aid had been fastened was no more. Presumably it had vanished into the depths along with the piton ripped out by Sepp Mayerl's fall. I had neither the possibility nor a free hand to be able to bang in a fresh piton in this exposed position. And where was I to put it anyway? One can only fix ordinary pegs in holes or fissures, yet here in this rock neither the one nor the other was available. In theory I could have drilled a hole, in order to secure myself to a bolt. But Heini and I rejected this technique. We never carried a drill. Either the section went without this technical aid or we turned back. After all, the first men up the route had not used a drill.

Below me the face fell perpendicularly for 400 metres to the cirque. Breathtaking, this downward view. On tiny rugosities I stood on the vertical face, like a four-legged spider on a house wall. The scenery impressed me but could not intimidate me. I took care to keep my weight on my feet. My arms and fingertips were, as far as possible, only for keeping in balance. This climbing technique was customary at that time on big walls. Nevertheless my upper body had to be braced if I were not to fall over backwards off the face. Instinctively I placed both soles flat on the gaping walls of the dièdre and leaned inwards. Thus I was standing more or less bent over forwards and held myself in balance by friction. Bridging wide, in turn I pressed the moulded rubber soles of my clumsy climbing boots and the palms of my hands diagonally on the rock. I climbed according to the three-point rule: first I took the weight off a foot and placed it higher. Then the other. First of all—with my right foot and left hand fully weighted—I got my right hand free in order to place it higher.

What wouldn't I have given up there for a real hold! Still more for a solid piton. Often I could not shake off the feeling of slipping. Don't panic! 'No sudden movements,' I said to myself, 'just don't panic.' For that would have paralysed me.

I needed minutes for those few holdless metres. I climbed at the point of falling and had lost all sense of time. I was concerned solely with not falling off the wall. Getting up was secondary. Besides, at this moment there was no going back.

There were still two metres to go to a small recess—the next stance—which I had already spotted. These two metres, however, were not only smooth, they were brittle and overhanging. It appeared to be impossible to climb any further. My fingers were sweating. A trembling went through my body. I gazed down. The rope hung freely beneath me. When a stone broke loose from the rotten wall it fell hundreds of metres down the precipice without hitting anything. 'Careful does it, keep calm,' I said to myself—and 'there's no going back.' Otherwise I would have done so.

Onwards therefore. Three firm points. Everything around me was forgotten, my whole attention was concentrated on fingertips and boot soles. Right foot lifted, sole placed, weighted. Suddenly I no longer had the courage to stand up straight. At each attempt I had the feeling I was slipping away down. Enough to drive one to despair! I didn't curse, I didn't pray, I only hoped. Was the friction insufficient to hold my ten-stone weight? 'Flying!' I bawled suddenly. That calmed me and was to warn Heini that I was about to fall.

However, I did not fall. I knew that the slightest false movement would be my last controllable action. Whatever move I made next I must manage before my strength ran out, otherwise it would be too late. I risked a balancing act, straightened up, made the big effort, forgot once more myself and everything around me—was just boot soles, rock, friction—and was up. A glance down at the rope to my companion calmed me. I had straightened myself and it had worked—perhaps only because I had known that my friend was standing below belaying me.

The overhanging roof which arched above us required something like death-defying courage, using the layback technique. It went horizontally for two or three metres. That much we knew from stories. Was that just climbers' talk? Many had turned back from these two pitches. A few had fallen. Nevertheless we tried it. We had got this far, now we were attempting the Schuppendach.

Pressed close together, Heini and I stood on the stance, sizing up the overhang. We weren't gamblers playing with our lives, we were playing with our abilities. Nor were we idealists, offering ourselves up for a higher concept. We were two young men, full of the joys of life, who plunged themselves into the unknown, in order to get acquainted with dimensions of existence beyond college and work. No, it was not the appeal of danger that thrilled us. We tried to reduce it to the minimum. In climbing to the limit of the possible, it is still always about living.

Heini led the next pitch. Once more he fingered the karabiners and pitons, which dangled from his climbing harness in order of size. With a casual glance he examined the knots by which the two ropes were secured to his harness. Then he untied himself from the stance. Briskly he climbed away over me up to the roof. A cleft the width of a fist separated the projecting roof from the face. On pencil-wide ledges, arms wedged in the crack in the roof, Heini worked his way leftwards, puffing and panting. In practised fashion he went round the seemingly impossible overhang and disappeared behind the edge of the rock. Only his legs could be seen for a few minutes longer. Regularly the rope ran through my fingers. 'Not too fierce,' Heini

On the South Face of the Torre Grande in the Cinque Torri group. At the age of eighteen I was fascinated by pitons and rope-ladders.

(Overleaf) The mountains of my childhood, the Geislerspitzen, with the Furchetta left, and the Fermeda Towers where Father taught me to climb.

called to me. He yodelled on his stance, as always when he had shaken off anxiety. Truly, it was a lovely bit of climbing, this roof traverse, and the rock was firm.

An exposed traverse and a succession of cracks brought us to the big couloir in the headwall. A dark throat with water, ice and snow lay before us. The route wasn't over yet. Over rock with good holds—albeit rather muddy—we climbed higher. Still more than ten pitches separated us from Quota 2992 IGM, as Punta Tissi was shown on the maps at that time. The tension, as each puzzle unravelled before us, dissolved time and again in joyfulness. Without uncertainty one does not have these redeeming moments.

The mud and the water in the summit shoot gave us more to do than the climbing to reach it. We wished we were on the summit, yet we felt scarcely tired and not the least need for intermediate belays. The feeling that there was no connection between body and brain, that my movements were automatic, made me feel secure. It was a blending of flowing movements.

Suddenly Heini stuck fast while leading. In an unsafe spot, thrown out of rhythm by an ice flake, he clung to the wall forlornly. Helplessly he scraped at the water ice with his left foot. 'Damned icing-up!'

It was deathly still in the summit couloir, the only sounds the drip of water and the wind. At each anticipated movement from Heini I held my breath and gripped the rope tighter. 'Look, there's a dry spot left of the roof.' I said it as if I wanted to excuse him the anxiety which I sensed.

'I can manage.'

'Bang in a peg.'

'It won't go in.'

Nevertheless each word was a help, an encouragement.

Suddenly I noticed a determination in Heini's movements. He bridged to the left, still further, made it! There was life in the rope once more. Regularly it ran through my fingers. 'On stance!' sounded from above. 'Come on!'

I untied, knocked out the belay piton and began to climb.

'Coming.'

Not only joy at success, but a blissful feeling of freedom swelled up in me, as after a bad experience which does no permanent damage; as if an air balloon was carrying us aloft.

After a final overhang we stood on the summit ridge. All the tension fell away from us. For a few moments I was sure I would do everything, but

Climbing free on the Heiligkreuzkofel in 1969.

53

everything. At that time I did not suspect that in the wide beyond there was a world of faces and summits of which I scarcely knew.

ON THE WALKER SPUR, on the Grandes Jorasses in the Mont Blanc chain, Fritz Zambra, Sepp Mayerl, Peter Habeler and I needed two days, so iced up was the second half or the face. That is why I nearly arrived in Bolzano too late for the re-examination. I arrived in time, but failed nevertheless. What now? I didn't want to go back to college. My father refused to support me any more. So I laid down the tools with which for more than a decade I had made hen-houses at home in the holidays and looked for a paid job.

My elder brother Helmut advocated that I teach for a year as assistant master at the newly opened secondary school in Eppan. There was a severe shortage of secondary school teachers in South Tyrol at the time which was the only reason I was taken on, as a stop-gap, to teach maths and nature study for nine months to three classes of eleven- and twelve-year-olds, a circumstance which was only bearable on account of my inherited inclination for teaching.

I had found myself a room with the Pattis family near Eppan and also ate there when I was not away. In the spring I wanted to make up for the failed matriculation by studying privately and then to go to university to study surface and underground construction engineering or architecture. I still felt myself unready for a six-day week and eight-hour day.

Each weekend now I went climbing. My pay as a secondary school teacher was modest, nevertheless financially I had never been so free. On the mountain, too, I wanted to progress a step further now.

In October I gave in to the allure of my first solo ascent of a 'sixer'. Here I could do everything for myself: I selected the route, determined on a style and was then player and referee all in one. After sixteen years at school, after pressures of all sorts, notes and punishments I was finally free of teachers. Free for more self-responsibility.

The morning was grey and cheerless. Reluctantly I passed the Sunday morning in my little room in Eppan. Suddenly the mist tore apart. The sun was out. A short time later I was on my way to the Sella Pass. Alone. It was already past midday. Beneath the southern walls of the Piz-de-Ciavàces I rummaged a rope, some belay slings and karabiners out of my rucksack and climbed away. I climbed as usual, only there was no partner on the other end of the rope. The start was easy. In a big chimney crack I thought of the rope

My first solo 'sixer' was the Soldà route on the South Face of the Piz-de-Ciavàces.

for the first time. However, there were no pitons there and I felt strong enough to overcome the place without safety.

On the Gamsband (Cengia dei Camosci), the Chamois Ledge, in the middle of the face such a joy came over me that, without stopping to rest, I stormed on up into the yellow overhangs which make up the crux of the Soldà Route. The exposure increased.

Between the overhangs I climbed higher, almost always using bridging technique, the loose rope wriggling free in the air. To outsiders this scene must have looked dangerous. Yet, like the jackdaws in their play, I too progressed—safe and free. They climbed, glided through the air, plunged straight as an arrow downwards. Often they let themselves fall for a hundred metres and more, before catching themselves again. A light puff of wind and already they were floating higher again. Scarcely a wing-beat.

This game with nature, with my own abilities, above the void was, by myself, somewhat more intense. The smallest error would have been fatal. A last overhanging dièdre and I was standing on the slanting summit slope. I was up.

Alone, I sat there in the rubble. I was still suspended above the abyss. Again I looked at the jackdaws as they danced above it. I thought of Gino Soldà, the first man to climb this daring free route, and of my future. In 1947 a youngster no longer, Soldà had yet summoned up the courage to climb this overhanging couloir dièdre, without knowing whether it was possible. One can go climbing for a lifetime, I thought, and also alone if one always identifies completely with oneself and the rock. Concentration is so important.

Later I climbed down. And when, in the afternoon, I looked for the jackdaws on Piz-de-Ciavàces, from the road between Canazei and the Sella Pass, I found them not. I saw only yellow overhanging walls, and a desire to set out seized me. There were new dimensions. I saw now that something in me had changed. An examination was not important, rather the identification with one's own goals. I had to give my life an unequivocal direction.

4

WINTER FIRSTS

1966–67

IT WAS QUIET AGAIN IN CISLES. The funicular and the cable car had been still for a long time. We rambled up from St Christina to the Regensburger (Geisler) Hut. Amongst the dark pines stood red-yellow larches. The sunny south faces of the Geislerspitze peaks rose sharply from the yellowy-brown upland meadows. There was not a soul for miles around. This was Cisles, the Cisles Alps, as I knew them from my childhood.

Abruptly the walls of the Stevia rose above us. There ought to be a Vinatzer Route there that was still a 'sixer' in its original sense, so it was said. Hans Vinatzer was a Grödner climber. In his youth, at the age of twenty-five, he climbed brilliantly; especially on poor rock and in cracks. His first ascents—the North Face Direct on the Furchetta, Marmolada di Rocca South Face, the Stevia-Riss—rated still, thirty years on, as touchstones for every Dolomite climber.

Curiously I searched the walls for a crack, the Vinatzer Crack. There, where the face overhung most, he had climbed up the white-yellow flight of rock and under a roof he had lost his way. Now we understood why this crack rated as one of the fiercest of Dolomite climbs.

In the hut, we met the mountain guide, and partner of Hermann Buhl, Kuno Rainer. In his time—shortly after the Second World War—he had twice prospected the Stevia Face. However, after the first few pitches he had given up. Too friable, too difficult. He encouraged us nevertheless to risk an attempt, gave us some good bits of advice, then set off down to St Christina. That was quite usual with mountaineers: no one was so mad that he never found another madman who understood.

It was already light when we quitted the hut next day. Heavy clouds hung in the sky and on the Langkofel there was a grey cap of mist and everything far below the Pichlwarte, on top of the North Pillar, was obscured. The eaves of the roof went and in just an hour Heini and I were standing at the foot of the overhanging crack. After the first hundred metres it already overhung by ten metres. And that was to be all free climbing? I bridged up the outside and so reached a deep hole in the crack. Each handhold was loose. The rock could not be pulled on, one had to press it with one's hand. Footholds fell away as scree as the weight came off. There were no intermediate pitons in. Only on the traverse of the roof did we find two spikes for safety: one deep down inside, the other, a mammoth piton, on the edge of the roof. The climbing there was still 'more criminal' than the first pitches. From the roof it went on vertically and free. Below me I saw only the boulders in the cirque, and it was the drop which roused new powers which opened my eyes to the danger. It was breathtaking. It had rained slightly and the last hundred metres were wet and mossy. Luckily the rock here was not so smooth. Under the big final overhang we traversed right and finished up on an alpine meadow. We lay down on the grass and were devilishly pleased with ourselves. We had learned to admire a man, who had first climbed this and many other routes in the Dolomites before Heini and I had been born.

THE ELEVENTH OF FEBRUARY used to be a national holiday in Italy. In 1967 it fell on a Saturday, so on the following Monday I had no school. These three days were the only ones during the winter which allowed me a longer excursion into the mountains. I was still working as a schoolteacher and was conscientious. On the ninth I sent a telegram to East Tyrol worded as follows: 'Am ready. Agnèr. Friday evening.' Sepp Mayerl came. As the undertaking was risky with only two, we looked for another 'madman' who wanted to join in. My frequent partner on the rope, my distant relation Heindl Messner, now a farmer in Villnöss, came along. For once someone else could milk the cows.

Winter ascents at that time were no longer the latest fashion but just as hard as when the first winter ascents of the north faces of the Eiger and Matterhorn had caused a stir in the press. I wanted to gain new experience. It is much harder to climb a Dolomite face in winter, not only because it is cold and the days are short but above all because snow and ice lie on hand- and footholds. On the following Tuesday I was obliged to be absent from school without permission. We didn't get back from the mountain with the long edge for four days.

I dozed, slept, was shaken awake. Again I dozed, slept. Sepp was driving. The back seat of his Volkswagen was my bed. It was night-time. Soon it would be morning, a cold morning. The name 'Pellegrinon' tore me from my more or less gentle sleep. Sepp had asked a passer-by for the whereabouts of the well-known mountaineer Pepi Pellegrinon. So we must be in Falcade.

In the bar into which the stranger led us we met Pepi's mother. 'Where is the great Pala climber?' I asked.

'*Dorme*'—He's sleeping.

'That doesn't matter, he's to get up, he's our friend,' we explained to her.

He came. Sleepy and unshaven but curious. 'What have you been doing recently?' That was his first question.

'Not much, but we have something on now.' We asked for a sketch of the Agnèr Nordkante.

Pepi went quite quiet. Anything we could have from Pepi, but a sketch of Agnèr, in the middle of winter, that was asking too much. His expression was at first hostile, then quite calm. Had we thwarted his plans? We invited him to come with us. He was to be the fourth, the missing man, I assured him. He had no time, he said, he had to work at the Italian long-distance skiing championships. So we remained a trio.

Pepi made us a sketch, as only he could: simple and clear. He had already tried the North Ridge in winter and been turned back. He wanted this winter ascent too—we understood that, it was his Pala, he was at home there, the local matador, but we wanted it too.

Goodbye and good luck! It was 11 February: we had a sketch.

There was no more doubt. The blue sky, the highly trained Sepp, we would do the Agnèr Ridge, now in mid-winter. Caviola, Forno Canale, Cencenighe. We drove through derelict villages, over broken-down bridges, past broad, silted-up stream-beds. The storms of November 1966 had devastated whole tracts of land here.

Heindl wiped the misty windscreen. 'Agnèr!' Sepp stopped the car. We had talked previously about the long buttress. Now we said nothing. No one asked. Each recognised the peak. We pressed our noses against the windscreen. We all three were amazed.

I had become faint-hearted. Big I had pictured it to myself, but not this big. From the valley bottom it rose 1600 metres into the air, all almost vertical, finely drawn silhouette. It was lightly covered in snow and stood completely in shade.

I shivered at the thought of the days to come.

In Taibon we found the small road which leads up a narrow valley between Monte Agnèr and the chain of Pale di San Lucano. We followed this as far as the woods at the foot of the ridge. No one said a word. We had the mountain before us. Under an old tumbledown hut we packed our rucksacks, sorted climbing gear and changed our clothes. Now at last it was time for the 'long edge'.

A farmer was dragging his sledge valleywards. As he passed us, we threw him an orange. A contemptuous smile showed fleetingly at the corner of his mouth. He exuded incomprehension. We were part of the affluent society, yet did not stay home in the warm. He didn't understand us, he took us for mad. He saw the Edge every day and yet he never looked at it.

It was midday by the time we set out. Just under the base of the plinth we picked up Pellegrinon's route. Up that we climbed to the little notch below the first rise.

To the left of the notch I spotted the best place to start the ascent. I set off. This was not proper rock-climbing: icy, grassy terrain, often dwarf pines served as running belays. We had to cross gullies full of deep powder snow. Sweat dripped off us. By four o'clock in the afternoon we were standing at the start of the ridge proper. Beneath lay 300 metres of the climb. More than four times as much lay ahead of us.

Sepp wanted to brew tea. The spot was favourable so we did some quick unpacking. 'Lighter, please.' The little petrol stove didn't want to burn. Damn! We warmed it, tried everything. In vain. Burning wooden wedges wouldn't get us far either; we had only two. Nearby stood an old weather-beaten larch. We could have felled it; it would have provided us with wood. But tomorrow . . . and the day after. . . . That was the first setback.

Sepp decided to go back down to Taibon to procure a cooker. Without one it was hopeless carrying on climbing. Tomorrow he would climb up after us. With two great rucksacks Heindl and I broke trail up through the deep powder snow. Often we sank up to our stomachs in the snow between the pines. Again we reached a step in the ridge. With our rucksacks, Grade III and IV climbing became a problem. Far away we heard Sepp calling. He was down; tomorrow he would bring a cooker.

Meanwhile Heindl and I had reached the first big steep wall. The sun went down. Its last rays hung over the Civetta. We dug a deep hole in the snow and threw pine twigs into it: straw for a mattress. Then we lay down to sleep.

Soon the first stars were glimmering in the sky. Night brought extreme cold and dark anxiety. Slowly we became stiff in our snow hole. All we said to each other was: 'Sepp will be back tomorrow', or 'Tomorrow we shall be far above'. We could not sleep. So in our thoughts we climbed higher up the edge—to the sky, to the morning.

One by one the lights went out deep down in the village. Above the mountains to the east lay a red glimmer. The stars vanished, morning came. At last. Still it was too cold to think of doing anything, let alone climbing.

It was daylight, 12 February. As we had not slept, there was no need to wake up. We stood up and took a swig from the flask which we had kept warm in the sleeping-bag. Where was Sepp? The village was a long way off. A shout! We looked about. Slowly Sepp was climbing up our tracks. He would be here soon! He was bringing the cooker! We waited. Then he was with us and made steaming-hot tea.

After a few pitches we pushed up over an overhang then, unroped, we climbed over both the big fields of dwarf pines where there was a lot of powder snow. Above the second pine field the ridge was steep and unfriendly. Now came the ramp. Clearly, the only possibility of progressing here was a broad ramp to the right of the knife-edge. The lot fell to me. I surrendered the rucksack and led off. This ramp was many rope-lengths long, in part iced up. Up above I found the correct traverse back to the ridge. Up this we now made good speed.

Then for the first time on this mountain the sun reached us. 'The sun!' All three of us shouted at once, yet we knew it would soon be dark again. Long before we could get warm, the sun was gone. After several pitches we stood under the headwall. Here was the last possible bivouac site. Heindl began to clear a small platform while Sepp and I prepared the completely iced-up traverse to the summit wall, which presented the main difficulty of the whole route.

For a long time we sat, chatting together over tea, buckthorn juice and fried bacon. One of us told of another hard camp in the open in the middle of winter.

It was very cold, 20°C below zero. We sat leaning against the rock wall and waited until it was morning. I felt uneasy. I shuddered at the prospect of further ascent, at the same time I was scared of going back down. Nonetheless I awaited the morning full of impatience. The cold stuck in our backsides, it crept into our boots, it sat in the bivi sack. It shook us.

Morning dawned at last. Sepp led up a smooth dièdre, sticking his big fist over and over again in an iced crack and thus hoisting himself upwards. He led us safely, he came through everything.

In the afternoon sunshine we climbed up the last pitches. Up above we untied and climbed wearily, each for himself, step by step, to the summit. For a whole hour we sat on the top and thanked each other. I was happy to have taken part—even if on account of my tardiness I were to lose my job as schoolteacher.

THE FURCHETTA WAS ALWAYS my ideal peak. Steep, vertical walls—and such a shape! When I was a small boy I had gazed at it a thousand times, at first from St Peter, then from the Gschmagenhart meadows.

I still remembered a walk with my father. We stood between the forest and the cirque and stared up at the North Face. It seemed to be endlessly high. The sun strafed the uppermost part of the face, and in the vicinity of the summit floated many small white dots. They must have been birds.

As I gazed down from high up on the North Face for the first time, I did so with horror. I did not dare to step on the edge of the precipice. Ten years later I was able to climb this face, on a summer's Sunday. Now it was my ambition to climb 'my' face in winter too. And to be the first to do so at that.

Some weeks after the winter ascent of the North Ridge of Agnèr, I met Heindl in Villnöss. We decided nothing definitely and separated with a 'Perhaps'!

One morning at the beginning of March it was so warm in Eppan that I couldn't bear it any longer. I drove to Villnöss and found Heindl. He was standing at the stable door and when I saw his resolute grin, I knew that we would be setting off next day.

The evening was clear and cold. Yet once more we trained our binoculars on the North Face. Snow lay on it, an unreal amount of snow. The risk was high. I passed a restless night. I was about to realise one of my dreams. On my home ground no one was going to forestall me!

We set out at three o'clock in the morning. Walter Troi, a friend who had got up specially, took us in his vehicle as far as the last farmhouse in the valley. There we shouldered our rucksacks, buckled on our skis and sped away.

The Furchetta was always my ideal peak. I gazed out on it in wonder every day as a small boy and in 1967 made the first winter ascent of the North Face. The most accessible of the Dolomites, just east of the Brenner Pass, the Geisler group deserves to be better known by visiting climbers.

A Volkswagen with Munich plates was standing by the roadside. What did they want here then? We flashed our torches inside the car. There were slings and wooden wedges, a helmet. Others were on the way to the North Face. Were they already up? We felt heavy, tired and clumsy—we would have liked to sit down. All on account of a wooden wedge in a Munich Volkswagen.

On the Glatschalm it became light. Nevertheless we noticed a lamp shining between the rough log timbers of the barn. So they were sitting in there. Without a word Heindl and I slunk past the hut. When we were about a hundred metres further on, the others were putting on their skis in front of the hut. They followed us. I was glad I hadn't overslept this morning. In the cirque, immediately under the face, we got to know each other. Konrad Renzler, Siegfried Hilber and Ernst Steger were climbers from the Pustertal, a strong team. At the start of the climb we all stood together briefly: the then best climbers in South Tyrol, plus Heindl and me. Heindl and I climbed as the first pair. It was icy and snow lay in the holds, but we had soon climbed ourselves warm and gripped the icy rock more securely. Nevertheless we had to safeguard every metre. Of the others we saw nothing more. Where were they? Towards midday we reached the Dülferkanzel, a rock ledge. We had trouble getting our cooker going. However, that was the least problem. What really worried us was the knowledge that dry snow was lying on the headwall. I felt uncomfortable. That headwall was steep and difficult and now all the hand- and footholds were fully snowed up. From below the conditions on the headwall had looked so good!

We climbed on at once. The weather deteriorated. On the horizon stretched long white strips of cloud and with them the first snow flurries. The first vertical cracks soon lay beneath us. The precipice opened up. I had to clean the exit from the big cave passage before I could find support. I admired Heindl who bridged across this spot with his twenty-kilo rucksack. The traverse of the row of cracks from left to right gave me no trouble.

I stuck just on the friable crack under the final roof as, far below, I saw the Pustertal men skiing away, stem-turning in the snow. Climbing the completely vertical wall, I knew that they had failed. I felt no gloating, the wall demanded my total ability. Heindl lugged the heavy equipment and food for three days on his back: we had provided for two bivouacs. Although the few firm holds were covered in snow and the pitons were loose, although the exit roof was iced up—we made it. In a day. In the exit chimney we lost time because the cram-full rucksack jammed. At six o'clock in the evening we were finally standing on the same stone on which we had stood years before. We had to smile at the thought of how inexperienced we had been then.

The ordinary route on the south side was largely free of snow. Quickly we reached the notch between the Furchetta and the Sass Rigais. By now it was dark. We abseiled off and plodded down the couloir on good firn snow.

5

CLIMBING FREE

1967

LOOKING AT THE DIRUPI DI LARSEC from Pera di Fassa, the eye comes to rest, inevitably, on a large and conspicuous triangular-shaped rock roof. This prominent roof—it is easily the biggest in the neighbourhood—had been climbed, as I came to know during those months in which technical piton climbing gave us more fun than free climbing. On the Drei Zinnen (Tre Cime di Lavaredo) we had got up some faces which overhung from bottom to top. Now we were burning to try out all similar routes in the Dolomites. Only one repeat of this huge roof was known up to then, and so we put this route on our programme.

In May we met up on the high pasture beneath the dry south walls of the Larsec group. Günther and I made up one rope, Heini Holzer and Heindl Messner the other. We discovered that one of the hay barns was not locked, so all four of us installed ourselves inside. Early next morning we climbed up through the sparse pine wood to the start. Unexpectedly quickly we reached the rise in the ridge under the huge yellow roof. Here it began to snow. We could have easily abseiled off. But we were climbing under the mighty overhangs. Outside the flakes whirled. As I hung in ètriers, a rope-length beneath the big roof while Günther belayed me from below, I watched the snowflakes. They fell quietly, a light puff of wind whirled them upwards again, but they did not come as far as us.

Soon Günther was hanging beside me. He was warm and enthusiastically started on the next pitch. But it was not long before he began to complain. The rock was rotten, the pitons held badly. Big stones broke away and clattered down 200 metres into the scree.

Günther advanced slowly. 'Frightful rubbish,' he kept saying, as he banged away at crevices and holes. He was glad when he could drive in a peg. Then he fished up one of the rope-ladders, with a "fifi" hook attached, which he had tied to his harness by two thin cords, and hung it from the piton. Carefully he placed a foot on the ètrier, weighted the middle rung, rocked a bit to test the piton and then climbed on the top rung. Then he repeated the process all over again. With the aid of this technique, one can 'unlock' 1000-metre walls, as we called this technical climbing. If there were no fissures one could, if one went in for that sort of thing, drill a hole and drive in a bolt. On our route there were a few such bolts.

Meanwhile the wind had got up. It drove the snowflakes against the face, blew them under the roof. Heini, who was climbing below me, was already quite white. His appearance amused me, for he was by trade a chimney-sweep. For more than an hour I stood in the same spot and froze. Meanwhile Günther climbed on doggedly. He cleared away debris and stones. He did not think of retreating, not for the time being.

What would it look like above the roof? Would the snow be lying there? Was retreat after the roof pitch still possible? My thoughts revolved around my duties as schoolmaster. Heini too had an anxious face. Almost simultaneously we burst out, 'We had better . . . ' 'Yes, we ought to turn back!' We didn't want to become the prisoners of this wall and I had to go to work again next day.

The following Sunday we were back in the barn under the Dirupi di Larsec. We were the same team. This time the keyed-up feeling, which gives such a route a large part of its attraction, was lacking for a long time. We knew the way, we knew the difficulties. Here a handhold, there the piton with the battered eye. There were no more unexpected places. Mechanically we climbed high using our ladders. I was almost bored. Already by early morning I was putting in a sling stance under the huge roof. Now everything changed.

The roof was stamped into our brains. Eight metres horizontally the rock projected. Here our strength must not desert us. With mixed feelings I began the dance on the ceiling. To begin with I could still reach the face with the tips of my toes, further out I hung from the roof like a marionette. Four hundred metres below in the cirque I could see isolated pine trees. From hook to hook, like a gymnast, I worked my way outwards.

It went more quickly and smoothly than I had imagined; also it was not so strenuous. Climbing a Grade V pitch free was harder than this game with ropes, karabiners and 'fifis', providing the pitons went in first time. When I was over the edge of the roof and had found two permanent pegs, I let Günther follow. As I was watching him, I thought of the final examination which lay ahead of me once more. Günther punched me on the arm and said, 'This artificial climbing is a joke,' and then, 'When you've done it once, the fun goes out of it, it's always the same after that.' I replied absentmindedly and thought of the bolts, which actually make anything possible. . . This was the day we decided to carry on from where we had been a year before, on the great free climbs. Silently I decided never in my life to place a bolt, never to take one with me.

We kept to the right and reached the summit ridge after several rises. The sun shone and we lay down to get sunburned. The only roof above us was the blue sky. And the only rules of mountaineering were our own.

WE HAD ALREADY TRIED the South-East Face of Cima Scotoni once. After the third pitch we had to give up. Lack of time was our excuse.

It was Heini Holzer who had told such horrid tales of the first ascent of this face. Shortly before he had read a report about it and could not sleep for three nights. There were places where one could hold on only with fingernails. A pendulum traverse, he had read, was indispensable, and that on a single, loose peg. A three-man pyramid was the crux of the face.

Meanwhile I had also been rummaging through all available alpine journals for reports on Cima Scotoni. In an old *Rivista Mensile* of the Club Alpino Italiano I found an informative article. Luigi Ghedina, a member of the original party, in a comparison of the then most difficult alpine faces, represented the South-East Face of Cima Scotoni as 'the face with the hardest climbing situations'.

Two attempts preceded the first ascent. In the summer of 1951, two of the strongest 'Scoiattoli' (Squirrels)—as members of a famous climbing club in Cortina d'Ampezzo called themselves—got as far as the centre of the face after fourteen hours of climbing. A smooth, crackless wall compelled them to turn back. Together with a third member of the club, they succeeded in making the first ascent a year later. Never before had they risked so much. The technical data of the climb were: thirty-eight hours' pure climbing time; two bivouacs on the face; top limit of the sixth grade; 140 ordinary pitons. Only two of them had been left in.

Of the first repeat of the Scotoni face we knew next to nothing. Only that Ignazio Piussi had been on it, a Dolomite climber as audacious as he was strong. Too much, yet too little we knew about this face. Too much to forget about it; too little to be able to plan an ascent in detail. We knew the start, but up above, what did it look like up above?

A week after our first attempt we were back again. The weather was good and we started climbing early. I was glad that we had left some pegs on the overhanging pitches during the first attempt. Then I had had to chip each hole in order to get the necessary belay pegs in. The rock was smooth and particularly unreceptive to pitons. Past familiar places we reached a stomach traverse, along which we crawled out on the first big ledge.

A pitch above the ledge it began to get extremely difficult. Via a steep wall with small handholds, I reached a yellow dièdre, which I climbed to a rock roof. With difficulty I was able to insert a reliable piton above the roof, the only one in the whole pitch. To the right began one of the notorious traverses. Part of it I could see, then an edge barred the view. 'If there isn't a handhold behind the edge, I shall have to jump off!' I shouted to Sepp, who was belaying below. Then I began to traverse to the right. With my fingers on the narrow ledges I progressed without problem. Behind the edge there was a handhold, a big one even. This sort of climbing pleased me: firm rock, small handholds and a single, free-climbing line, the only logical route.

At that time there were two directions in extreme mountaineering: technical and free climbing. Some people used all imaginable aids to achieve their goal. Others—among whom I counted myself—imposed limits on themselves, so as not to make the relationship between man and mountain too incongruous. A mountaineer can, through training, skill and experience, raise the limit of his performance and climb extremely difficult rock faces free, or he can overcome everything with technical aids without much risk and climbing skill. On repeat ascents I endeavoured always to bang in fewer pitons than the original climbers had done. A new route was for me only justifiable if I managed to find a line on the face which was possible with slight use of pitons. Ideally, in my view, a route would have been one which was climbed in a direct line, under the greatest difficulties without any technical aid, and leading to an 8000-metre summit. I knew this ideal was beyond human grasp; we could however approach it. In attempting that I see a possibility for the future development of mountaineering.

Over vertical places on the face, we had reached the crux. To the right of a completely blank wall, I laybacked up to a leaning flake, put a sling around the top of it and tried to pendulum to the left. Nothing doing. I could find no handhold, no crevices. It was impossible. Here, therefore, the first climbers must have used their human ladder.

I had another go at it, peering about for holes, ledges and fissures. Then I found by chance an eye in the rock, a tiny hole in the wall. In our jargon we called it an hour-glass. With much patience I was able to thread a sling and had won the day. Some quite small handholds, scarcely counting as such, were there. I climbed nimbly and stood on a narrow ledge. 'On stance!' I shouted with relief.

The face above us overhung considerably. Only an open dièdre permitted further progress. On the first ascent they had put in almost thirty pegs; Sepp Mayerl managed with five or six. After each reliable running belay he bridged up boldly—five, six, eight metres.

Above that was a second widish ledge. Things became easier. Without having to bang in more than one piton, we climbed higher. Mist came on. Heini Holzer and Renato Reali, who made up the second rope, and who were still climbing far below, lost track of us.

I struggled up the iced-up exit crack. For a while I forgot that it was snowing hard outside. Up on the summit ridge I saw the whirling flakes for the first time.

We had reached this summit by many detours. Only traverses, once right, once left, had made a free climb possible. The route was longer, to be sure, but a free climb. A technical direct ascent would in this case have been laughable. That the long free route was better than the short one, forced with pitons, no one could deny. But artificial direttissimas were the fashion. People who knew the free route, but didn't dare to do it, counted for nothing with me then. I had become a fanatical free-climber, without sensing that this fanaticism was eating up my inner freedom.

SOMETIMES, WHEN THE SUN SHONE for weeks, when a certain tune caught my ear, when my fingers had healed again after my last mountain trip, I was seized with such high spirits. My mother always used to say, 'You're full of beans!' This spring I was studying for matriculation and I had other things on my mind. But I knew that tomorrow, or the day after tomorrow, or on Sunday this face, that pillar, or a long snow ridge would be in good condition, so that I would be climbing again.

I used to be accused of escaping from reality in these climbing trips.

However, I had much more the feeling of escaping into reality. When I was up aloft, especially at the limit of my powers, I was doing my own thing; and this gut feeling is truth, reality.

The Via Ideale on the Marmolada d'Ombretta I had known about for years by repute. 'It is probably the hardest and most dangerous rock route in the whole Alps'; so the first man to make the ascent had written in one of the alpine monthlies. In this statement there stood much rebuff and much attraction.

Four of us met at the Falier Hut in July. Meanwhile I had passed my matriculation and considered this summer of 1967 as a sort of respite. In the autumn I would enrol in Padua. The guardian served us soup and tea in spite of the late hour. He enquired about our project: 'Via Ideale—*attenti all' acqua!*', Look out for the water, he warned, both enthusiastic and startled at the same time.

'*Due giorni basteranno?*' I asked.

'No, two days will not suffice—impossible!'

Aste and Solina had spent six full days on the face during the first ascent and had nailed their way out. Only six ordinary pitons and fourteen bolts were still in. Meanwhile several attempts to repeat the route had failed just above the start. Next morning we stood beneath the tremendous slabby massif of the Marmolada d'Ombretta. All four of us were impressed.

We started up the face just to the left of a big, leaning pillar. Straight away it was the hardest free climbing: chimneys, slabs, smoothly polished cracks. Not knowing where Aste and Solina had ascended, we searched for our own route. After several hours we reached a system of steep cracks and gullies that allowed a rapid advance. Where the cracks ran out, a serried flight of slabs built up. Far below me was the first peg, a bolt; I had climbed past it, without clipping in the rope. So we were on the right route. I found a second bolt somewhat higher up this pitch, then once more nothing but grey, holdless slabs.

It had got hot but suddenly we were in shade. Luckily the sun was no longer burning down on the grey south wall but, over the Ombretta Pass, mist was coming up—that could mean a thunderstorm. 'With a change in the weather, the Via Ideale becomes a dangerous trap,' Aste had warned. For the time being, however, there was nothing we could do except to look for a place to bivouac. It was too late for retreat.

Above a short bolt ladder we reached a spacious cave at the start of the final third of the wall. Inside it was damp, outside water dripped. We decided

The North Face of the Lankofel, where I was tested to my limit making the first solo ascent of the Solda route in 1969.

(Overleaf) The Civetta from the north-west.

to bivouac, although it was only five o'clock in the afternoon. The cave offered us protection from rain and security from stonefall. Perhaps it was the only safe spot on the Via Ideale. We didn't know.

We made ourselves comfortable in the cave, each arranging a little place for himself, for squatting or lying down. A night up there lasted a long time. In a bottle we found a slip of paper, on which Aste and Solina had scribbled good luck wishes to those who would come after them.

It was still dark when somewhere stones rumbled. Was it raining? The others were awake too. Sepp Mayerl shone the torch outside. No, it wasn't raining, it was pouring. In front of our cave a waterfall leaped down the face. From time to time stones whirred through the darkness. Now we knew the real worth of our shelter.

Many hours passed before we could decide it was morning. The mist rose. Out of the summit couloir waterfalls poured down. A retreat in these conditions would have been extremely risky. Water poured over the grey-black streaks of the ascent route below us. Pieces of ice and stones, which certainly would have carried us away, leaped in great bounds across the face. 'The weather can only get better,' said someone, so we decided to carry on.

First we had to pass the waterfall coming out of the summit stone shoot. Luckily the ground there was easy. We only kept dry by keeping a good lookout and climbing quickly. Detouring to the right, we reached an overhanging area of the face. 'Traverse left,' it said in the description. On a sloping shelf, I inched my way to the left and hoped that my soles would not slip. Here there were no handholds, a single running belay in forty metres. Up above it looked still worse. Out of a couloir shot a thick stream of water, enough to drive a small generating station. We had to go through it!

Sepp climbed up, first of all, to the cracks to the right of the waterfall, then disappeared into the couloir. The rope paid out slowly, very slowly. It must be hard, very hard. Through water and overhangs he had forced himself higher until he was just under an inclined gully, down which once more water was pouring. On the outside edges of the gully, I bridged up past this stream and so avoided getting much wetter than I already was. Then the couloir was barred by a steep step. The only weakness consisted of a crack in which all the water was collecting. In and up! A horrible thought. Retreat was unthinkable.

On the Neuenspitze, South Face. I had made the first direct ascent with Günther.

'Careful, Sepp!' I cried quickly and already I was standing under the icy shower-bath. It took my breath away. Struggling for air more than with the difficulties I gained a few metres. Stuck in the crack, I even managed to bang in a piton. The water ran down my collar and over my whole body. My boots overflowed. Finally I could see the handholds again, my head was above water. A little later I stood dripping wet and shivering with cold on the stance and belayed Sepp. He had knotted two slings on the rope in front of him. The water ran along the rope and dropped off the knots. Now it became easier, for a short stretch at least, and we got warmed up.

Again the couloir rose up steeply, again it was full of water. Far above an enormous icicle hung in the chimney. Aste had climbed to the right of a crack, using many pitons. To us it appeared hopeless. Too much water, too much ice, too awful weather. We had to reach the top that day, if we wanted to get out of here safe and sound. The wet was terrible. The waiting on the statices became unbearable. We could not have survived a night's bivouac in this condition. We were hypothermic and wet through . . .

To the right of the Aste-Solina Route, Sepp found a fairly dry crack. It went—or rather we made it go—with pitons, wooden wedges, knotted slings. Each of us, including Heini Holzer and Heindl Messner, who the day before had climbed in front, led a pitch, as his turn came. We surpassed ourselves in order to escape from this hell. In these conditions it did not bother us one bit that we were climbing up the refuse chute of the cable car station.

The crack went up an icy gully. It was full of filth, with splinters of glass everywhere, but we scarcely noticed. We had to get out of the wet cold. On top, for the first time, at the hut, someone said; 'What a rubbish tip!' And all at once we realised that we had climbed the last pitches through faeces from the sewer of the summit hut. For once, this Sunday, the guardian had not emptied his garbage pail down the gully. What a bit of luck!

IT WAS SATURDAY. We wanted to travel to the western Alps. However, a depression which struck the north side of the Alps made us wait and see. The western Alps were more exposed to storms than the eastern Alps and in the Dolomites the weather promised to hold. Sepp Mayerl and Renato Reali wanted to repeat the Aste-Susatti Route on the Punta Civetta. Renato, an Italian from Merano, was young and a brilliant climber. He was a friend of Heini Holzer. Heini and I had still not decided.

Towards nine o'clock in the evening we entered the Coldai Hut. What a surprise! Heinz Steinkötter, a successful limestone climber, was standing at the door. Heini and I liked him a lot. What was up with him? The usually friendly Heinz made a sour face. Our presence was obviously unwelcome. What lay behind that? Guess. No. Again. Yes, what else!

'Civetta-Direttissima?' I asked. No reply. Problem. His problem. My problem, for many weeks.

For years people had been looking for a new route between the Philipp-Flamm and the Solleder routes on the North-West Face of the Civetta. Two German groups had been on the face, then some 'Ragni di Lecco' (Lecco Spiders) tried and later a team from Trieste.

On the previous Sunday I had been to the Civetta with binoculars and no rope. I had discovered three possibilities in the compact middle part of the face: a crack on the left, directly above it a dièdre system, and to the right, cracks and ramps which led to a pillar left of the Solleder Route.

Possibilities for finding new ascents in the Alps had become sparse. Apparently all the big walls had been climbed, many even by several routes. Technical aids were to blame for that, they had made anything possible, which was why I had imposed restrictions on myself, renouncing bolts and hoisting systems.

It is maddeningly difficult to work out a free climbing route on a wall from below. I preferred to make compromises in the line rather than the style. If it was impossible to manage without bolts, I was ready to abandon the first ascent. Other, better climbers would come along and resolve the problem by fair means. The attempt at a first ascent was for me nothing other than an attempt to test, metre by metre, whether a wall would go. Often it was only a question of a single route, this being the ideal line. Whether it led directly, or by detours, to the summit was of lesser significance.

A year before the idea of a Civetta-Direttissima had not yet occurred to me. It developed in my mind as I saw the possibility and, while I studied it, the decision grew to climb it.

Nevertheless, for the time being I did not want to tie myself down, did not want to proceed rigidly up a line on a photograph. I wanted to be free of any 'once-and-for-all-line', free for unforeseen possibilities. On first ascents there are basically two ways of going about it: either one forces a wall up a particularly difficult line, or one follows the line which the wall prescribes by its shelves, cracks and dièdres. I was a mountaineer in the classic mould and always looked for this second solution.

Now, however, others were here with the same aim. Perhaps they wanted to proceed in another style, but on 'my' line. There could be no more waiting. I had waited perhaps too long already.

Next morning we set off. My friends removed the last doubts. Luckily Sepp had the equipment for our planned trip to the western Alps in his car. He and Renato fetched gear, provisions and bivouac equipment. Renato, who had no leave, called home and fixed things with his place of work. In the hut kitchen we filled the rucksacks, weighed everything. Anna, the guardian's wife, helped out with whatever was lacking. Around two o'clock in the morning all was ready. We could snatch an hour's sleep. At four o'clock sharp it would be time to go.

The last quarter of the waning moon lighted our way to the start of the climb, throwing our shadows on the scree. On this first day, Heini and Renato were to be the first rope. As the second party, Sepp and I undertook to carry the equipment.

We climbed the gully, with which the Philipp-Flamm also begins, traversing right to a crack and dièdre system, and used this as far as a shelf below the yellow wall. Just as three men from the Tissi Hut approached the start of the climb, we reached a chimney in which two ropes hung. The three, who were from Trieste, asked us to throw their ropes down. They had been on the face before us and had given up. No, they didn't want to go on. As we had only thirty metres of rope in reserve in the rucksacks, we asked the Italians whether they would lend us a rope. 'Gladly!' We were to leave it afterwards at the Coldai Hut. How generous! *'Molte grazie'*—many thanks. The men from Trieste wished us luck in our further ascent and collected their gear.

It was beautiful free climbing, with only the occasional isolated pitons left by our predecessors. Towards midday we reached a shelf on which we took a short rest. Our way led us now over the dièdre to the right of the wall: again with cracks and handy places on the face.

I had made a sling stance on a vertical rock pillar. Sepp was able to follow. A single peg stuck in the traverse between him and me. Shortly before he reached this, a flake broke off suddenly, to which he had been holding firmly with both hands. He lost his balance. At this moment he was still holding the flake, which measured perhaps half a square metre. He lifted it over his head and threw it behind him, simultaneously pushing off from the face with his feet. Then he fell.

The yank came before I expected it. His falling body tore a few metres of rope through my hands, then I was able to hold him. The stone slab, which, quick-wittedly, Sepp had thrown behind him, could have severed the rope.

Only when Sepp stood beside me did I feel relieved. We could not detect any injuries but a fall was always a dangerous thing, its consequences on such a big wall incalculable. Never yet had I fallen while leading, and it was my ambition to keep it so. For that reason I selected my climbs where I knew I was up to the difficulties.

About five o'clock in the evening we reached the top of the pillar to the right of the serried wall, up which ran a broad crack. Not the ideal route! The fiercely overhanging dièdre system above us looked very rotten. A lot of water dripped down. To take the wall direct would have been a major battle. We would have had to knock in a hundred or more pitons. So we began to study the third, the right-hand, possibility.

While Renato and Heini prepared the bivouac site, Sepp scouted towards the right to the edge. 'It'll go!' was his opinion. 'All free.' We did not ask ourselves how the line would look in a picture afterwards. We were looking for the logical way on the ground, not on paper.

Heini had plaited himself a small mat out of rope, a little bivouac nest. Sepp and Renato lay on a rock ledge about forty centimetres wide. I sat above them on a narrow knob of rock.

It was not cold. From time to time stones whirred past us. Otherwise there were only wind and clouds, mist and rocks. Even so it was a long night. As it began to dawn, we were all four awake. We cooked, ate, packed up. We hurried so as to be able to set off in good time.

On this second day, Sepp and I climbed first. Just to the right of the yellow pillar we ascended a broken crack, then crossed smooth slabs and finally climbed a difficult crack to the top of the pillar. There was still a slightly overhanging step, which Sepp, the senior member of our team, did partly with aid, partly free. Then the main difficulties lay behind us. After a few pitches we joined the Solleder Route, into which our new route merged 200 metres below the summit.

Slowly we began to rejoice.

IT WAS ALREADY AUTUMN. I knew that the Livanos-Pfeiler was difficult. It was madness to think of an ascent in one day—but bivouacs in the autumn were cold.

We should not have gone.

And yet we went, Günther and I.

I was anxious about the friable, vertical walls above us and would gladly have turned about in order to lie in the sun all day or to look for chamois. Soon the academic year would begin and I wanted to go to university in Padua. But I knew that, instead of sunbathing, I would rather be up there on the Kreuzkofel Wall; and that by evening I would have been dissatisfied if I had foregone the adventure.

After the initial broken pitches we climbed on, as retreat was still open to us. The rock deteriorated with each step. I don't know whether one of the few intermediate pitons on the white dièdre would have held a fall. One out of five perhaps, I don't know. We didn't test them. Every time when I drove a peg into the back of the dièdre, rubbish trickled out of the holes and fissures far above me. With patience and luck we reached the Conca (shell, basin), the first big terrace. Above that the Face seemed no less rotten than the white dièdre.

We were puzzled as to where Livanos had actually gone. However, on the upper left-hand edge of the Conca, there was a wooden wedge stuck in a prominent cave overhang. Up there, therefore.

Climbing free—on decent rock—we climbed during the early afternoon to the shoulder, a big shelf running across the face. A rope-length above this were three rock roofs, one above the other, like an upturned giant staircase.

We chose to bivouac on the shelf as we didn't want to spend the night in slings between the roofs. At the outside right-hand end of the shelf we found a humble cave. Just ten metres away a thread of water trickled from the overhang. We filled our flask and noticed for the first time how thirsty we were.

By the light of the setting sun we knocked straight the bent pegs and counted those remaining. Still thirty-one. We had brought forty with us. Forty pitons and two wooden wedges, which we had already used. One was sticking in the yellow dièdre, the second we had had to sacrifice in the cave overhang above the Conca. We had also only two more U-pitons. That was not much!

We did not wait until dark before we lay down in the cave. At regular intervals water dripped on the bivouac sack. I followed the drops as they formed, released themselves, fell. Out of nothing into nothing. Always the same game.

Now in the darkness a feeling of uncertainty sneaked up on me. Was the weather holding? I mapped out a retreat because I hoped the weather would be bad next morning. Time and again I looked at the stars. In between I slept.

And I froze. It was morning and already the end of September. I pressed closer to Günther. I don't know how long we still lay awake. Was it three, four or five hours? As it finally got light we crept out of our cave. Unconcernedly we stuck the bivouac sack and the flask in the rucksack. The weather was good.

By eight o'clock in the morning we were standing once more under the big roofs. After forty metres the rock became firm and blank. A single fissure allowed progress. Under the second roof I constructed a sling stance. While Günther was knocking out our pegs again, the wind played with the ropes, which swung over the first roof. The second roof above me barred all view upwards.

Time and again my gaze slid back down to the cirque, where the shadows slowly shunted and five chamois grazed. When I looked again from the next stance—a narrow ledge above the third roof—they were lying on a tongue of snow at the start of the climb, exactly below me. The sun came sparkling round the corner. So I was able to watch the chamois and sun myself!

The ridge relented, and magnificent free climbing predominated. The sun still stood high as we dried our sweaty shirts on the summit blocks and counted the remaining pitons.

There were still nineteen.

As we descended to the hospice, our eldest brother was standing there and shouting at the face. He was relieved to see us. It was time to drive to Padua if I wanted to enrol. 'Yes,' I said. 'I know. But up there we wouldn't have been able to hear you.'

6

NORTH FACES

1968

SNOW, BRUSHWOOD, FOREST, THE Agnèr-Wand above. Darkly it stood over the Lucano valley as we trudged up to the start. It was 29 January 1968. There were three of us, Heindl Messner, Sepp Mayerl and me. Sepp was breaking trail. Suddenly he stopped. 'Lot of powder snow,' he said dryly.

Some days before it had snowed. The storm had blown away almost all the snow from the North Ridge which looked more inviting than the row of chimneys, pregnant with ice and snow, on the North Face. They were filled with ice cascades and packed snow. 'This will be a hard winter ascent,' I thought to myself half-aloud, and groped a few paces forwards, eyes fixed on the face all the time.

The weather looked set to hold, so I tracked on. On a ridge far below the start we stopped. The view of this 1500-metre soaring rock wall was very good from here and we would not be able to inspect it from close to. We decided on the most favourable route, in our minds linking cracks, pillars and ledges into a line until the route became too long for our courage. Should we give up? 'No, we'll give it a try at least,' encouraged Heindl. We deliberated as to which of the two ascent possibilities in the first 200 metres seemed the more repulsive: the main chimney bursting with ice and snow, or the cracks and slabs to the right which were grey-white, as if freshly sprinkled with sugar. We agreed to decide on the spot.

The decision was spared us. At the start we came across a fixed rope, a sort of 'via ferrata', or protected climbing path. Had a team from Trieste already prepared the face that autumn for a winter ascent? We got the details later. We chose the prepared route to the right of the main chimney and quickly gained height. After about a hundred metres the fixed rope came to

I made the first winter ascent of the North Face of Monte Agnèr with Sepp Mayerl and my cousin Heindl Messner (right) in January 1968.

an end, as if to say, it's up to you now. Iced-up gullies, new snow everywhere. The ground was not too steep, our climbing speed correspondingly brisk and regular. As far as the first flight of slabs all went smoothly.

Suddenly all way forward seemed barred to us. I climbed up a few metres and back again. Just in time. 'No good, too much snow!' I called resignedly to my two companions, who were belaying me from a gully. But there was no other possibility, so I made another attempt. New snow terrain I was familiar with; it took patience and courage. Slowly I climbed higher. Now and then I chiselled notches in the hard frozen ice underneath with my peg hammer, in order to have handholds for my clammy fingers.

After eighty metres the wall became so steep that free climbing in the present conditions was no longer thinkable. And nailing? Out of the question. Like a giant belly, the grey-yellow Dolomite rock arched itself over us. From below,

83

with a worm's eye-view, everything looked foreshortened, but I knew that there were still far more than 1000 metres to the summit. Placing pitons metre by metre and hanging ètriers that would have remained there for ever was not my thing. Either we got up free or we turned round. This face was too big for anyone to be able to overcome it other than in classic style.

Everything around us was steep, drops everywhere, yet we were all but lost. Since we had started up the face, we had orientated ourselves only bit by bit. From below, from a good distance, the face had appeared to us as a graphic whole. Now we were on it, we were lost like travellers in the desert. Beginning and end were not visible. The world around us, nothing but valleys and mountains, seemed to me as far away as the universe is from the earth.

We tried to orientate ourselves by a photograph. If we pendulumed to the left we must reach the couloir of the main chimney. It seemed to be less steep.

We needed photographs, even though no one had ever captured all the details of such a gigantic wall. We reached the deep chimney and stamped out a stance there. Lumps of snow vanished down the cliff. Above us there were icicles on the smooth walls. Pitch after pitch we bridged our way higher. Already it was beginning to get dark, and still no sign of a bivouac site. The chimney was now vertical.

I would have gladly given up the lead. I kicked footholds in the packed snow, was able to fix a reliable piton. Then I bridged my way up the smooth chimney walls. I felt secure. All anxiety and all faint-heartedness were shaken off. Dutifully I climbed upwards. Small, rounded footholds were the only positive holds; my hands I pressed flat against the gaping chimney walls. All the pitons from summertime lay buried under ice and snow. There was no sort of belay for there were scarcely any piton cracks available. Finally I was able to knock a small peg into a natural hole. That was all.

The first stars showed in the sky. Onwards! Time was running out. Once more I climbed free, legs and hands pressed against the chimney walls, until it became too broad and bridging was no longer possible. What now? In balance I stood in the chimney and chopped at all the holes and cracks. No peg wanted to hold. I threw a questioning glance at my companions, who were standing twenty metres below me, following all my movements. My calves hurt. Should I go back? That would have meant a fall, perhaps an accident. I persevered, with the last of my strength.

Immediately in front of me the ice armour in the chimney was interrupted by a hole, the underlip of which was a snow balcony. Would it hold my weight? Quickly I knocked away the loose firn snow with my foot, clawed my fingers into its hard compressed surface. If it did not hold, it would bury my companions below, perhaps me too. I was less afraid at this moment of the fall, than of having to climb up again. 'Slack rope,' I called, 'and watch out!' I swung myself into the hole and rolled into a roomy cave. I was safe. If the snow balcony had not held, would one of the pitons have held, I thought, as I searched in the darkness for two cracks to make a stance.

Sepp and Heindl were not a little amazed when in the hole, through which my legs had vanished, my head now emerged. A safe cave and just before nightfall! We decided to bivouac in this eagle's nest, though the space was too small for sitting, too small for standing, too small for lying; we could only squat there, sipping lemon juice as we took stock of the situation. The ground beneath us was, according to the description, easy in comparison with the second half of the face. This twenty-metre overhanging chimney had been merely one of the crux pitches of the wall.

In its bed we constructed ourselves a bivouac. We had made 300 metres height. That was little enough. If we continued thus, it would be at least four or five days before we reached the top.

After a while we settled ourselves down; like sardines in a tin we squatted together. Each movement had to be announced and carried out simultaneously by all three. At intervals we also slept. It was as exciting to get out of our nest in the morning as it had been to get in the evening before.

A jammed block made the ceiling of our cave. I knew that, because now and then snow dust came down from above. A weak beam of light suggested a hole. Perhaps it led up the chimney? I tried it. After a good ten minutes I was outside. But it was tight.

After some difficult chimney pitches I reached a wide couloir. I was just constructing a stance on the right-hand wall of the couloir, when suddenly a snow balcony far above me broke off. That will take me with it, I thought, gripping the piton frantically. Everything went dark. I noticed something tugging at the rope. It had to be lumps of snow sweeping down the chimney. When I dared to look around, the chimneys above me were as before, quiet and gloomy. Sepp and Heindl, who had secured themselves on separated stances, shouted excitedly to each other. I looked like a snowman, covered all over with powder snow. I shook myself and banged in two pitons. Now the pair below knew everything was okay.

Sepp took over the lead. Above a row of cracks on the left wall of the couloir he climbed to the top of a pillar, as described in the guidebook. From there a slightly inclined gully led up the middle part of the wall.

We were now waiting longer on the stances and getting cold. On the opposite side of the valley we saw the shadow of Monte Agnèr. So it must be noon. Sepp surmounted an overhanging crack. His streaming breath indicated that it was difficult.

The shadow of Monte Agnèr moved on. Heindl and I climbed after Sepp, pulling up the rucksacks. That warmed us but we were soon chilled through again. Meanwhile the shadow fell on the deserted villages of Listolade and Taibon; soon it would disappear. We had used the shadow as a clock because the sun never got to us on the North Face. Just as Sepp had reached a favourable bivouac site—another cave—a few sunbeams strafed the North Ridge to our right, seeming to touch the rocks at one point only.

Next morning the principal difficulties would start. We had to rest and recover. My gaze glided along the cave walls out into the starry sky. The remaining 600 metres of face stood in my mind's eye: slabs, cracks, overhangs, ice and snow. Again no sun. Since we had set off from home, we had been living in shadow. Or in the dark. What was it that had made this winter ascent seem so desirable? A few happy days, the sun, the mountain? Probably only my daydreams in the grey university town of Padua. Now it was night and I was alone with two sleeping comrades and still not up the climb. No one knew the way ahead. I wondered whether there was a route this way, or whether insuperable difficulties would stop us.

Again the shadow of Monte Agnèr stood completely behind the Lucano valley. We had already climbed several pitches. Hoar-frost lay on the slabs left of the main chimney. Here the rock was swept clean by the storm and only in the lee fine snow crystals clung to the handholds. From the east the wind blew across the topmost third of the face.

Meanwhile we were at about the same height as the Spiz d'Agnèr, the easterly neighbour of our peak. Time and again I compared our height with that of the Spiz. Two rope-lengths to go.

The Spiz d'Agnèr itself is no dwarf in the summit crown of the Pale di San Lucano, but Monte Agnèr overtops it by quite a bit. The shadows projected across the Lucano valley showed this distinctly. What a picture! The whole mountain massif was sharply etched on the other side of the valley: Torre Armena, Monte Agnèr, Spiz d'Agnèr. The individual summits were clearly recognisable by their shapes. Only their colour was uniformly grey.

Above us a pillar now built up, steep and impressive. We consulted the guidebook: 'Up very steep slabs, until the vertical wall forces a return to the main chimney.' This was where we were now. I traversed from a snow ridge to the chimney and came straight back. Out of the question. Here there was no going on. The chimney was full of snow balconies.

The conditions on the original route compelled us to choose the vertical pillar left of the chimney; the wind had performed useful work in clearing it. I did a pitch directly up the pillar on the smallest hand- and footholds. Grade VI difficulty. Above us rose a steep gully. It became easier again.

Then carne a shallow, snowed-up crack. Again things went slowly, while the shadows pushed more quickly forwards on the other side of the valley, falling on the sharp edges of the Pale di San Lucano. Our climbing speed increased once more. Now I felt the strength in me to master all to come. A childlike ease came over me. There was nothing which could stop me. There was only the conviction that we would succeed! Already the shadow of our peak was pushing round like a wedge in the direction of Torre Trieste. The sun must therefore be very low.

We were about 200 metres below the summit. Here we had planned to bivouac, but could find no suitable place. It would be dark in two hours. They must suffice to get us as far as the summit slope! Of the two possibilities mentioned in the guidebook, we chose the right-hand one. A giant dièdre system—and the summit couloir. Placing only one piton we thrust a few pitches higher.

Still a last broken overhang. 'Bang in another peg,' I heard Sepp scolding me from below—and I was up. Off the North Face, out of the shadow. I stood there in the light of the setting sun. 'I'm up!' was all I said. I could not believe it. The summit was quite near and the sun was shining on it. By the time Heindl and Sepp stood beside me, the sun was away, set. Only a red gleam still lay on the horizon.

Report by Günther Messner

My eyes slid once more up the face. Quite slowly they searched, compared, appraised, harmoniously joined up the line point by point. I held a creased North Face postcard in my hand. I scribbled on the other side next to Reinhold's address: 'Peitler, the tops—well studied—all free—1 day—expect you Saturday.'

Reinhold came. He had a hard week behind him, exams, little sleep. My plan seemed somewhat daring to him—he thought the face could scarcely be done without a bivouac—nevertheless I insisted on one day. Monday I had to be back at work. In the afternoon we travelled to Coll. From there we rambled, past the Gungan-Wiese, up to Würzen. A beautiful light over all; the North Face bright. Unbelievable that this face was still unclimbed.

The morning was clear like the evening. As we picked bits of pungent hay off each other, a few sunbeams struck the summit. It was time to set off. The slabby North Face seemed bigger than ever. Would one day really be enough? We stumbled on over loose stones to the start. The first pitches we climbed fast until the dièdre became steep. We chose the free way, traversed to the right and climbed higher on the slabby right wall of the dièdre, thus reaching a broad shelf under huge yellow overhangs. Here we allowed ourselves a short rest. We knocked straight some bent pegs, had a drink from the full leather bottle.

It was ten o'clock. A little later Reinhold bridged up over a somewhat friable dièdre. He stopped. The dièdre overhung. Could it be climbed free? I was excited. Reinhold began to traverse left, and I saw nothing but two big black boot soles, which got bigger and bigger before they vanished beyond the edge.

Beautiful pitches followed as far as the huge roof. We kept shouting encouragement to each other. The sun was still high when we reached a vault under the summit. We paused briefly.

A small blunder cost us time. Reinhold retreated, tried further to the right . . . it went . . . we had done it. The North Face Direct on the Peitlerkofel was to become a classic.

FOR ME SPEED PLAYS a subordinate role in mountaineering. Speed is only important if the safety of the climber depends upon it, if objective dangers require a climb against the clock. According to the old school of climbing, objective dangers are stonefall, avalanches and changes in the weather—as opposed to subjective dangers which, in the first place, can be attributed to over-confidence. But dangers which depended on laws of nature were for me not objective dangers. It lies with the mountaineer to recognise these dangers and to plan accordingly. Random dangers one can avoid or take into account. There no speed, no safety is of use: only patience to choose the right moment to climb, or just stay at home.

Each stone released a whole avalanche. From the summit rocks, on which the sun now shone, a black dot detached itself, rolled at first, then skipped across the dark ice surfaces, shot like an arrow into the rock islands in the lower half of the face. This stone brought the whole face into movement: crashing, splashing, whizzing.

It was summer 1968. Günther and I sat under the wall which we wanted to climb: the North Face of the Gletscherhorn in the Bernese Oberland. It was steep, in part blank, more than 1000 metres high. Up until then it had allegedly been climbed only six times. Towards noon the stonefall had set in. Therefore we had to be on top by midday—or not start at all. This calculation was simple.

We started up the climb and did the first hundred metres unroped as the face was not yet steep. One would not kill oneself if one fell here. After that we roped up and belayed each other. From rock island to rock island we climbed upwards. That way we saved time because we could fix belay pitons quickly. Besides, stances on rock were safer than on ice.

In the crevasse under the summit rocks we allowed ourselves a short rest. An hour later we were on top. The weather changed. Mist came up. In order not to run any risk of going astray on the other side of the mountain, we followed the ridge from the Gletscherhorn to the top of the Ebnefluh and climbed down its North Face.

In the early hours of the afternoon we sat in front of the Rattal Hut, from which we had set out that morning. Now the stonefall was crashing down on the North Face of the Gletscherhorn. There were people who at that time had bivouacked on this North Face and reproached us—for our speed! They chided us for our tactics, saying, with stonefall one had to belay doubly well. 'Why,' I asked, 'when one can also climb without triggering off stonefall?'

WITH A LETTER IN MY POCKET, Günther and I left South Tyrol in my cram-full car to try our luck in the Bernese Oberland. I had bought myself a Fiat 500, the smallest possible motor-car, and so was more mobile. It was the end of July and all the big Dolomite walls were snowed-up or wet, mostly both. In the completely iced-up Schmitt Chimney on the Fünffingerspitze (Punta delle Cinque Dita) I had broken some teeth the day before setting off. Leaving the Dolomites at this time was not hard for us. The conditions could not be worse in the western Alps and then there was this letter: Toni Hiebeler had invited us on 'something big' in the Bernese Oberland: '1800 metres! Mixed ground'—no more details in the letter. The notorious intriguer was giving nothing away. I hardly knew Toni Hiebeler at that time, but I respected him as editor of *Alpinismus*.

In Stechelberg, at the end of the Lauterbrunnen valley, we put up our tent. I had not deceived myself, the ice conditions in the Oberland appeared to be quite good. The weather promised to hold. In the late evening I was able to speak on the telephone with Toni, who lived in Mürren. Next day he came to our tent. After three hours everything was ready—for the Eiger North Pillar!

The Eiger has become world famous on account of its North Face. For all that, this wall is not especially difficult and the summit is less than 4000 metres high. This North Face, however, 1800 metres high, is not just the highest face in the Alps. It has a dramatic climbing history and often bad ice conditions. Many parts of the wall stream with water, the upper part is exceedingly friable and the stonefall danger undeniably great. On account of its position, sudden weather changes on the Eiger are far from infrequent. Many parties have been surprised by snowstorms or hit by stonefall, while not a few have frozen to death. The North Face of the Eiger is one of the few faces in the Alps on which luck is almost as important as ability.

To the left of the North Face Route, up the North-East Face, was the Lauper Route. Between the two walls is an indefinite buttress, the North Face Pillar. It was scarcely touched by stonefall and I estimated that its difficulties would not exceed Grade IV. We were not long weighing it up. Naturally this buttress was an overwhelming line.

Toni had had this climb in mind for many years. He had brought some pictures with him and now introduced us to his plan in detail. That same afternoon we travelled with Toni to Kleine Scheidegg. Fritz Maschke, our fourth man, followed on foot in the late evening.

The conditions on the Eiger were not the best: a lot of new snow, with avalanche danger and water. Nonetheless such a route was to my taste: 1800 metres high, mixed ground, logical line and relatively free from stonefall. In the Alps, as a rule, such opportunities were no longer to be found.

Without torches, early in the morning we looked for the way to the start. For a short time four lights above Alpiglen aroused our attention. It was about an hour before dawn. Did they want to do the Pillar too? Who were they? Then they approached the start of the North Face. We calmed down and marched along beneath the North Face to our buttress.

It was full daylight as we built a cairn at the foot of the climb. Without roping up, we climbed up for several hundred metres. The ground was not steep and the rock was good, unexpectedly good even. Here and there there was a snow rib to cross. Quickly we gained height. We could not tell what lay before us, but were moving too quickly to care. We hoped that it would go as well further up. If we had known about the two terrible bivouacs which awaited us, perhaps we would never have started climbing.

Toni grumbled. He sank deeper into the snow than us, as he was bigger than we were and carried a heavy rucksack. Below the first steep rise—Günther and I were ahead—at Toni's request we roped up, which made the rucksacks lighter. The rock was either iced up or steep. Too steep to be able to climb with crampons, too icy to do without them. When my turn came to lead I tried with, then again without.

Our pace was extremely slow. We climbed with all four of us on the same rope, at Toni's express wish. Two, often three, belayed while one climbed. For many pitches we climbed obliquely upwards to the right. Fritz was often 140 metres behind me. How was he getting on? I had not spoken with him since nine o'clock in the niorning.

In the late afternoon I came on fresh tracks in the snow. Who had made them? There are no yetis in the Alps. They caused a lot of speculation.

On a snow ledge Toni and Fritz began to construct the bivouac. Together with Günther, I climbed three more pitches. We followed the fresh tracks and found the bivouac site of our predecessors. But this was smaller and less comfortable than ours lower down. We left the rope hanging and climbed back down to our companions.

Toni and Fritz had shovelled away the snow beneath a slightly overhanging pillar. The flat space was just wide enough for two men to lie side by side. Günther and I squatted nearby. Time and again snow slides came down from above. Bits of ice and sleet pattered down upon us. We crawled into our bivouac sacks. Cooking was out of the question. Our mood was depressed. The fact that it was not particularly cold was no comfort. Everything was wet. On top of all that were these puzzling tracks. I couldn't get them out of my head.

In vain we hoped that it would freeze during the night. From the overhang it began to drip: plop, plop, plop . . . It was not long before our duvets were soaked through; everything else was already dripping wet. Freezing cold, we squatted next to each other. The silence was only broken when one or the other asked what the time was. I dreamed of warm days. Days full of work, days studying, days at home, all better than these wet cold nights on some alpine face.

On the morning of the second day the weather did not look good. We could have given up. The choice was ours—up or down. We all four knew that the danger in bad weather would be great. But no one said 'Back'. We were not finished yet.

With Günther alone I would have climbed to the top in a few hours. But we were a party of four and, after all, it was Toni Hiebeler and not we who had developed the idea for this first ascent. The Eiger North Pillar was certainly no glittering prize but easy it was not under these circumstances. Luckily the ropes which Günther and I had fixed up the day before were hanging on the face. With these we were able to climb quickly and get ourselves warm. Toni found a cigarette stub in the old tracks and identified our predecessors as Poles. A few pitches later their tracks joined the Lauper Route. All was made clear.

We continued up the buttress. Above a steep rock wall I found a pleasant resting place. The sun broke through the clouds briefly and we decided to cook. First hot soup, then buckthorn juice. Fritz had laid hintself down on a sloping rock slab and gone to sleep.

As the sun left us, it began to turn cold. I leaned against a block of rock and gazed down at Grindelwald. The air above the village was filled with warm haze. But the sky was a discouraging grey colour and was shot through with bright streaks. Oppressive, dense clouds hung over the hill country to the north.

Reluctantly we moved on. First we plodded through wet snow. Further up we came to rock again. Late in the evening we were climbing up the right-hand edge of an ice-field. The thought of finding a good bivouac site was our only comfort. We hoped we would not have to freeze like the first night. Time and again I scouted for a flat place by an overhung rock ledge. The others were silent. It was high time to find a campsite.

On a rock island I managed to bang in two pegs. That exhausted the inadequate belaying possibilities on the rocks. After a short reflection I began to hack away the hard ice under the rock. I could not let Günther come up before both of us had a platform to stand on. It was already dusk. The others stood far below on the face, listening to the blows of my axe.

Hours later Günther and I were sitting on a narrow ledge of ice. The situation was not unusual but hard. Again it was wet, again we froze. Toni and Fritz had set themselves up in the middle of the ice face, as far as they could. Leaning on the ice, I squatted with feet drawn up and waited. I did nothing, thought nothing, just squatted there. It felt as if I had been squatting there for ever.

In the morning it was snowing. We did not know whether this would be our last bivouac on this Eiger buttress. Laboriously I put on my crampons, as Günther shook out the red bivouac sack. Slowly I traversed to the left on the steep, rotten ice. Then I began to climb up the slope to a stance.

It was a long time before Günther could follow. The wind blew sharply in my face. It was still snowing. I wiped the snow dust off my knees. It was an hour before our chain, our four-man rope, got into full swing and I was able to warm myself up a bit.

Far above I removed my crampons again; the steep, badly layered rock demanded it. In the afternoon we climbed in mist up the summit ice-field and the Mittelegi Ridge to the highest point.

The hours of daylight remaining were just enough for the descent, I reckoned, while Toni and Günther prepared a hot meal: broth, a bit of bread. Our demands were not great. We had become more frugal during these days on the Eiger.

IN THE SUMMER OF 1968 I opened up two new routes on the Marmolada: the Südtiroler Weg with Konrad Renzler, who had become my friend after our morning meeting below the Furchetta North Face, and the Slab Wall to the left of the Soldà Route with Günther.

In three days, from 7 to 9 September, I found three new routes: first with Heini Holzer, the Renato Reali Memorial Route on the Klein Vernal. Renato Reali had fallen to his death a few days previously while soloing the East Face of the Capucin.

Then with Günther I climbed the North Face couloir on the Wasserkofel in the Geisler group. Finally I managed a new variation on the South Face of Piz-de-Ciavàces with Claudio Barbier.

Each weekend Günther and I climbed together. During the week I had to look for other partners as Günther was working at that time as a bank clerk in the Gader valley. I was a student and the summer belonged only to my dreams. Turning ideas into facts completely filled my life.

Above Stern in the Gadertal, where Günther worked, stood the grey-yellow wall of the Heiligkreuzkofel: several kilometres wide and up to 600 metres high. In climbing circles this sweep of wall was then unknown and no one went there. Only a few local South Tyrol climbers knew that there were ideal possibilities for first ascents there.

In 1967 Günther and I had repeated the Livanos Buttress. A year later we were on the central buttress of the Heiligkreuzkofel. We set off at eight o'clock in the morning. After three short pitches the buttress became yellow-coloured. Only to the right was it possible to continue climbing free. We traversed as far as we could. I knocked in a ring piton and abseiled pendulum-fashion to a rising ramp on the right. Above that we reached a small ledge on the vertical edge of the buttress.

Up to here all had been clear; nature had given us the route and we had followed it. But now?

For two more metres it still went free. Extremely difficult, but it went. Then it was beyond me. I found a tiny hole, two or three centimetres deep and put in a short knife-blade peg, which held. On a bit more. Yet another belay piton. A bit further. A third. Further. A fourth...

At last, a few big handholds. I stuck my hammer in my pocket. In a narrow crack in the back of a shallow dièdre I was able to wangle my way higher by free climbing. I reached a narrow little shelf—just in time. By now my strength had gone.

A smooth slab, in which there were no fissures and scarcely any handholds, barred my way. Four metres further up, a crack. I must reach that. I stood on a foot-wide shelf, on a ledge, below me an overhanging drop, very airy. Straight up was out of the question. Obliquely to the left was too smooth, the handholds too small for me to be able to lift both feet off the shelf.

After thirty minutes I was not one centimetre higher. Retreat was hard too; I endeavoured in vain to climb down. It was impossible and I didn't have enough courage to jump off.

Already standing on the ledge was hard work. I asked myself whether I would be able to stand on the tiny notches higher up—that was the only way out. Time and again I got ready, tried to push myself off from the shelf. Time and again I retreated with the idea of still trying to go down. As soon as I was standing on the shelf again, my ability to think logically returned. There was no going back. No, there was no hopelessness, no fear, no doubt. But also no way out.

Again I dried my fingertips; we did not use chalk in those days. It had to go! Just these few metres! This command was buried in my brain.

I must risk all and have a go. Above me was a small handhold. Once I had that, I could not retreat. Next I would have to place my right foot quite high and simply stand up—a balancing act—then reach the sloping ledge with my left hand and pull up. In my head was only the one thought: up, handhold on the right, then grip to the left . . .

To this day I do not know how I did it. I only know that suddenly I was standing up there—relaxed, full of joy. And afterwards it all seemed simple. A few hours later on the summit Günther and I did not speak of this spot, rather of the situation below. And when today I think of the Central Buttress, I see everything as it was then. Only the way out is an open secret, a dream realised. It was twenty years before this crux was repeated, by Andreas Orgler and Otti Wiedmann from Innsbruck. A good feeling and a lasting moment in my memory.

A smooth slab in which there are no crevices and scarcely any handholds. Four metres further up, a crack. A foot-wide shelf on which I stood. Below me a lot of air, an overhanging drop. An impression which stays in the mind for a lifetime.

THE FARMER IN COL DI PRÀ only shook his head as he divined our intention. He sat on the doorstep, killing time. He had got in his hay and the cow had to be milked again first thing in the evening. There he squatted now and looked up at Monte Agnèr, which took the sun from him.

Three days later we were back and the man was again sitting in the doorway. Or perhaps he'd never moved away.

Our tent stood on a small patch of meadow by Col di Prà, directly under the huge Agnèr face. Günther and Heini wanted to stay there. Erich, another of my six brothers, and I decided to carry on homewards.

A car stopped next to us.

'Are the climbers already back from the North Face?'

'Yes, just.'

'How long did they take?'

'They bivied for the second time on the way down, in the bivi box under the summit.'

'Where did they start?'

'Over there, where Aste tried a few years ago.'

'How do you know Aste tried it?'

'They told us in Taibon.'

'How far did Aste get?'

'Not far: about 400 metres.'

'What's it like?'

'Long, free, not without danger. It's similar to the Via Ideale on the Marmolada d'Ombretta…slabs, waterfalls. No, not as hard! But still a big climb.'

'Do you know the Via Ideale?'

'Made the second ascent,' I said proudly.

'What's *that* like?'

'Without doubt one of the most splendid climbs in the Dolomites, if not in the Alps as a whole. What a line Aste put up there!'

'Careful! Aste *sono io*'—I'm Aste, said the man with the stubbly beard, which could have been a week old.

Strong handshake! In no time there was a friendly atmosphere. He was going to climb the North-East Face tomorrow, if... On the Civetta we had already snatched the new North Face Route away from under his nose.

'*Ci dispiace*'—Sorry about that, I said and thought: We got here in the nick of time. As if we had known he was in Taibon when we went to the North Ridge in winter. He too had wanted to make the first winter ascent.

'And now, have you climbed the North-East Face?'

'Yes.'

'*Complimenti.*'

'Thanks.'

'The early bird catches the worm,' he remarked somewhat sadly. 'You have a good eye and more luck than us. How did you get to know about it?'

'In the winter, when we were starting the North Ridge, I saw this possibility to the left of the Jori Route. The snow lying in all the hollows gave me a clear picture of the difficulties. Then on the ridge I forgot about the face but I studied it again this summer.'

'And how was it?'

'I got here three days ago with Heini Holzer from Merano and my brothers, Günther and Erich. That's our tent over there.'

We had set off on 17 August with outsized rucksacks. Erich acted as porter and carried the heaviest things up to the start. The first 400 metres we did quickly. Grade IV at the most. There, just right of the black streak of water, we found some bivouac gear, a cooker and food. During the whole ascent we puzzled over who they belonged to. Only on the descent did Erich come out with: 'Aste must have been here already before us.' The old man laughed somewhat bitterly. 'Yes, Aste has also tried it—your face,' he said and I understood that it was his face. The bearded Aste did not smile. However, he wasn't cross with us. 'How was it up there?' he wanted to know.

We had climbed straight on, at first up the buttress, which rises above Aste's bivouac site, another 400 metres of beautiful climbing. Only the rucksacks made life hard for us.

Via a chimney, late in the afternoon we reached a small ledge under the steep, grey-yellow slabs of the North-East Face. There we set up a nice bivouac site. We had time in hand.

From the west, however, a bank of dark clouds pressed towards us. As a precaution we stretched the bivouac sack over our sleeping place. Rather wait for morning cold than wet, we thought in a sort of gallows humour. We were afraid of a thunderstorm. We thought of the report by Gino Buscaini who, with Silvia Metzeltin, had been stuck for five days on the Jori Route to the right of us. Incessant rain had made each further attempt to climb impossible. Retreat through waterfalls and under avalanches of stones was out of the question. Cold, hungry and wet... A wonder the two of them had survived.

'*Attenti all'acqua*'—Beware of rain, the landlord at the Locanda al Sasso in Taibon had warned us. It won't rain, we had thought. No, it did not rain, it poured, it hailed. Lightning flashed, thunder crashed. A wild thunderstorm had broken out and did not leave off again.

As the first stones landed on our bivouac sack, we hastily deserted the little place we had laboriously made, fumbling our way down the chimney in the twilight and cowered together under a jammed block for half the night. We were afraid, and how!

Behind everything which we call adventure, experience, joy of climbing, behind all this stands fear. Our situation was so tight and full of doubt. We didn't want to be afraid, not of the waterfalls, not of the slabs above us, not of a fall. We had been courageous, down in the valley, before setting off.

Nevertheless we were afraid. For the time being only of the rain, of the lightning, of the stones. The overhangs only came later. Towards midnight the thunderstorm had passed. As we groped our way up the back of the chimney to our little nest, no stars were visible.

This night lasted a long time. Nothing happened anywhere, yet we were rattled. The weather had not improved. We bided our time. At nine o'clock in the morning we continued the climb because the return seemed to us too long and too dangerous.

The slabs were easier than we had thought the day before. With only six intermediate pitons I climbed over the 200 metres of armour-plated slabs, once to the right, then to the left of the streaks of water, always following the best of the free climbing.

Under the last steep step we paused briefly. Heini it was who led and nailed the overhanging crack in the exit couloir. Above us a small stream leaped out of the couloir and rippled over us as we were climbing. It was like being in the shower. The summit ravine was not particularly difficult, some wet spots, friable chimneys.

On the other side of the mountain, in the bivouac box under the summit, we settled in for the night. As we dried our clothes in the morning sun, Erich came up. He was surprised to meet us at the bivouac box. Down below in the tent he had been so impressed by the bad weather, that he had no longer believed in a happy ending to this adventure.

We wanted to get on. 'Perhaps I'll find another face problem for this leave,' said the great Aste. We seconded his wish for him.

'*Arrivederci—auf Wiedersehen*, Aste.'

'*Auf Wiedersehen*, Agnèr.'

The farmer was still sitting in front of the hut and looked at us aghast.

Report by Günther Messner

I gather that someone wanted to use bolts on the North Face of the Second Sella Tower. At any rate it was planned. When now I look back on the day on which we climbed this wall, I have to laugh. Secretly I am ashamed because I too talked of nailing it. I certainly did not consider bolts but I laughed at my brother when, at the start, he obstinately maintained that this 200-metre face was possible without aid climbing. I would like to bet that he himself did not believe it; and had I not been there when he proved it, I would still be sceptical today.

It was on a Saturday morning. I came home from work and Reinhold got me enthusiastic for the North Face Direct of the Second Sella Tower.

'A nice short thing,' he enticed. We didn't get away until midday. At three o'clock in the afternoon we began the climb. 'Too late, much too late,' I grumbled. 'It won't go like this . . . We need a whole day here . . . Actually, why don't we come back? . . . I don't want to have to bivouac!'

Our failure seemed a foregone conclusion to me. In my vexation over Reinhold's stupidity I could scarcely pay out the rope, as he climbed up the first thirty metres. Infuriated, I grumbled away to myself: 'So and so many first ascents he has already done and yet he will not see that this slab wall is not possible free. He thinks he can get up here with a dozen pegs, the block-head. He fancies he has a good nose for a climb. He's welcome to his notions. It's all right by me if he falls off.'

The first pitches Reinhold did without any intermediate pitons. Only as

I followed did I notice how hard it was. Arriving on the stance, I asked whether he really wanted to do another pitch… Reinhold pressed the rope into my hand and disappeared behind a rounded edge. A piton sang: peng, peng, peng. It held.

'How's it going?' I asked.

No reply. The rope ran out a few metres, came back again. Again the rope moved: forward, back. 'Look out, I'm trying to the right,' I heard him say. I couldn't see him. I knew that it was pointless talking about pitons. So I shut up.

Reinhold tried it to the left, then right and once straight up. 'Testing a face', he called it. Five tries, ten tries.

But before he gave up it did go and indeed without pegs. 'A pegged pitch is one which the first climbers weren't good enough for.' Yes, he was right. And I was all for that, too. If one wasn't up to a face, one ought to give it up. Others would come tomorrow, later, in ten years' time, who were.

Reinhold must have done it. Completely free. The rope ran quickly, then stopped again. 'That's the place—just right of the peg…undercut hold…really quite easy.' Disconnected words floated down to me.

Another belay peg, more attempts. Just above the streaks of water he was still going strong. A roomy cave provided him with a good stance. I followed, it was hard, but fantastic climbing.

The third pitch seemed from below to be the smoothest. 'I want to climb a few more metres,' remarked Reinhold. Then we'll abseil off, I thought, and try again tomorrow.

But Reinhold did not come back—he climbed ever higher, cleanly, free, mostly without pitons.

The cave passage got me in the arms. Then came more marvellous pitches. Firm rock, unexpected big jug-handle holds, the rope dangling free in the air.

My irritation had long since passed away. It was a joy to see how Reinhold climbed towards the evening sky!

THE BURÉL IS A PEAK in the Schiara group, a quite inconspicuous mountain, 2281 metres high, and completely unknown until a few years ago. Only from the Val di Piero does this peak look enormous, inaccessible. Burél means 'precipice'. Chamois hunters must have coined this name, thousands of years ago perhaps.

Overnight the Burél was a mountain which the alpine world knew about. Everyone was talking about the South-West Face. The ascent of the wall was a sensation. In ten days, and with 120 pitons, a small Polish party did the top half of the face. The lower part, up to the big shelf, was then done by two Italians. As yet no one had climbed the whole of this 1400-metre concave rock wall.

The huts were shut. Some way from the start we bivouacked amongst the pines, in a small hollow.

The way via the Rifugio 7° Alpini was long and our rucksacks were heavy. How quickly we had fixed it all up. Telephone call to Konrad. His refusal. Three minutes later his return call and acceptance. Konrad always said yes when it was about mountaineering. He was a businessman and had little free time. But always, if I asked him whether he wanted to come for three or four days, he made time.

Konrad liked bivouac nights. He understood something about open camp-sites. Our nest was soft, the floor warm. Above us stood the Little Bear, with the Milky Way clearly visible. Now and then a shooting-star. Above us also stood the mighty South-West Face of the Burèl. In three days we wanted to be home again.

The rock was treacherous, the pegs were bad. We had been on the go for several hours already. The sun blazed down on the face where only a few shady stances were to be found. We had two and a half litres of tea in our flask and already our throats were parched. Climbing in the blazing sun and breathing heavily took it out of us. Our thick lederhosen stuck to our legs and the sweat ran off us while hoisting the rucksacks.

The difficulties were less than made out by the first party but the rock was not good. No, the rock really wasn't good. By the early afternoon we had reached the big shelf in the middle of the face, where we planned to bivouac. Another swig from the flask. No, it was several swigs. We still had two litres, two litres and a hellish thirst. Each of us could have emptied it in one go. We had to economise. Above us stood 700 metres of wall, with one roof piled up above another.

The summit was still a long way off. If we were to carry on, we must find water! From a report by the first ascent party we knew that via the terrace one could reach the Alpini Hut. We hoped to find a good bivouac site on the ledge—and, above all, water. I ran on ahead. The shelf was first broad, then sloping. Later we found some dwarf pines and Konrad was able to see chamois. I hurried across gullies, climbed over short steep steps and listened tensely in the quiet evening. Time and again I could hear water gushing. Only quite gently but still I found nothing but dry holes. Was I hallucinating?

In the end we compromised and made our way to the Alpini Hut where we could drink, fill our flask and next day, very early, traverse back on the face by torchlight to begin the climb again fresh in the morning.

At seven o'clock in the morning we were ready to climb, having left some of our equipment in the hut. We were climbing now with only one rucksack. After two pitches it became extremely difficult. Grade VI it said in the sketch. At once it became clear to us that the definition of a 'sixer' had changed. On the second half of the face the Poles had done some neat work. Cracks, roofs, smooth wall pitches, all free climbing. A technical traverse took us leftwards on the upper face. Now we were cut off with huge roofs below us. An abseil was out of the question. Reverse the traverse? Rather not. We did not want to go back, we wanted to continue. But we would have welcomed the opportunity to retreat.

Fenced in between the roofs, we climbed on. Now for the first time I was conscious of the whole problematical nature of this face. And the height! And the overhangs above us! And the drop! No one could help us here, neither from above nor from below.

There were just the two of us, climbing up there, as if on another planet. Today was Tuesday. 'If we're not back by Thursday,' I had said at home, 'then…' What then? We would be back Thursday at the latest.

We had delivered ourselves up; to solitariness, to the Burél. Our lives were hostage to our ability, to our will. That was the sum total of things.

I still felt up to the situation, in fact I felt myself superior to it. Nevertheless I was anxious because a bad accident could mean the end here. It would have taken all of ten days for a mountain rescue team to find us. It is not my custom to humanise mountains. Nevertheless, sometimes I caught myself doing it, as I talked to a handhold, or implored a loose block on the face not to choose this moment to lose its balance.

The roofs of the Burél could throw stones at us and slay us or let us live, as they wished. A buttress could crash near us and tear us with it. A handhold might break off, or a piton fail. Just a single piton and it could all be over. A fall, a broken leg, and we were prisoners of the Burél South-West Face.

A single muscle with cramp, and already a fit person was climbing with an injured one on this huge face, and neither would have been able to help the other, because one was not enough.

Caution was thus the watchword. Slowly we pushed higher. Each trusted the other and, on that account, going on was bearable.

We did not know how far it was still to the summit. The fifty-metre roof just above us barred all view upwards. There was more than 1000 metres of space beneath us. And, lower still, a stream escaped at the foot of the face, a real stream near the path from Val di Piero. On this path people walked in summertime and could have seen us and known we were there. But this was the end of October. There was nobody about. We were delivered up to the Burél and Burél meant 'precipice'.

We had always hoped to get off the face on this second day. After each dangerous place we thought that it was the last. The flask was empty and the evening cold made us shiver. It got dark early. We squatted anywhere to bivouac. Our thirst tormented us. Then I must have fallen asleep. I knew we were sitting on our bivouac up on the summit. I woke up and hollered out: 'Water!' And the mountain answered. Konrad laughed over it. He too was thirsty and frozen stiff.

A constant falling asleep and waking up—that was the night on the summit. Anxiety and joy alternated. Fear of the precipice, of a bad accident; joy at success, joy at living.

7

EXPEDITION TO THE PERUVIAN ANDES

1969

I WAS DEEP IN THE STUDY OF MECHANICS. In Padua, I had been living for weeks in a world of lectures, studies, examinations. In the midst of this, I was surprised by a telegram from Innsbruck. It was an invitation to join the Tyrol 1969 Expedition to the Andes. It struck me like lightning! At that time I still thought that everyone must have a 'proper' job and I wanted to learn a breadwinning profession, so as to be 'free' to go climbing.

I made telephone calls in all directions. 'Nonsense,' said my father.

'Start 25 May, Innsbruck Airport, 1600 hours,' explained Otti Wiedmann, the leader of the expedition. 'The equipment is supplied. You need only bring a rucksack, storm matches, three pairs of boots . . .'

'I'm coming,' I said over the telephone without knowing whether I could meet the deadline. Passport, visa, inoculations, insurance—I had to do all that in three days. It was crazy. And the mechanics examination? That no longer existed for me.

With the aid of some friends and a great deal of luck I was ready in time. On the way from Venice—I had obtained a visa there—to Bolzano, I fell asleep at the wheel of my little motor-car and went over the embankment. A lorry driver took pity on me and pulled me out of the orchard back on the road. At midnight I was home in Villnöss. 'The flight goes from Innsbruck via Zurich, Dakar and Rio de Janeiro to Lima,' I told my parents.

A few days later in Lima we were making the final preparations for the expedition. I loved foreign cities, the climate, the people. The social distinctions in Lima were incomprehensible to us Europeans. Here hundreds of thousands lived in corrugated iron huts on the edge of the city while a few others lived in luxurious residential districts.

In the afternoon we went to see Señor César Morales, head of the mountaineering section of the Instituto Nacional de Recreación. He was himself a climber and an expert on the Andes. He showed us pictures, made arrangements with the porters and made notes for a short newspaper article:

Expedition leader and climber: Otti Wiedmann
Expedition doctor and climber: Dr Raimund Margreiter
The team: Sepp Mayerl, Peter Habeler, Egon Wurm, Helmut Wagner, Reinhold Messner.
Expedition goal: East Face of Yerupaja Grande, one of the steepest ice faces in the Cordillera Huayhuash.

We had to wait several days until our expedition luggage could be released after hours of customs' formalities. Everywhere in the world, there is this bureaucracy!

At the beginning of June we set off northwards in a rattling bus, along the Pan-American Highway, that famous road which runs down the west coast of South America. We turned off from this luxury highway on to a dirt road and reached Chiquian, starting point of our expedition into the mountains. Several thousand Indians lived there in the most miserable conditions. At the end of the road a narrow path led up through wild gorges into the Andes, up to the last settlements.

We wanted to set off early next morning for Pocpa. We stowed our equipment in sacks and loaded three mules but not until ten o'clock were we able to get going. Far away on the horizon we saw the Andes for the first time. Soaring above all the other peaks stood Yerupaja, our goal.

I had difficulty keeping pace with the mules. They raised so much dust that it was better either to walk in front of them or far behind. Now and then we met a peasant family, carrying maize and potatoes or driving cattle to sell in the market in Chiquian. The children were barefoot and dirty, and they stared at us, never before having seen Europeans. The valleys were wild, stony gorges, often without vegetation. The Indians had their villages near the few springs, where they cultivated maize, oats and other cereals. Their small mud huts gave the impression of everything being temporary. Nonetheless these hamlets were welcome oases on our march through the summer heat. After six hours we arrived at Pocpa and were lodged in the parish hall. One of our drivers invited us to supper. So much hospitality was possible only in a poor country. Slowly our mistrust of the local inhabitants relented. They lived by stock-farming and agriculture. Their expressions radiated contentment and a peace such as I did not know with our farmers in the Dolomites. On the bare earth floor we set up camp for the night, for wooden floors were unknown in the mountains. The people slept with their dogs and pigs in one room.

For two days we marched on, over plateaux, alongside lakes, over passes and through valleys. In rain and mist we arrived in Caruacocha. During the crossing of the last two passes it had been snowing. We were tired, wet through, filthy, hungry and freezing. We were many thousands of kilometres from home.

By some stone blocks the height of a man, near a spring, we set up our base camp. The altimeter showed a height of 4150 metres. We dug ditches, put up the tents, dug a hole for our provisions. Next to one of the boulders we constructed a kitchen. The thin air made the heavy work an ordeal. It continued to be rainy. We only saw the East Face of Yerupaja once. As it rose out of the mist far above us, it seemed higher and more unfriendly than it really was. A kilometre away stood a few round stone huts, with roofs made of reeds. It seemed to me as if nothing had changed here for thousands of years.

After two days the weather improved. We climbed up to the edge of the glacier, just below 5000 metres, where we found a favourable place for our first high camp. High camps should always be about 500-900 metres above each other and offer the greatest possible safety. At that time I knew this only from theory.

It was the middle of June. One morning four of us set out from Camp I which stood on the left-hand, lower edge of the big icefall, up which we had previously marked and trodden out the way. Up the fixed rope, which Peter and Sepp had fastened to the start of the South-East Buttress of Yerupaja, we gained height quickly. Then Sepp and I fixed another hundred metres of rope. Peter and Manni, our doctor, brought up gear behind.

In the afternoon, opposite the first buttress top at a height of 5350 metres, I found an ideal place for the second high camp. We fixed a rope cable-way from the top of the buttress, then brought everything up to the campsite. Meanwhile Sepp had chopped clear a platform.

Again it began to snow. Sepp and I put up a small tent, then stowed away all the gear susceptible to wet and descended the fixed ropes to the foot of the buttress, before burrowing our way back to Camp I through new snow. Here we met Otti and Egon who had been filming in the icefall. Heli and our high altitude porters had arrived in Camp I from base camp with equipment, exactly as I had always pictured an expedition to myself. 'All for one and one for all.' How naïve I was then. Everyone contributed to the common aim, and worked to produce the conditions favourable for an ascent.

It was a week later and everything was ready. From Camp 2 we had made a track to the foot of the East Face and there put up a medium-sized tent, East Face Camp. It stood at a height of about 5300 metres.

The face proper was 1300 metres high. It led to a height of 6634 metres above sea-level. I need hardly mention that up there the air was thin, and the exertion correspondingly great. The right-hand part of the face had been climbed already by an American party. Now Peter and I wanted to climb it up the summit fall line. The rocky summit pyramid, eighty metres high at its greatest point, was yellow and white, a rubbish tip. A stonefall gully started 300 metres lower down. Left of that, the ice face was bordered by a huge rock buttress. An ideal and safe ascent line but in all probability extremely difficult. Seen from the front the buttress rose slightly to the right and ended on the ridge to the left of the summit. From it icicles, up to thirty metres long, hung over our face.

During the day the chances of getting up this face alive were slim, on account of the danger of falling stones. The expanses of ice were concave and ran up together like a wedge. Only the 300-metre-high wedge under the summit ridge was climbable without great risk after sunrise. Therefore we had to reach its lower point, at a height of 6300 metres, before the first rays of the sun touched the summit rocks, i.e. at six o'clock in the morning. My plan to climb up and down this steep and sinister face with a light sack in one day seemed to us all somewhat audacious. But when now I reflect on it quietly, I am sure it was the only correct plan: I had applied this tactic on many ice faces in the eastern and western Alps with success.

About an hour after dark, Peter and I left the tent at the East Face Camp. It was cold and starry clear. With our head torches we climbed swiftly upwards. We must have made 200 metres an hour. We were continually checking time against altitude. By daybreak we must be off the face. At six o'clock in the morning we were up in the stonefall-free cone as planned.

The first half of the face had been firn snow and our aluminium pegs, which were up to eighty centimetres long, had performed good service. From the middle of the face the ice was blank. Nevertheless we continued in the summit fall line.

As the first rays of the sun reached the face it came alive around us. Stones whirred away down, ice began to fall. In the central gully we would not have survived! The ice above became ever steeper. At the top was ribbed firn snow like huge, downwards-tapering pillars, glued to the face.

Still three rope-lengths, still two, still one . . . we were on the summit ridge! The East Face, our expedition goal, lay beneath us. It was still morning as we climbed on over the heavily corniced ridge. As far as the start of the rocks all went well.

From below, the summit pyramid had made not too much impression on us. Now, however, we established that the vertical rocks consisted of detritus and the summit cornices of soft snow. After twenty metres Peter came back. Impossible! The altimeter showed 6612 metres. By going around the rocks to the right, it would have been possible to reach the top. But there wasn't enough time.

We decided to abseil. At three o'clock in the afternoon we began the descent of the steep ice slope. The sun had disappeared behind the West Buttress and on the face it was quiet. During the day it would have been suicide to climb here. Now, however, in the night-time frost, the descent was justifiable. We climbed, we ran down the face. As Peter abseiled over the enormous bergschrund, night fell. We were amazed at our speed, at the race won against the clock. We holed up in East Face Camp and lay awake for a long time. Now and then we heard stones crashing at the foot of the face.

A few days later Peter and I climbed the South-West Face of Yerupaja Chico (6121 metres). It was a strenuous ascent. From East Face Camp we had chosen an intricate route, over several steep steps. We had to go through a maze of crevasses. After nine hours and the hardest route-finding, we reached the top. We gazed around, over there to the East Face. Our attention, however, was concentrated on our friends Sepp and Egon, who were attempting the South-East Buttress. A Scottish expedition had had two goes at conquering this, but in vain.

Sepp and Egon had set out from a third camp. On the same evening they had reached the forepeak. There they bivouacked. Now they were making slow progress, where Peter and I, coming from the East Face, had got on the summit ridge. The linking ridge from the forepeak to the main summit must be more difficult than expected.

Meanwhile Peter and I had descended to base camp. Now we waited tensely to see how the pair were doing. The binoculars went from hand to hand and the excitement became ever greater. At last Sepp and Egon set off again. It was the morning of the third day. They traversed, as we had proposed, anti-clockwise round the summit rocks to the right-hand ridge. Now they speeded up. Our joy in base camp grew with each step.

Like a radio commentator, Otti, who had the glasses, described their passage to the summit. Now both were up. They embraced. Even without the binoculars I could recognise a black dot. Our eyes filled with tears.

It was two o'clock in the afternoon. Sepp and Egon started down at once. We heaved a sigh of relief but the descent of the East Face progressed hesitatingly. Towards midnight we saw a head lamp flash on the face, followed by lots more flashes, then no more. So they were bivouacking.

None of us slept. First thing next morning we were able to welcome them in East Face Camp. They were completely exhausted.

At base camp it turned out that both had badly frozen feet. There was nothing for it, we had to descend. Thanks to our excellent expedition doctor, Raimund Margreiter, their toes were able to be saved.

8

A MEET AT CHAMONIX

1969

I WAS INVITED BY L'ÉCOLE NATIONALE de Ski et d'Alpinisme de Chamonix (ENSA) to participate in an international climbers' meet in Chamonix. Back from the Andes, I was in top form and no longer interested in studying. Mountaineering had become for me the most important thing in the world. Father and Mother accompanied me. They wanted to take advantage of the beautiful weather and to combine the journey with a visit. Three of my brothers— Erich, Siegfried and Hubert—were working that summer in Switzerland, earning themselves pocket-money for the school months as herdsmen and shepherds.

The journey via Mailand, Chivasso and Aosta flew by. Father told stories about the weeks he had spent there at the end of the war in 1945 while trying to get home. Some villages he still recognised, although in the meantime much had changed. From Courmayeur we had our first glimpse of Mont Blanc. A welcoming light lay on the massive firn slopes of the Brenva Face, and on the summit I thought I could see a snow plume.

As we drove in a column through the great mountain to France, I was steadfastly thinking of the Pillar of Frêney. In my thoughts I had just got up to the big roof, when the tunnel came to an end. Before us lay Chamonix, the town of climbers, at that time meeting point of all the great alpinists of Europe.

In the evening we listened to the weather forecast. It was good, and I was without a partner. Once more we strolled through the town. The summit slopes of Mont Blanc were touched by the last rays of the sun. Above the gloomy Chamonix Aiguilles the gleaming summit looked friendly. Yet, even after my experience in the Andes, I could not look at the peak, whose torn glaciers crept down as far as the valley, without a shiver.

This particular evening the fascination of the Droites North Face filled my thoughts. I could not recall having thought of making a solo ascent of this face before. Now, however, as the sun went down the plan suddenly crystallised for me. I saw before me the dark wall and the long serrated summit ridge and was at once attracted to this 'problem'. I wondered to myself that as yet no one had had the idea of soloing this face. I had tried it in 1965 with Günther but we had failed.

I wanted to jump and run. No one else was even talking about this face. They were all going around with everyday faces: their holiday faces, their office faces, their factory faces. They smoked their cigarettes or sipped their coffee in front of a bar. I had to walk about and avoided everyone on the street—out of fear they would be able to see my 'Droites-Face'.

Next morning we drove to Argentière. From there I climbed up into the snow basin and my parents drove on, into Switzerland, to my brothers. It was ten o'clock. I was up on the flat glacier, which has to be traversed below the Aiguille Verte. The sun blazed from the sky and the snow reflected the heat. A small watercourse bubbled near the dirty tracks. The man who was in front of me wiped his sleeve more and more frequently over his face. Then he stopped, knelt down and drank greedily from the icy stream.

From the face came a dull crashing. The stranger looked up as if someone had called him. Some blocks of stone which had melted from the summit ridge plunged down the North Face of the Droites. I was as scared as if they had got me. The man sank his mouth in the clear water again. 'By eight o'clock I must be up on the vertical part of the face,' I said to myself, 'then I can still turn back if necessary.'

It was quiet again in the Argentière basin. Once more I scanned down the face. The unbelievably steep bulge at the beginning was blank; in the Basin, an indentation in the middle of the face, narrow strips of snow rose as far as the first rock island. Above that the face was vertical. New snow lay on the tops of the buttresses and some rays of sunshine caught the summit ridge. Half an hour later I pressed my way into the crowded hut.

I threw off my rucksack and went into the kitchen to find Michel. He laughed all over his face as I stretched out my hand to him. 'Droites?' he asked at the same time, and then, 'Where's your brother?'

I shook my head: 'I'm alone.'

Michel, the son of the hut guardian, was a longstanding friend, and spoke some German. Günther and I had got to know him when we gave up on this face four years ago after 200 metres. 'You must come again!' Michel had said as we departed. Now I was here.

'Droites?' asked Michel once more.

I nodded.

'Solo?'

'Yes, I want to try it.'

'Hard!'

'I know, I want to try it.'

Michel laughed, he was filled with enthusiasm for my eccentric plan.

'Don't say anything,' I begged him, and would he next day scan the face from time to time. Michel took the binoculars and then showed me my bedspace. He excused himself and disappeared again into the common room. I sorted out my rucksack, and went downstairs. In the day-room, I fetched out the hut books, settled myself at a table and leafed through them.

Near me sat a guide, who was relating one of his experiences. Everyone around listened. I didn't speak a word of French but I understood that, all of a sudden, the talk was about my planned solo ascent. I stood up, left the books lying there and pushed my way through the back door into the open.

Outside on the balustrade in front of the hut sat Michel. I simply could not be angry with him. Why had he betrayed my plan? Without a word he handed me the binoculars. I looked up at the Droites Face. Michel's small brother, however, placed himself in front of me and grinned. For a while I boxed with him, then went to the dormitory, in order to check over my equipment once more. My crampons were blunt.

Michel brought a file, and the three of us sat down in front of the hut to sharpen my crampons. The guides who were sitting there exchanged a quick glance. The guides' course was based at this hut, a fact that had not escaped my notice. I would have a critical audience. One of the men clapped me on the shoulder, then went into supper.

Only Michel remained. He sat himself by me on the railings in front of the hut. Now, with the darkness, a feeling of uncertainty crept up on me. As always in the night!

'Michel,' I said, 'Michel, I shan't do the climb tomorrow.' As he smiled in astonishment, I said I had had second thoughts.

That evening I could not get to sleep for a long time. Several times I went from the day-room into the dormitory, then back again into the day-room. It was not the thought of the face that had unbalanced me. It was my firm intention to climb it alone which bothered me.

At one o'clock Michel woke the first climbers. It made me jump although I had not slept.

Two o'clock. Again some went out: For the Argentière, Verte, Triolet...perhaps even Courtes. Michel shone his light once near my pillow. I shook my head. The thoughts circled around in my brain like will-o'-the-wisps. I had my eyes open and lay with my thick breeches under the covers. His candle painted shadows on the wall.

When all the other climbers had set off, I got up, dressed myself, took the rucksack and slipped out into the morning. There I saw lights approaching the North Face of the Triolet, three of them. A guide lit a lantern in front of the hut. In the east already the morning was coming up. As I stumbled down the slope to the glacier basin, I toyed again with the idea of the Droites North Face. What did I think? I don't remember. I was in top form and the weather was good and I had no worries, even though in the night nothing had made sense and this doubt lingered as I plodded up to the start.

I sank into the snow up to my ankles. On the North Face of the Verte two lights were already high up. Lower down were still more, six or eight it would be. As I stood under the bergschrund, the day dawned. The vertical part was extremely difficult. Far to the left I found a dièdre, via which I reached the first ice-field. I climbed obliquely upwards to the right until I was under the first rise. There was only a thin layer of ice on the rock slabs which soared up alarmingly steeply above me.

Three times this face had been climbed up to then. My predecessors had needed from two to five days. Above the next rise the angle of the ice relented again. If I could get that far...

It comforted me to think that I was not yet committed, to leave things open. I could still go back, could still climb down.

I knew that I had no time to lose. By eight o'clock I must have reached the summit rocks or have climbed down, for then the stonefall would start. I could not abandon myself to chance. My observations of the day before and my form were what counted. I knew that the stonefall began on the face when the sun touched the summit slopes.

The alarmingly steep gully above me was blank. The ice, however, was soft and the gully so deep that I could climb it as if I were in a dièdre. I climbed without resting. I concentrated alternately on the front points of my crampons which I carefully jabbed into the ice, on the pick in my left hand, for which I looked for small bright stains in the ice and on the axe in my right hand.

On ice, I climbed according to the three-holds principle. Only when I had found good holds with axe and pick did I climb three paces. On slopes as steep as this I would not have been able to cut any steps without losing my rhythm and balance.

Actually, after about a hundred metres the face was less steep and I could rest properly. Then I climbed on, dragging one rope after me, the other on my back. Not until I was just below the rocks at the beginning of the last third of the face did I tie the second rope around me too. Less than two hours had passed since I crossed the bergschrund and not one falling stone had menaced me.

Over mixed ground I climbed obliquely upwards to the right. Before an overhang I secured myself with my different-length ropes. The rock was slabby, with all the cracks filled with ice. Only once did I come across a piton, probably left in by Wolfgang Axt and Werner Gross on the second ascent of the face.

Further up I went too far to the left, so that I lost Axt's variation of the route. At all times I climbed where the face seemed to me easiest. The original route ran further to the right and had seemed too dangerous, given the amount of verglas.

A steep, compact slab barred my way upwards. Further to the left it was impossible, to the right too friable. I would have to climb back to the Axt variation. Before doing that I decided to try the hands-breadth crack which went up the granite slab. As I had only two big pegs with me, I banged one in and secured myself to it. Then I climbed as far as I could, banged in the other and abseiled down to the first one, pulled it out and climbed up the fixed rope. Between the pitons I climbed free and assisted myself with big knotted slings, as necessary. I had cut off a piece of my longer rope in order to be able to belay myself.

This crack cost me a lot of time and concentration. It was more than a rope-length long and extremely difficult. Five times I climbed back down and up again, before I reached the top. A slanting ramp led me to the right to less steep ground, thus bringing me back to the original route. The powder snow, which lay on the ice here, required the most extreme caution once again. So long as I could hold fast to a bit of rock and grip the ice with my crampons, I felt safe. However, as soon as I got on a snowed-up stretch of ice without any rocks, I felt the tiredness in the calves of my legs, and the sleepiness which suddenly came over me.

I sat down on a stone block which reared out of the steep ice slope like a pulpit, banged in a piton, tied myself firmly to it and went to sleep.

When I woke up I tried not to think about things. I was scared as I looked down my rope into the void. I was about 900 metres up the North Face of the Droites. There were two people going along the glacier. The sun must be exactly in the south because the shadow of the Droites was falling on them both. I pulled out my gloves and took in the rope. I did not want to wake up. I shut my eyes and tried to doze. I had the feeling that falling asleep would be the most wonderful thing in the world. But I could sleep no longer.

Again I estimated the distances and steepness.

An hour to the summit, I thought. I stood up, completely rested. Without any problems, I traversed an ice-field obliquely up to the right and quitted it where a steep wall, interspersed with rock, led to two towers on the summit ridge. From below the two dark rocks had looked like horns. Crampons on the ice, hands on the rock, I climbed to the gap between the horns. Without stopping to rest, I went on and reached the highest point.

It was one o'clock. Away to the south the sky was cloudless. I descended by a gully on the opposite side. It was the most dangerous part of the trip on account of the crevasses. The snow was like thick soup and I crawled across the slush whenever I suspected there was a crevasse underneath me.

At the edge of the glacier, and out of danger, suddenly I was all choked up. I pulled myself together and tried to laugh. Over there was the hut! By a spring of water, about a hundred metres above the path, I lay down on the grass. Once more strong emotion gripped me. If someone had come across from the hut now, I would have had to avoid him. I had not wept for many years. Now, pushing my rucksack under my head as a pillow, suddenly my defences were down and the tears flowed freely. I had the feeling of being free of something. I thought of nothing more. I sensed, however, that these tears had given me a clearer understanding of myself.

IN CHAMONIX ERICH LACKNER was waiting for me. He was back from the West Face of the Petites Jorasses and brimming with energy. Erich was big and stocky, a bear of a man. He had switched over from boxing to mountaineering. His arms and hands revealed a terrific strength. In temperament he was good-natured and gave up boxing for that reason. He was studying mathematics and physics at the University of Vienna and was exactly the type, according to the reports, who usually falls on his first hard route. Erich, however, already had hundreds of extreme rock routes behind him without the slightest accident.

The day after my ascent of the Droites North Face we climbed to the bivouac box at the Col de la Fourche. Our plan was to climb the Central Pillar of Frêney.

In the evening we studied the glacier basin, which stretched across to the North-East Face of the Aiguille Blanche, under the mighty Brenva Face. Nevertheless, in the early hours of the morning we had trouble orientating ourselves. Two more parties set off at the same time and started up the Route Major. We descended gullies and snow slopes and traversed the flat basin under the south flank of Mont Blanc. It was still so dark that we could not recognise the individual ribs and buttresses on the gigantic slope above us. We could have mistaken the lights of the climbers above for stars. While ascending the steep ice couloir to the Col de Peuterey we got into a maze of crevasses. Only as day dawned behind the Grandes Jorasses did we find a way out. One behind the other we hurried upwards. Without belaying we climbed over several crevasses. On the Col de Peuterey the snow was hard. The sun shone on the three compact Frêney pillars, giving the granite a friendly appearance. The bluish, glistening bergschrund, which twisted and turned along the foot of the face, had only two weak places. We chose the left-hand one and crossed the intermediate plateau. An old track could be perceived. The July sun had nibbled at it, so that the separate steps, which the night frost had filled with grains of snow, were scarcely still to be seen. Minute by minute the sun became stronger. The reflected light masked the structure of the granite wall above us. The air—previously icy and clear—was now pleasantly warm and the rocks were shimmering.

A voice sounded from the enormous, smooth rock buttresses above us. At first it was only scraps of words, then we heard rope commands. We put our heads far back, but could not spot any climbers. On the upper third of the Central Pillar, where the rock arched in overhangs, the air was so transparent that each crack and each ledge could be recognised.

'There's one hanging from the big roof,' said Erich excitedly. At the same moment I saw him too; some 600 metres above us he was dangling in the air. The rungs of his étrier shone metallically. The tiny figure jerked and quivered, as if racked with cramp. Suddenly he pendulumed back from the edge

115

of the roof and hung like a sack in the air. 'He's fallen,' I said. For a long time he was quiet. Then he stretched, hoisted himself slowly, stretched, kicked a few times with his legs and in two moves climbed up to the platform above. More than an hour he had needed for this crux at 4700 metres. The pair—they were Bulgarian and likewise guests of ENSA—had started up the face the same day I had been on the North Face of the Droites; so they were to tell us that evening in the Vallot Hut.

It was now six o'clock in the morning. The rocks at the start of the climb were covered with a thin glaze of ice. The sun shone on the back of the first dièdre. Sometimes a piece of ice crumbled away, leaped down the steep wall and lost itself, in the crevasse between rock and snow. We were climbing, leading alternately, exactly up the edge of the pillar, when a piton to the right lured me on a tremendous flight of smooth wall. I had lost my way and could go neither forward nor back.

Only with difficulty was I able to retreat from a small ledge on which I was standing. Slowly I climbed higher. I placed my heavy double boots on tiny ledges, emerged over a projection and with my right hand gripped a rounded, warty knob of rock. There were still two metres to go to reach less steep ground. For some time I clung on, looking for handholds. I clawed at the rock, panting, and was able to climb back just before it was too late.

For some time I stood on the small ledge and could find no way out. Momentarily I felt exhausted and, for that reason, did not risk a second attempt. By chance the only crevice near me took a piton, so that I could belay Erich.

Erich did not climb up to me. Instead, he remained on the edge of the pillar and mastered this extremely difficult piece of face. Secured from above, I was able to follow without any problem. Around midday we struggled up a ridge poor in handholds below the Candle. Meanwhile, the Bulgarians were past the main difficulties and on their way to the summit. We could no longer hear their rope commands. Now, however, we saw a Yugoslavian party on the Harlin Pillar. The pair were at the end of the difficulties. They were climbing within earshot to the left of us, level with us. However, we had the main difficulties still in front of us. The second on the rope stood in a waterfall and talked to us. They would soon have the second ascent of that route under their belts.

Erich led the first pitch on the Candle. Powerfully, he climbed hand over hand up a projecting flake. Handhold by handhold, he tested the pitons carefully. Under a big overhang he took a stance. The traverse to the right out from under the big roof fell to me. In a sling stance I watched Erich, as he climbed up the dièdre to the big roof. Legs widely bridged, he crept up into the fissure which ran through the roof. Then he jammed himself inside with his arms. His legs hung wriggling in the air.

It was so still that I heard his every curse, his breathing . . . The granite in the back of the dièdre was poor, wrinkled and with cracks that divided and subdivided. Luckily the pitons held.

Beyond the blindingly white snow-fields, the woods stretched blue-green. Once more falling stones disturbed my gazing. Erich twisted and turned his way up the cleft. Shoving and gasping, he worked his way outwards until he found two good handholds on the left-hand edge of the roof. The most strenuous pitch was behind him. Those which followed gave us no more trouble. Exactly at sundown we stood on the summit of Mont Blanc. Like a gigantic cone the shadow of the mountain fell to the east. The easy northern slopes beneath us were bathed in light. We threw off our rucksacks, then freed ourselves from rope and climbing harness. Some pitons which had survived the repeated banging in and out, I stuck in one of the outer pockets. There were only a few of the belay slings left over.

9

CRAZY SOLOS

1969

Livio, the guardian, sat outside the Tissi Hut as I tied the rope on my back. We were old friends.

'Werner,' I said to my small brother, who had accompanied me this far the previous evening, 'Werner, about four o'clock I shall be up, about five o'clock you can cut along to the Coldai Hut.'

Then I asked Livio to look at the face now and then through his binoculars. 'What are you going to do?' he wanted to know. 'Diedro Philipp,' I said. 'Solo?'

'Yes, alone. Ciao.'

I ran down the slope, past some tents, towards the start. As I turned round to wave, Livio was still sitting on the bench, staring.

In the cirque under the face of the Civetta I hopped from stone to stone. Now and then I stopped and gazed up at the huge wall. Mist played around the triangle of snow on the face and a dampness clung to the cracks. Sometimes I could hear the voices of the Czech climbers who had started up the face about six o'clock in the morning.

From my worm's-eye view, the face looked less steep than from the Tissi Hut. Only the big yellow dièdre, the middle third of the face, looked terribly smooth and unfriendly from underneath. The Czechs were traversing now to the left into the back of the dièdre. The crack up it was dry. All the same I felt uneasy. To my right I heard the rushing of waterfalls, and isolated lumps of stone crashing into the snow-field under the Solleder Route. In the summit couloir the ice appeared to be melting.

The first gullies, up which I climbed obliquely to the left, were scrubbed smooth by stonefall and water. After the first vertical pitch, I overtook the second Czech rope. The first lot was still at the place where the route bends sharply to the left. There was no way of climbing past them. I waited on the stance until the second was on easier ground.

I had used the waiting time to throw out one of my ropes, so that I pulled it behind me now like a long snake. In friendly fashion the Czechs let me past but when my rope got caught on a rock tooth and I asked them to free it, they declined, made some rude remarks and recommended me to turn back.

The overtaking manoeuvre and the confusion of the rope had shaken me out of my composure. I no longer acted instinctively but climbed hurriedly and deliberately fast.

Messing about with the others had put me off balance, not bodily, that was still there, but mentally and I now failed to find the correct crack. On an overhang I lifted my foot too high and couldn't get any further. I had to go back. Not until I was standing at the beginning of the big dièdre had I pulled myself together again. The others were out of sight.

It was raining now, at first only quite lightly. On a ledge I stopped and looked down. The others had begun to retreat. Now it was coming down in big drops. As the face overhung a lot that did not matter to me. I climbed on. The rain will leave off, I thought, and pushed on over smooth slabs. I was relieved when I was able to slip into a narrow cleft. The Dolomite rock on the left side of the crack was so smoothly polished that it was like a mirror. The rain in the air, however, had moistened it, so that my boot soles only held when I placed them on small ledges or sills. I supported my back against one wall, my feet on the other. Often bits broke off from the splintery rock. Under pressure, however, hand- and footholds held.

On the next pitch, which earlier had been the crux, there was a bolt. It was the second one which I had found on this once feared free-climbing route. Walter Philipp and Dieter Flamm had made the first ascent in 1957 with only a few pitons and without bolts. Up to 1966 all those repeating the climb had done without bolts. When the route became famous and people who were not ready for the difficulties tried it, it became 'overnailed'. By the use of many pitons and above all by the two bolts, it was degraded. For a pure climb on extreme rock a sporting spirit is a prerequisite. I know it is not easy to turn round in the middle of the face but it is not climbing 'by fair means' to carry on using all available aids.

I had often given up on quite big climbs. Once, because the weather was bad. Then, because I was not sufficiently in training or the day left something to be desired. Often I was too cowardly or anxious. To me giving up had always come easier than going on. That was true of a solo attempt on the Cima Scotoni South Face and of the first ascent of the right-hand buttress on the Grandes Jorasses, as much as for the Eiger North Face.

Under the Schuppendach, once more I felt like going back. It took some will-power to bridge up out of the cave to the overhang. I belayed myself tying two pitons together, and let one of my ropes run through doubled. With a Prusik knot fastened to my climbing harness, I could pay out rope to myself and keep any fall as short as possible.

Under the roof I traversed on small footholds to the left edge of the roof where I released my self-belay and continued in the crack, until overhangs forced me further left to the slabs. The big traverse to the summit couloir I took higher than the route description gave. Although the rock there was wet with rain, I found the climbing easy. On the other side I put in two pitons for a stance, tied on the second rope and climbed the few smooth metres to the couloir mouth, as if I were in a roped party. Alternately I let the ropes run through the karabiners which I had linked into the available pitons. Before each new move I pushed the jammed knots along the belay ropes so that the free ends shortened. From the highest piton, I roped back down to the stance, took off the belay sling from the last part of the traverse and climbed up again on the fixed rope. In this way I collected my karabiners.

As I took off the rope, a dreadful feeling of being at the mercy of something crept up on me. A retreat from above the traverse would have been extremely problematical, if not impossible. There was nothing for it but to continue to the top.

Two-thirds of the face, for which I had needed little more than three hours, lay beneath me. Before me rose a deep, wet couloir. It looked un-friendly, repulsive.

Thirsty, I sipped the brown water falling from the couloir. I had under-estimated the rain. My long cord breeches were now so wet that they hin-dered my climbing. I ate a slice of fruit for I anticipated that I would not be able to eat anything more for a long time.

Heavy mist hung on all the mountain massifs. I noticed isolated snow-flakes in the rain. It was too late for turning back. Feeling chilly, I got under way again. After several easy steps I left the couloir on the right and stood under a cave entrance. It was the hardest part of the route and, with the thought that here some good climbers had fallen in years gone by, I got quite hot, as if anxiety had sharpened all my senses. This steep step was horribly friable. I could only press down on the handholds. A piton came away in my hand when I grasped it. I banged it in better, tied it to a second one which I had driven in myself, and belayed myself to both.

Above the cave the rope ran out and when I tried to pull it in, it was stuck. Despairingly I tugged with one hand at the springy cord. With the other hand I clung to a flake. The rope did not move. I shook it as much as my exposed position allowed, and tugged again. Tugged for so long that my left hand got cramp. That was dangerous. My fingers were more necessary for the summit couloir than a piece of Perlon rope. With my hammer I cut it off and so freed myself. I could continue climbing.

Now it was hailing. My clothes were dripping wet. I had traversed back into the summit couloir and was standing in an abominable waterfall. Anxiously I looked up the gully. It was grey, wet, slippery and full of hail. Suddenly a crash above me—lightning had struck. I lay against the wall as stones whistled past. Then step by step I climbed up the waterfall.

A feeling of being at something's mercy brings terrors with it. There are many such couloirs in the Dolomites but only this one sticks in my memory like a choking snare. I did not want to confess to myself that I was afraid. 'Bridge, keep bridging,' I said to myself, knocking in a piton with studied calm.

I had hoped to find a protecting cave somewhere and thought frequently of bivouacking. I could not have held out in this wet and cold for a whole night even in the bivouac sack I had tied as a precaution under my pullover. I did not fetch it out now. In my subconscious I still hoped that it would stop raining before nightfall.

I belayed myself carefully now, taking hold of each piton individually to check that it would hold. My wet breeches and shirt stuck to my body, making all my movements more difficult. As I stood in the water while knocking in pitons, I began to freeze pitifully. But I was a conservative climber and could help myself with the simplest aids. Neither bolts nor down clothing would have been any use to me now. In our technical age, old-fashioned methods can often improve progress and safety.

Under the chockstones on the topmost terrace I waited for a while. I knew the route, so was able to find the hole to climb through in the top corner of this giant cave despite the thick mist. I crawled out and climbed on. The mist was uniformly thick. Only once, when the rain stopped for a short time, did I see the Tissi Hut. My breeches were now so heavy that I took them off, wrung them out and tied them round my middle. My instincts and my body worked automatically. My judgment, however, worked more slowly. My eyes saw something, my hands gripped for something. My body led without me thinking out the proper movements. If I had had to consider each handhold I would have been flushed away by the water.

The short technical pitch under the summit held me up for so long that I was trembling with cold. As I hurried up the last metres into the flat notch between Punta Tissi and the main Civetta summit, I began to steam again. I slipped into my dripping breeches and was exceedingly pleased that I was not going to have to bivouac.

At the start of the Via Ferrata degli Alleghesi, on which I descended, a stranger was waiting for me with a thermos flask of tea which he had carried for three hours up to the start.

WHEN I GOT UP in the morning my car was gone. The police commented laconically: 'Sometimes we find vehicles again, sometimes we don't. We must wait and see.'

So I was chained to my attic and to my practice rocks at an old sawmill five minutes from the village. During the summer months I was now living at home again with my parents. Although I had still no profession, I was once more on good terms with my father. He interested himself in my climbing, which as he put it, I had developed into an illness.

Every time I went to my room, I fetched out a photograph of the South Face of the Marmolada taken by Jürgen Winkler, and looked at it for hours on end. The huge flight of grey slabs above the ledge was shot through with many shallow gullies. There were also little caves and holes there. A crack appeared to lead directly to the summit of the Punta di Rocca. Jürgen Winkler really took pictures on which one could study routes with a magnifying glass.

I was playing with the idea of doing the route on the Marmolada di Rocca, the South Face Direct, by myself. I had spoken with several climbers about this possibility but no one had thought it practicable.

This route was my idea. I had thought it through and would need two days. For many hours I would have to work my way up narrow cracks, bridge broad dièdres, grope across smooth slabs. For the descent an hour must suffice. I had already become a fanatic, I lived on this face, without having started up it.

Next day I had to go to the police. My car had been recovered. While the policeman telephoned I played with a squeeze-grip which I carried in my jacket pocket for finger training. The officer laughed.

'And what is the point of this?'

'For climbing.'

'You're suicidal!'

'Driving is much more dangerous,' I said. But he did not understand. When, half an hour later, I had my car again, I would have liked most to drive straight to the Marmolada, but it was too late. I would start next morning. At home I packed my rucksack. My mother was not horrified. 'Take care of yourself,' she said; as always.

I spent the night in the bivouac box on the Ombretta Pass. As it was cold in the early morning I had no desire to climb and did not start until late morning. 'I shall have to bivouac in any case,' I thought aloud.

For the first two pitches I carried the rucksack. The Vinatzer Route was familiar, but harder than I remembered it.

In the cave on the shelf I set up my bivouac. To the left of that I discovered some water that I mixed with lemon juice. The pitons from 1968 were still there. Günther and I had bivouacked here exactly a year ago. We had wanted to climb straight up to the summit, but during the night twenty centimetres of new snow fell and we were glad to get up the Livanos variation finish. Then Günther and I had deposited a bundle of pitons for a second attempt. My brother was not with me this time. He disapproved of my 'crazy solo ascents' and so we climbed our separate ways.

I hung the pitons in order of size on my climbing harness. In good time I lay down to rest. In front of the cave it got dark, the air nippy. I pulled my legs up closer to my body and drew the bivouac sack over my head.

When morning came again I had no desire to get up, but I was familiar with this period when my spirit was dull and my body thoroughly chilled. In my dozing during the night I had thought more than once that it would be impossible, perhaps, to climb to the summit alone. These moments of night-time doubt I could overcome—but not the inertia of the morning.

A fly sat on my rucksack. It rubbed its legs, first the front ones, then the back ones. It rubbed them two by two against each other, apparently pleasurably. I sat up. When the fly had gone I too massaged my arms and legs before getting up. Then I stowed the bivouac equipment in the rucksack and tied on my climbing harness.

Some ten metres to the right of the bivouac cave I put a piton in the

overhang. Secured to it, I climbed straight up a steep step and on over slabs, without having to place another peg. I was relieved to find that the climbing was simpler than expected. Beneath a vertical rise I stopped. The wall had holes, but they were too far apart. Further left I thought I recognised a greasy crack. I traversed left on rock columns like organ-pipes. Over there, however, the rock was vertical and disjointed. The piton which I managed to get into a crevice held. Belayed to it and two further ones, I climbed strenuously up over the slab.

This spot was one of the most difficult I have ever climbed. Next I climbed upwards over a long slab. Every time it got difficult I looked around for suitable stopping-places—and found them.

'You're doing something wrong,' I said to myself when I became unsure. After a brief reflection I changed a hand- or foothold, and was off again. Only as I was climbing a series of cracks and dièdres obliquely upwards to the right did I notice that the sky had darkened. It was sleeting already.

I now turned off somewhat from the direct line and located a crack which led to the ridge right of the summit. At the limit of free climbing I reached this, then nailed my way up it for some twenty metres. My rope ran through the karabiners as if I were climbing with a partner. Where the wall was climbable free, I put in two abseil pitons, then roped down and collected my karabiners. I left the pitons because I no longer needed them. Satisfied, I climbed the last steps up to the summit.

For two days I had climbed on this face, probing it out with my fingertips. For me a face was not only a mass of stone, it was an organism which I studied, and with which I lived. This first ascent will perhaps remain my most important. It satisfies the nature of the mountain and at the same time the ideal of the direttissima.

I WAS STANDING AGAIN under the North Face of the Langkofel. Three times I had been there this summer and three times I had come away. I was having yet another look at the Soldà Route which was not properly described in any climbing guidebook. 'I ought to have started climbing this morning,' I said to myself.

I climbed the last scree slopes to the start. It was past midday and I was in

Jürgen Winkler's superb photography (left) helped me plan a new solo route on the South Face of the Marmolada di Rocca, a variation of the Vinatzer Route.

a hurry. Each time I got out of breath I stopped and gazed up at the face. Above a broad plinth the rock towered up. I was too close to be able to register its whole height but I could recognise details: cracks, ledges. The wall was possible. A waterfall poured down the big couloir in the middle. Now and then small stones exploded on the hard snow cone which lay at the end of the couloir. Involuntarily I clutched my helmet.

After two rises the climbing became easy. I was climbing solo and without a rope. Across a ramp I reached a slab from which I had to traverse into a deep stone-shoot. Now for the first time I got out a rope. Next to the existing piton I knocked in a second, tied them together with a belay line and threaded the rope through the sling. Thus secured, I traversed obliquely upwards to the right. Then I roped myself to a third piton in the big gully. Once in the bed of the gully, I pulled in the rope, thereby cutting off my retreat.

I left the couloir after a few pitches on the right wall and soon got into extreme difficulties. I was climbing on wet, fragmented rock. Previously everything had been firm. I felt insecure. Carefully, I fingered a piton from my harness. With some tentative hammer blows I succeeded in driving it in a few centimetres. I must hurry. I was standing on small footholds, my left handhold was damp. I hammered in the iron peg vigorously. Suddenly a cracking sound gave me a fright—the handle of the hammer had broken. Luckily the hammer head was still dangling from some of the handle fibres.

I could not grasp the implications of this incident straight away. I tried to climb on, free and unbelayed and in a manner that would allow me to reverse my moves, but I did not get far; one, two moves, then I had to come back. It didn't go. I was in a trap. Twice I tried to climb away from the piton—in vain. I had knocked it right in to be able to belay myself. Just this bit, further up it would become easier. Between thumb and forefinger I held the stump with the hammer. 'Made in Italy', it read in English. I tried to hammer. I would be able to abseil if the piton would hold, I thought. It would not hold. Now for the first time I knew the true worth of a piton hammer. My whole body was sweating, particularly my fingers.

It would have been impossible for me to stand for hours on this same spot. 'I must shout for help,' I said out loud. For the first time in my life I had to think of that. But who would have been able to hear me? A shepherd perhaps or a rambler. It was late afternoon. Was anyone going along the bottom of the face?

The more absurd the situation the less bearable is the thought of death. I must act before it was too late. Great difficulties lay behind me, still greater perhaps before me. I would have been ready to let myself be hoisted out of the trap but there was no hope of that. My position was bad and I must do all I could to free myself. Going up would be easier than going down. Doubly carefully, locating small resting-places, I pushed myself upwards. With the knowledge that it was all over if I did not make it, I went from ledge to ledge.

I was so tense that I forgot everything around me. When the rock became less steep I stopped, standing now on a platform as big as a chair. I leaned my forehead against the face and closed my eyes. Slowly I began to forget where I was. I forgot the dangerous situation which I had just lived through. I forgot the broken hammer handle. Figures rose before me. Faces, staring and immovable. When I opened my eyes I saw, quite close to, the grey Dolomite rock. Delicate mosses swelled out of the crevices, marvellously distinct. Pointed, glossy and glistening, the unevennesses of the rock grew towards me. Crystals interweaved with the mosses and formed themselves into fantastic pictures. Then everything dissolved in a grey billowing mass.

When I could see clearly again, the rock was back to normal. Left and right of me arched the two buttresses, yellow and overhanging. When I recalled that the face below me was five times as high, I clung more tightly to the handholds.

Below me, in the dark, narrow couloir, a piece of ice broke off and fell noisily, bounding from one wall to the other, into the depths. Minutes later all was still again. The trees below in the cirque looked tiny and their needles flickered in the sun. Nothing stirred, all around me was quiet: the cirque, the faces, the couloirs. They lay there, as if there had never been people.

A mighty overhang barred the exit dièdre. I was able to turn it unexpectedly easily. Relieved, I drew a deep breath, as I climbed leftwards round the edge to less steep ground. Via an ice gully and broken rocks I reached the summit in the early hours of the evening.

My whole body was keyed-up. I was too tired to rest. I sat down and noticed for the first time that my hands were trembling. 'One can only fall once,' I said to myself, 'after that, never again.' Perhaps I understood for a moment what 'never again' meant.

As I stumbled down from the col in darkness and over the Langko-felkar to the Sella Pass, I reflected that everything would be the same without me:

mountain, cirque, stars. I sensed that something in me was missing which I must win back: the ability to smile at myself.

CAREFULLY I STUCK A knife-blade piton in the fissure, then fished my hammer out of the leather loop on my harness with my free right hand and tapped gently on the head of the peg. It held. At the first heavy blow, however, it jumped out, past my head into space. Involuntarily I shrank back and clutched the rock with my left hand as the steel spike bounded clinking down the face. A feeling of falling seized me. I was attempting a second ascent and first solo of the Meranerweg on the North Face of the Furchetta. I had climbed obliquely upwards to the right to some wooden wedges and would have reached less difficult ground before long.

It was no good lamenting now over the lost piton. In order to progress I must insert another and quickly. My ability to concentrate stretched as far as my fingers and boot soles which stuck to the rock.

The most difficult climbing situations captivated me so much that I lost track of time. I behaved as if my life would continue into the unforeseeable future. Naturally I knew, when I thought about it, that I too must die some time. But that lay in the far distance. It had no reality. First came something other: this climbing situation, this route. I was ready for each hazardous enterprise because I was confident that I would survive. I knew fear of bodily and spiritual breakdown at a decisive point, also fear of objective dangers. But not fear of death. Not because I had become so brave, but because death for me did not come into question.

Meanwhile I had stuck a second piton in the crevice, having previously secured it to a safety line, just to be on the safe side. Again it jumped out and again I was frightened. When a spoon falls from the table, one stoops and picks it up. That is a commonplace. Who is scared by that? However, on a steep face, far above the cirque, was something else. A whirring piton, a falling stone, a jackdaw in plunging flight, fleetingly brought the giddy drop, the possibility of death nearer. For a split second I identified myself in my subconscious with falling. Falling acquired a new meaning.

After this critical spot, I progressed faster. I climbed on up to the right, to the edge, and followed this until it merged in a yellow buttress. Now, partly climbing, partly abseiling, I traversed over into the Soldà Route, which the Meranerweg joined in the second third of the face. The rope which I had used occasionally to belay myself, I now took off again and tied on my back.

I was climbing the last part of the face for the fourth time. Soon I was on the broken wall under the final overhang which I did without a rope. On the first winter ascent, three years before, Heindl and I had used no pitons here although the rock had been snowed up and cold. Now I found myself in much better form. The wall was dry and pleasantly warm. In the narrow crack I pushed myself outwards and reached the icy final chimney.

As I scribbled my name in the book, I weighed up the possibility of a solo ascent of the Vinatzer Route, which today is still outstanding.

10

ODYSSEY ON NANGA PARBAT

1970–71

AFTER THAT SUCCESSFUL SUMMER of 1969, for the first time the Alps had become too small for me. I was twenty-five years old, I had made more than fifty first ascents and twenty extremely difficult solo ascents, and I was curious to go further.

In late autumn I received an invitation from Dr Karl Herrligkoffer to take part in his next expedition to the Rupal Face of Nanga Parbat. It was to be called the Siegi Löw Memorial Expedition. Was this not the new dimension of which I dreamed? Until then I had been an alpinist, the trip to the Andes just a welcome chance to get to know another continent. Now it had come to a fundamental decision.

For the mountains of the Himalaya I had previously summoned up no particular interest. Judging by the photographs and reports, the ascents there seemed to me to be too flat. Snow-plodding I did not want.

There was, however, one wall which had fascinated me for years: the Rupal Face on Nanga Parbat. It was almost 5000 metres high, steep and unclimbed. Hermann Buhl, the first man to climb Nanga Parbat, had described it in his book as 'unclimbable'. He had climbed Nanga Parbat from the north and from above had been able to peer down into the fathomless depths of the southern face.

I promised to go. I knew that the expedition leader, Dr Karl Herrligkoffer, was not himself a hard climber. The arguments between him and Buhl after the 1953 Nanga Parbat expedition I knew of from hearsay and there were a few mountaineers who warned me to 'Be careful!'

But Dr Herrligkoffer was the only one at that time who had a key to this face and I wanted to go there. One big problem was the financing of the expedition. Each participant had to make a contribution and as a student in Padua I saw no chance of raising the necessary. So I applied once more for a post as secondary school teacher in order to earn some money. Also I could train better at home in the South Tyrol.

Around Christmas-time Günther also received an invitation. Peter Habeler and Sepp Mayerl, who originally were to have been in the party, had dropped out. We were both very happy. Günther travelled with the first group in the truck, I with the second group by air. We met up in Rawalpindi, then flew to Gilgit, 400 kilometres to the north. Next by jeep, then on foot, in three days we reached base camp at a height of 3600 metres in the Rupal valley and stood in front of that immense wall. When I saw it for the first time, my courage deserted me: it was almost three times as high as the Eiger North Face!

Our equipment, transported by 300 porters, arrived in the main camp. It was mid-May. The first week the weather was beautiful. Everything went well setting up the first camp at a height of 4700 metres. Camp 2 we erected a few days later at 5500 metres. Then it snowed. It was three weeks before we could set up Camp 4 at 6400 metres.

In the storm, Günther and I spent a bad ten days in Camp 3, with daily snow and avalanches, returning to base camp to restore our strength on 15 June.

The storm had passed but the weather was still not good. We decided to climb up again. The weather improved. Was this our chance?

All the camps were occupied except Camp 5, with five of us in Camp 4 on the Rupal Face. At midday I spoke over the radio with Dr Herrligkoffer, who was in base camp. The weather seemed once more to be turning bad. A broad cloud bank to the south was rolling irresistibly nearer. I arranged with the expedition leader, who was to hear the weather forecast in the evening, the following signals: blue rocket meant the weather remains good. We would be able to equip the Merkl Couloir with fixed ropes in peace and then four of us could try a summit assault. Red rocket meant the weather becomes bad, we have no more time, this is the last chance. In this case I wanted to venture the ascent alone. To climb as far as possible, eventually to the top. Blue and red rockets meant doubtful weather. The decision was to be left to the spearhead group.

In the evening, as we were climbing straight up the upper Merkl Ice-Field, we saw a red rocket climb into the sky. There was no doubt! Three of us had climbed to Camp 5 and now had no more radio contact with base camp. It was all agreed: I would climb up next day and go as far as I could. Gerhard Baur and Günther would secure the bottom part of the Merkl Couloir.

I had set the alarm for midnight, but I didn't wake up until two. I was ready quickly, for I had lain there fully clothed. All I had to put on were over-trousers, boots and anorak, in which the day before I had packed the most necessary things for the 'summit storming': a packet of fizzy drink tablets, dried fruit, a Minox camera.

As I left the tent, Günther and Gerhard were still asleep. The moon illuminated the upper parts of the face and the Merkl Couloir. Uncertainly, I fumbled my way up the Merkl Couloir by the light of my headlamp. The moonlight came to my aid at last and I could see where I was going. I climbed slowly. At first I trudged over steep snow, until a step barred the way in the long gully. I took off my outer gloves, so that I could climb in silk gloves up this steep rock barrier. Further up there was a second step which also was not overly difficult. Climbing free, I got over the obstacle and continued. Suddenly I was standing under a bulge which could not be overcome free. I climbed back down and traversed to the right-hand edge of the Merkl Couloir. I had to try to get on the ice-fields which led up on the right to the South Shoulder. I felt very calm.

The moon had moved on and my shadow on the snow became longer. The couloir was icy and a great deal of powder snow was lying on top. It was similar to the exit couloir of the Philipp-Flamm on the Civetta. On that occasion also I had been alone. I could see that here there were no comparable difficulties.

I traversed across a steep snow ledge to the wall on the right-hand side of the couloir. Over a snow-covered rib which bordered the couloir, I thought I could reach the South Shoulder, which I had studied from base camp with binoculars. I reached the rib, but had to admit that there was no safe possibility of crossing the snow slope. Somewhat higher perhaps? No. Finally I had to turn round. I tried another place. No good. The terrain was climbable but the snow dangerous; in part powdery, in part frozen. I must turn back. Should I give up the whole thing? Then I discovered, somewhat higher up in the Merkl Couloir, a half-concealed ramp by which it was possible to turn the obstacle. A rocky wall, rather smooth and snowed up, led to a new ramp, which led in turn under the ice slope below the South Shoulder.

The difficulties eased although, naturally, it needed care. I was climbing with crampons and the rocks were awkwardly layered. The way to the summit seemed to be open. Once more I looked the steep Merkl Couloir up and down and was startled as suddenly I saw someone below me. Was it imagination or was I already suffering from altitude? Was that really a person? It looked like my brother Günther.

I waited and soon he was standing by me. I did not ask him why he had followed me. His voice sounded normal, not tired, not hoarse—just cheerful. Had he brought a rope? For six weeks we had climbed on this huge face together, had slept next to each other and cooked for each other. For fifteen years we had climbed as a rope in the mountains. It was clear that we would go on together.

The morning was soon gone. As we began the big traverse to the right under the South Shoulder, tiredness set in. But also hope. The summit ridge must come soon. We went slowly, in single file. All the time I searched for the best route up the steep and amply snow-covered rocks. The mist, which had hindered vision, had now vanished or lay beneath us and the sun was shining. The snow softened, and we had to rest frequently, with our bodies propped on our axes. Urging each other on, we tried to fight against tiredness. Below the ridge I stopped longer than usual. Günther suggested I have a rest. He wanted to lead now and went past me. The scorching sun was worse than our exertions. It made us weary, sleepy and slow. A sea of mist moved beneath us. Every time Rupal Peak, a small summit opposite Nanga Parbat, emerged from the mist I looked around me. Where was base camp? I looked for it in vain. We were far removed from the world below.

As Günther climbed up the steep snow slope towards the summit ridge, I took some photographs—they were to be among my last ones of him.

'The top," said Günther, taking a breather just below the ridge. As I caught up with him he was standing on it, taking a picture of the summit.

This arrival on the ridge was exciting. Everything was spread out before us: the summit, the plateau, the Silver Saddle, Rakhiot Peak. Günther and I were impressed. We spoke of Buhl. We saw his route of ascent. Seventeen years ago he had been here alone. We thought also of Merkl and Welzenbach, of all those who had fought for survival in 1934.

The summit stood before us, a gentle snow pyramid. It seemed to me to be quite near. Then a shred of mist covered it and the distance seemed to grow. Along a snow-covered ridge we approached the South Shoulder, 8042 metres high. Wind-crust snow alternated with powder snow. Several times my feet searched for holds and pressed into emptiness. Everything seemed to be quite near. I wondered whether I should go faster and climbed past a big rock tooth. Then I reached a hollow, the last slope. Only a few more minutes, I thought. These minutes seemed to me like hours. At last a snow dome; it was the summit of Nanga Parbat!

Günther, who had photographed my ascent, followed slowly. Now he was here, beside me. He took off all his gloves and stretched out his hand to me. I looked into his eyes, for we had taken off our goggles; I don't know why. So there it was—the first ascent of the Rupal flank lay behind us. We were full of so many impressions. We took pictures of each other and gazed at the panorama again and again. For the first time in my life I had the feeling of being above the clouds!

We had been there an hour already, we must descend. I tried to put on my Norwegian gloves again but they were too stiff with frost. I had a pair in reserve and left the lumps of ice that were my gloves on a rock to the east of the summit. Then we began the descent.

Günther did not feel up to climbing down the difficult sections which we had overcome on the ascent. We decided to go down to the notch at the top of the Merkl Couloir for the time being. One way or another we had got to bivouac. Next day we could shout for help.

The hours had passed without us being conscious of the danger we were in. It would soon be dark. We accelerated our descent. In single file we carried on as far as the South Shoulder. Once more we examined the descent possibilities. Going down the Merkl Couloir would be too difficult, Günther felt. I was aware of the seriousness of the situation. Could we descend westwards to the Merkl Col? According to a photograph of the mountain, which I had brought with me, we could reach the Merkl Couloir again from there below the principal difficulties. From this saddle it must be possible, moreover, to call for help from Camp 5. By way of a descent over a rocky ramp and a snow trough, we reached the saddle. It was already night. Under a rock outcrop I found a niche in which we squatted to bivouac. We took off our boots and wrapped our feet in space foil. Then we pulled our wet inner boots on over that and sat on our outer boots. Hour after hour. A long night with no end. Time and again we forced ourselves to wriggle our toes.

Several times Günther asked me to cover him up. He kept trying to pick something up. But there was nothing. We had neither blankets nor a bivouac sack. The temperature was well below -30°C. My brother's condition made me uneasy. In his state, and without a rope, the traverse from the saddle to our ascent route was risky. About six o'clock in the morning I decided to call for help. I went to a spot to the left of the saddle from where I could see directly into the couloir. I wanted to ask for a rope. Suddenly I saw someone below in the Merkl Couloir. Towards ten o'clock I saw two men in the couloir coming up our track. Felix Kuen and Peter Scholz! They were only 100 metres away from us and they had a rope.

I did not doubt that they were coming up to help us, and with relief shouted something to Felix who was in front. But he didn't understand me, and I didn't hear what he said. When I grasped that the pair of them wanted to go to the top and had not climbed up for our sake, I was bewildered. I shouted to them that they could come to us and go on towards the summit in our downward track. That would have been just as quick for them. Was everything all right, gesticulated Felix. I agreed. He climbed back into the gully, turned right and both of them disappeared behind a rib. I couldn't believe it. Why had they not come up to us? I had called for a rope! Yes, Günther was not injured, he was okay, only too unsafe for the descent and was sitting in our bivouac. It was stormy on the col, communication had been bad. We had misunderstood each other.

After Felix and Peter had disappeared and I knew that they were going to the summit, I traversed back despairingly to the bivouac to explain everything to Günther. I stumbled, fell a few times and hurt my hand. Then I went back again to the couloir. The sun slanted across me. For a moment a great uneasiness arose in me. It was as if I had gone mad. My thoughts eddied through each other. I plunged away and looked at my axe and myself, as from without. I wept, without knowing why. Günther caught me up and said, 'Now it's you who has lost his head.' His voice drew me up short. The moment of crisis was past; for a short time I had lost control of myself. Now decisions must be taken. Günther insisted on descending at once. No second bivouac at this height! Perhaps alone I could have gone down the Merkl Couloir to fetch help? But then Günther would have been alone all night. No, no splitting up!

So there was only one possibility for descent: the Diamir Face. This western face, up which Mummery had essayed an ascent in 1895, was much easier than the Rupal Face.

At home we had studied photographs of Nanga Parbat and I had Mummery's route clearly in my mind. If Mummery had managed to get up there in 1895, we ought to be able to do it without belaying. I did not find this plan exciting and mad, just feasible. I was sure that lower down Günther would recover again. As yet we did not think of going right down. At eleven o'clock we set off across a snow slope, left of a rock ridge leading to the summit. Below us a violent thunderstorm got up. Then it hailed. I went ahead to find a route in the mist. We found a narrow gap between the two séracs which separated the higher Bazhin basin from the drop in the middle of the face. We came to a rock rib and continued our descent along that.

Night was upon us but we climbed on down. From time to time I had the feeling that there were three of us, but knew that it was an illusion. Towards midnight we were somewhere on the top of the Mummery Spur and stopped to bivouac.

However, we did not stay long, for the moon had risen and Günther felt a bit better. In the moonlight we continued down into the valley and, around eight o'clock in the morning, reached a steep slope at the foot of the face. Slowly we climbed down, one after the other, first a rock barrier, then a big snow face. Tacitly we agreed to meet at the first spring; there one would wait for the other. At first we descended across a hard snow slope. I went very fast and stopped now and then to wait for Günther. The difficulties were not great but there was the threat of avalanches. Further down, at the bottom of the rocks where the glacier formed a terrace, I decided to go to the left, where a long avalanche cone made a fast descent possible. I came into the sunshine. Water! The ice was beginning to melt. At last there was water. Water! I drank and drank. Tiredness overcame me. Time and again I turned round to look for Günther. I waited. He did not come and, because I could not see him, I thought he must have gone down to the right below the rocks, so as to reach the greenery quickly. Perhaps he was already there.

I went on down, then stumbled across a glacier covered with debris and stones. Suddenly I saw people. They were coming towards me at the edge of the glacier, a horseman amongst them. I heard voices and waved. After a while I came to the edge of the glacier but there was nobody. I had another drink. Once more there were voices, known and unknown. I could hear Günther. But there was no Günther, no one at all. I kept feeling that Günther was behind me but when I looked round for him he had vanished. I began to look for him, at first at the edge of the moraine, then down the valley, up the valley.

I returned across the glacier. I searched and shouted at the fresh ice avalanche. I could not believe that my brother lay buried underneath it. I looked further. It got dark, I fell asleep, started up in alarm, called again. All my shouts died away unheard—a whole night long.

Then I went on down, leaden-footedly. I came to the edge of the glacier and walked along the last moraines to a meadow, across which a thin stream of water ran. I drank. There were the traces of an old campsite but no trace of Günther. I looked around to see if he had been there already. No sign. He wasn't there. I waited, he must come at any moment. I undressed and washed myself, had another drink. An hour went by. Günther was still not there. I shouted for him. No answer. I got dressed again but left pieces of clothing behind by a rock, so that he should know I had been there. Then I went to look for him. Shouting and searching, I retraced my route of that morning. The glacier was soft, everything in motion and I was wet up to my knees. I climbed slowly to the plateau where I had last seen Günther. There were no traces there. My tracks had disappeared too. It was now afternoon. I must find Günther before nightfall.

The sun had gone down by the time I decided to go down the glacier where Günther must have descended. Were those footprints? An avalanche! It filled me with horror. I climbed over the debris shouting all the while for my brother. Then I went along the glacier, calling, despairing. I went round in a circle. Night had now fallen. In the darkness I came once more to the avalanche. I dug with my hands, shouted, fell asleep. The cold wakened me. Or was it Günther's cries? I had gone insane! The whole night long I climbed over ice blocks, searching, calling. In the morning I was still there, shouting. But I no longer knew why. My wet breeches, my wet boots were frozen into lumps of ice. Once more I climbed up the glacier. As the sun streamed down on the face I went back to the moraine. Like a sleep-walker, and many kilometres distant from help, I felt more forsaken than ever before in my life. I called again and waited for Günther. An hour passed and he did not come. I went back to the moraine. I was too tired to think, at the end of my strength. 'Perhaps he went down on the side of the avalanche,' I hallucinated, 'perhaps he wanted to meet me down here.' I kept a look-out and my despair went round in circles inside my head.

It was the middle of the morning. On the Diamir side of Nanga Parbat avalanches were crashing down—perhaps twenty or thirty of them. I knew that I was in a dangerous situation. All shouting was pointless, yet I could not decide to go on. I waited by the spring. I called. Slowly the still of night came over the valley. With legs drawn up, I squatted there. I listened. I waited. I knew now that Günther was dead—yet I waited for him. Then I lay down under a big block of stone and tried to sleep.

In the morning I still could not make up my mind to set off. He could still come. As the sun shone on the Diamir Face, I packed my things in my anorak. I placed my red leggings on the rock under which I had lain all night and weighted them with two stones. Like a signal they lay there. Which was the way to the valley?

I did not walk, I dragged myself forwards. Now and then I took off my boots and socks, so as to bathe my feet in the mountain stream. My toes were blue! I went on between the mountain and the glacier, where I found some huts destroyed by a landslide. I shouted. No answer. I went on. When a big rock wall barred my way, I climbed down to a glacier tongue. Step by step, after several hours, I reached the opposite side. Wearily I climbed up on the moraine, which was covered with tufts of grass. There was a narrow path but my legs would carry me no more and I fell. As I picked myself up, I fell asleep. I was finished.

When I awoke, it was late afternoon, the sun low. I started moving again. There was a narrow clearing, then I traversed through an upland valley covered in scrub wood. At last I came to a meadow where some cows were grazing. A man was standing near the wood.

I called but he disappeared between the trees. I called louder. Nothing. Was I hallucinating again? However, the cows were real. I got to the spot where I had seen the man. Nothing. I listened. Then I heard someone chopping wood in the forest. I approached and met up with three wood-cutters.

They were poor peasants. Would they help me? It took an hour before I could make them understand that I was hungry. They gave me a piece of chapati, my first nourishment for five days. Then they took me to their hut in Nagatou, a pasture above Diamirai, where I also got a cup of milk. I spent the night under a tree.

Next day a young man accompanied me to Diamirai. I could walk only with pain. In the middle of the village I bartered my over-trousers for five eggs and a hen. Together with some local inhabitants I cooked it all in the open and then lay down in the temple. I tried to persuade some of the young people to carry me out of the valley. As payment I offered them the clothes I could do without. No, I had no money and for my last shirt the people did not want to

The Diamir Face of Nanga Parbat with an avalanche pouring over the Mummery Rib. Our route of descent was difficult to prospect and thus dangerous.

(Overleaf) Alone on the glacier (center top of picture). Immediately after the tragedy under the Diamir Face I had been too weak to go on searching, so I returned the next year to look for my brother's body.

carry me. I packed up my things and tried to stand up. With my axe in one hand, a stick in the other, I could stand and thus I dragged myself along.

At the end of the village I was all in. The front parts of my feet were black and blood oozed from my toes. I was barefoot. Then two men came along. One had a gun slung around him. I was scared. Did they want to help me or kill me? I was dependent on them, for I could do nothing but lie there. They agreed to help me. My feet were so swollen that I could no longer stand, let alone walk.

They carried me on their backs, in turn. When the path became rocky and difficult I crawled along on hands and knees. This descent lasted many hours. Only occasionally did we find any water in the narrow gorge. One of the men ran off down the valley before sundown and returned with more helpers. In the evening they took me into a peasant house, where once more I was given milk and a bit of bread. The following morning I asked the peasants to build a litter but they did not understand me. So I made it myself out of four branches and some rope, and they carried me on it to the Bunar bridge in the Indus valley. I was completely apathetic, lying there at the edge of the road. The sun burned down mercilessly and there was no shade. For a few hours I found shelter under a bridge, near the cool mountain stream which came down from Nanga Parbat. I was alone but I could think clearly again. I must get to Gilgit as fast as possible: the pain of my frostbite had worsened.

The first vehicle which passed was a jeep but it was going in the opposite direction. Then nobody else for hours. Suddenly the jeep came back and stopped. In it were two soldiers, one of whom, a Pakistani officer, spoke English. He took charge of me and took me to a barracks, where at last I could have a wash and have something to eat. This officer was the first person with whom I could make myself understood. Although he did not believe my story about Nanga Parbat, I gave him the details: that there had been two of us, that I must get back to the expedition. That night I set off in a jeep for Gilgit but, thirty kilometres from the town, the road was blocked by a landslide. We would have to wait in a hostel until the obstacle had been removed. By sheer chance Dr Herrligkoffer and the others, who had descended from base

In the 1000-meter Khumbu Icefall, the first major obstacle on the south side of Everest.

Bulle Oelz gives an injured Sherpa a drink of tea, after a close call in the Icefall in 1978. One has to ask oneself whether the use of porters is justified through this hazard.

camp and were on their way home, were waiting there too. Meeting up with them again that dark night, eight days after our last radio conversation, was very sad.

EIGHT WEEKS AFTER THE EXPEDITION I was sitting in the Innsbruck University clinic. It was a friendly room on the tenth floor. When I looked out of my window at the mountains I could see the Martinswand, the Hechenbergpfeiler, the Nordkette. This had been my world for six weeks. On a board at the foot of the bed my amputations were recorded: first to fourth left toes, first and second right toes partly amputated. My fingers could be saved. The magazine *Bunte Illustrierte* had printed a world exclusive picture report of our expedition. According to that, Günther had been too weak for an ascent to the summit. Yet, who in the team was stronger than he? When Peter Scholz and Felix Kuen, who had reached the summit on 28 June, returned to base camp, they were decked with flowers and hailed by Dr Herrligkoffer as 'summit victors'.

On 18 July a memorial mass was held for Günther in the parish church of St Peter in Villnöss. Neither Herrligkoffer nor Kuen were present. Shortly afterwards Felix Kuen gave his first lectures about our expedition. He had a predilection for quoting heights, numbers, hours which he had passed with others in Camp 3 or on the summit.

In the clinic I got to know some interesting people, among them Hias Rebitsch and Oswald Oelz, a doctor, who later became one of my best friends. He was visiting Gerd Judmaier, who for several weeks shared the room with me. Dr Gerd Judmaier, son of a famous doctor, had lost his footing on the

I lost my first to fourth left toes, and my first and second right toes after the descent in which Günther lost his life.

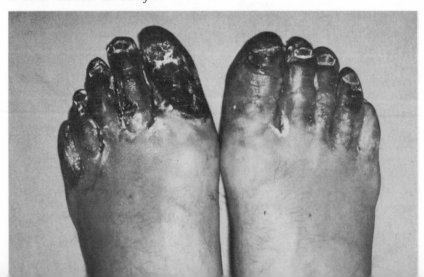

summit of Mount Kenya and smashed his leg in a heavy fall. His rope parmer 'Bulle', as Oswald Oelz was known to his friends, had been able to organise the rescue only after climbing up and down several times. It was a dramatic tale and a wonder that Gerd was still alive.

When I left the clinic I was a cripple. As I had spent all my savings on the Nanga Parbat expedition and could take no examinations in Padua, further study was for me out of the question. I had neither money nor right to a scholarship. Besides I was due for military service, which I could no longer defer now I was not a student. However, when I was examined in the autumn of 1970 the military authorities exempted me from service because of my amputations.

During these weeks I got a position as a secondary school teacher once again and for the time being I decided to stick at this job. I liked mathematics and my pupils and slowly got my life in order again. Sure I had a limp, and between me and Dr Herrligkoffer a bitter quarrel had broken out. As the expedition contract prohibited me from making an independent report, I felt myself frequently libelled and muzzled. To have been released for all time from military service was cold comfort in this dilemma.

The death of my brother weighed heavily on me. I had to bear the re- sponsibility for that. He would not have died if I had not encouraged him to come on the expedition. If I had not been his brother, he would probably not have tried to catch up with me on the last part of the Rupal Face. I had not sent him back. During the descent I had frequently gone on ahead. Seen in this light, I was responsible for his death and I must live with this tragedy. Slowly, I had to learn to come to terms with it. Hindsight could not undo it. It did not help my brother if I gave up climbing. It was my job to shape the future. So I lived with the tragedy and I didn't like it when people gave me well-meaning advice.

With the Nanga Parbat expedition, I had increased my experience of human nature. I had become mistrustful and my idealistic picture of the world had received some knocks; and that was a good thing. I now knew more about reality and when, in a year's time, I was able to run and climb properly again, and people smiled at me enthusiastically, I did not believe them.

In January I gave up my teaching position and became a sort of freelance alpinist, although really I had no profession. I did what I had to or wanted to do. So, against all the warnings of parents and friends, I became a moun- taineer and later a kind of adventurer. This word today has acquired an

In the Innsbruck University clinic recovering from my amputation after Nanga Parbat.

interpretation which plays down the total uncertainty which it encompasses. Adventurer is not a profession, rather a condition. One cannot earn a living by it, as my father had already explained to me in my late childhood. An avalanche might come and destroy the base camp or the monsoon set in too early and the expedition have to be broken off prematurely. There were torrents and crevasses into which one could fall. If you came out of it alive, your belongings were lost.

So I also became a lecturer and author in order to earn the money necessary for my adventures, and be as free as possible. I worked for six months in the year and travelled for the other six. Thus one adventure made possible the next. I was able to live quite well that way, but sometimes I had to be prepared to wait before I could go on a big trip again. I did not want to get rich either. All I wanted was to live as freely as possible and have time for mountaineering.

I came to like all solitary big peaks and felt myself at home on them, even though daily and hourly I had to weigh their dangers. Between expeditions I lived at home with my parents. As the night shadows of the Geislerspitze wandered slowly across the snowed-up cirque I would see myself in spirit once more in the Himalaya, in front of the tent at night. It was the same icy light which, on clear nights, lay over the great mountains, the same stillness, the same air. I could feel the storm tugging at the side of the tent, the frost crumbling on my face, as I crept outside. At home, I could not understand how I had endured all that and, still less, how I would endure it all again. Yet I knew that there was also security in the high camps.

11

NDUGUNDUGU

1971

IN SEPTEMBER SERGIO BIGARELLA and I flew halfway around the world to Djajapura, the capital of West New Guinea. This enormous tropical island is divided in two politically. The eastern part is administered by Australia; the western, also known as Irian Barat, is part of Indonesia.

After we had overcome all the bureaucratic obstacles in Djajapura, known in the old Dutch colonial days as Hollandia, we stocked up with provisions for three weeks, plus the thirty kilos of salt, machetes and steel axes, which we had brought to pay our porters. The Dani, who inhabit the New Guinea highlands, did not recognise money as a method of payment; they were still in the Stone Age, hunting with bow and arrow and grubbing up the jungle with stone axes. They had not learned to weave material for clothing and their tribal rites were cruel.

An estimated 1,500,000 people lived in Irian Barat. Of these, about 700,000 lived in the interior, in the highlands, at altitudes between 1400 and 1800 metres. The rest were coast dwellers. Most of the island was uninhabited, impenetrable jungle, where there were crocodiles, snakes and mosquitos. Roads were non-existent. With small Cessna machines the highland villages could be reached by air.

Skilfully, our pilot set down the two-engined aircraft on the slightly sloping, bumpy landing strip at Ilaga. The Dani, who were waiting at the edge of the field, fell back. But as we unloaded our bags, a hundred kilos of expedition luggage in all, they pressed around us, wanting to help. These small black people with their frizzy hair looked like merry dwarfs. With a grin I remembered the drawings of cannibals which, as a child, I had seen in books of fairy-tales. But these people were not frightening.

The men were almost naked. They wore only a penis sheath made from dried gourds, up to fifty centimetres long. Some of them had stuck bird of paradise feathers through their nostrils. Their faces were smeared with soot and pig fat. The women, who were clad only in a loincloth of reed-straw, made a peaceful impression.

This was Ilaga. The pilot confirmed the fact before he flew off. We understood not one word of the local people. We did not know where south was, or where we could get hold of reliable porters. We were standing in a broad valley surrounded by dark rainforests. I knew only an expression used by the Dani: 'Ndugundugu!' I tossed the word out like a ball. They took it up and with outstretched arms pointed across the jungle to the mountains up the valley. Their faces became earnest. Over there, therefore, lay the west, there lay the Carstensz Mountains. The highest peaks of these mountains were the goal of our expedition.

The Carstensz peaks are named after the Dutch seafarer Jan Carstensz, who in 1623 sailed along the south coast of the island and had seen peaks covered with ice and snow. Three hundred years later his sighting was confirmed by a British expedition. In 1936 a Dutch expedition explored this mountain massif, penetrating into the heart of the Carstensz range from the south. The highest summit, the Carstensz Pyramid, remained unclimbed. During the next twenty-five years several expeditions failed; in 1962 a small international group, led by Heinrich Harrer, succeeded in climbing the Pyramid for the first time.

The fact that, in the highlands of New Guinea, immediately above the warm and damp rainforest, there were glaciers, was for me both unbelievable and fascinating. In the Carstensz range lie the highest peaks between the Himalaya and the Andes. The rock walls are as steep as in the Dolomites. The approach march, however, would lead us through dense jungle. Also there were settlements of cannibals.

'Ndugundugu' was the Dani word for everything connected with ice, snow and cold. After they had looked at my amputations, they called me Ndugundugu too. To start with, at any rate, they had believed that I had cut off my toes myself, out of grief; for the Dani hacked off a finger-joint on the death of a relative, or cut off a piece of ear.

Ilaga was the highest settled region in the mountains of Irian Barat, first discovered by missionaries in 1954. In the east, soaring above all other heights, was Kelabo, its white limestone rocks standing in gross contrast to the deep green of the jungle spread out below.

The fields stretched out symmetrically on both sides of the valley. Here and there they extended like an outspread hand into the rainforest which hemmed in everything like a mysterious wall. At the southern edge of the settled area several thousand people were living then. However, most of the same 10,000 inhabitants of the valley were Dani, who claimed to have settled this region from the east. Flowers bloomed the whole year round. One crop followed another. There was no monsoon and no dry season, the birds sang continuously. There spring and autumn were simultaneous, rust-brown foliage fell near the young buds of giant rhododendron bushes. Year in, year out, the same temperature prevailed, a climate like spring in central Europe. Pines and palm-trees stood side by side, as almost nowhere else on earth. Were we in Shangri La? No, the chieftain explained to me, his great-grandmothers had emerged from a black hole. The Dani were difficult companions. They nourished themselves chiefly with sweet potatoes, sugar-cane, bananas, maize and pork. The men and women lived in separate huts.

That same day I tried to engage porters to accompany us into the mountains. I went from hut to hut and attempted to negotiate with the heads of the families. The huts were round, six metres across, scarcely more than the height of a man at the highest point, and roofed with reeds. I crawled inside through a hatch, to where often more than twenty men squatted round the fire, and in the flickering firelight their dark bodies looked uncanny. I had rigged up a phrasebook for myself which comprised in all about forty words and tried to hold a conversation with them.

The Dani were friendly to me. They offered me sweet potatoes and a kind of spinach. After visiting fifteen huts, there were ten Dani on my list who had promised to come to our campsite next morning. But when our column got under way next day, there were not ten but fifty porters. I ascertained that some of them were carrying potatoes for our porters. However, who really belonged to the expedition and who did not remained a puzzle for the time being. After an hour's march the confused crowd had shrunk to twenty-five men. On the way they had bought so many sweet potatoes, corn cobs, bananas and bundles of sugar-cane, that I feared they were carrying too much weight and that the expedition would be slowed down. I had taken over the bartering. For a net full of potatoes I gave a handful of salt, three times as much for the same quantity of bananas.

Abruptly the settlement came to an end and we were standing right in the middle of the jungle. The Dani led us up a scarcely recognisable path in many twists and turns through the thicket. Now we had to balance across slippery tree-trunks, to wade through streams and bog. The trees were often several metres thick and up to a hundred metres high. The mossy under-growth was so dense that sometimes I could only crawl forward. Sunbeams seldom penetrated to the swampy ground.

The Dani ran light-footedly from trunk to trunk. Their 'hu-hu' shouts sounded like the belling of young hounds. They did not get tired although each of them had twenty kilos or more to carry. I had lost my bearings completely. I could not have said where Ilaga was or in which direction we were going. With-out the Dani I would never have found my way out of this natural labyrinth.

Late afternoon they called a halt in a small clearing. We had been going eight full hours. They laid down their loads and ran into the forest. Crying 'Hu-hu' and swinging the steel axes, which I had given them in Ilaga, they ran around like spirits. Soon they returned, bringing with them trunks and broad strips of bark and in less than an hour two weatherproof huts stood there. They kept off the rain better than our new tent.

On the second day we saw our goal for the first time. We had crossed a pass and the jungle seemed to lie behind us at last. Before us there spread out an endless plateau which was bordered on the left-hand side by table mountains. Suddenly the Dani were running faster. They stopped on a rocky outcrop and shouted in chorus: 'Ndugundugu'. Then they pointed to the west. Between rocks and clouds a white stripe was visible. It shone. It was the snows of the Carstensz Mountains. It did not seem to be far. But four days' march still separated us from the mountains: many valleys, just as many high ridges, streams, bogs… Our enthusiasm threatened to capsize in tiredness. Tibetans believe that when we climb mountains we are looking for gold and diamonds. The Dani believed we were looking for snow.

'Ndugundugu!—Ndugundugu!' they shouted with joy as they saw the glaciers. In reality this chant was only a weak echo of the deep fear which moved them. Mistrustfully they went on. Tired and wet through, we reached the limit of the vegetation. Beneath a rock overhang we set up our camp; the Dani built huts again and squatting tightly together, they sat in a circle around the fire. I lay under a rock from which drops fell regularly on my sleeping-bag. Freezing, I awaited the morning.

With the first bird song the Dani began to come to life. They replen-ished the fire and pushed some sweet potatoes into the embers. For four days we trudged together across boggy plateaux. Every time the Dani found a campsite, when their hut was up, when one fell in the water, or when I gave them some preserves, they shouted, 'Hu-hu-hu'—a cry it seemed for both joyful and bad moments.

Having arrived at base camp by Lake Larsson, I decided to climb higher next morning and set up an advanced camp at New Zealand Pass. By six o'clock it was broad daylight. I got up, made tea, wakened Sergio, then tried to make it clear to the porters that five of them were to climb up with us towards 'Ndugundugu'. When I checked the equipment, two-thirds of the provisions were missing. We could only hope they and the porters entrusted with them would turn up. The Dani seemed to be peace-loving and good-natured, but they were as unpredictable as young dogs. Only two years before they had killed two missionaries with spears and literally eaten them. I was hardly afraid that they would make a feast out of us, rather more that they would all run away from us. Without provisions, Sergio and I would be completely helpless here. Far from any human habitation and dependent on ourselves alone, we would never have found our way back. When at last we left the main camp with the five most courageous of the Dani, to put a high camp on New Zealand Pass, the missing porters had still not arrived.

Two hours after setting off, we were standing on a pass directly above Lake Larsson. Before us stood the huge wall of the northern face of the Carstensz peaks. Enthusiastically the Dani kept pointing to the glaciers, which flowed down from the summit plateau in gigantic cascades, through gorges in the wall.

At the sight of the vertical limestone walls I was naturally reminded of the Dolomites. All these walls were still unclimbed. In my mind I drew lines up all the ridges, gullies and walls, estimating their difficulties and heights.

'Ndugundugu,' said the Dani, as if they were communicating with the spirits. Then they took up their loads again and ran on. They rounded a lake, then we marched along the North Face and called a halt by a big boulder at the foot of the wall.

Though they had got to a height of 4000 metres naked, the Dani could not climb to the snow-line without some protection. So when we stopped for the daily rain, we gave them shirts, pullovers, shorts, socks, boots and stockings. First they put on the shirts. We helped them by doing up the buttons which they took for ornaments. Only when I had promised to give them the things permanently, did they hesitatingly remove their penis sheaths, after we explained that the pants would not go on over them. We also tried to make sure that they did not put the gloves on their feet.

We had gone hardly a hundred paces when the first one took off his boots, placed them under a stone and went on in stocking-feet. The Dani know nothing of footwear. They have broad, flat feet with thick horny skin on the soles. Barefoot, they could run across slippery tree-trunks, gripping firmly with their toes. With boots on their feet, they staggered like drunks.

Later than anticipated we reached our campsite north of New Zealand Pass. Under a rock roof we found a tolerably dry platform. The porters' socks were worn out and they ran back to base camp barefoot.

One can compare the Carstensz massif with the Marmolada except that here ice and snow lay on the south side. The glaciers were arranged like an enormous horseshoe around the Carstensz Pyramid, which stood like a narrow knife cut off to the south of the main crest. In the range between the Pyramid and main crest lay two valleys, separated by a rock ridge.

The rock consisted of grey limestone, cut by innumerable gullies, and it offered firm holds, so a free climb was possible, even on long, vertical and overhanging walls.

Next morning we crossed New Zealand Pass to the North Face, descending into a valley of lakes and traversing the lower Carstensz Glacier. The snow which covered the glacier was soft and coarse-grained. Only at its edge did we meet bare ice where we could get a hold. The ascent made tiring route-finding. The glacier had shrunk greatly during the last forty years. In 1962 Heinrich Harrer had measured a retreat of more than 400 metres, compared with 1936. We established a further retreat of about 120 metres on the same glacier.

Early in the morning we stood under the long, jagged East Ridge of the Carstensz Pyramid, the highest peak in the group. What a climb! We climbed gymnastically over knife-sharp sections of ridge. We climbed tower after tower. Once we detoured on the north, once on the south side of the walls. It had begun to snow, but the rock was rough and firm. When we reached the summit just after noon, we were glad that the skin on our hands had survived.

I WENT ON TO CLIMB neighbouring Puntjak Sukarno, proving thereby that it is a separate peak and not the same as Carstensz Pyramid. Next morning we travelled back to the Dani in base camp. They were visibly disappointed that we had brought no ice with us, no 'Ndugundugu'. The missing provisions had not turned up; moreover, the Dani had eaten up all the stores: all that remained to us were four bags of soup, one per day. The return march became dramatic when Sergio was taken ill and could only drag himself along with the utmost will-power. The Dani complained of hunger too. If they couldn't hunt birds, they looked angry, and I was afraid of ending up in the cooking pot.

I went ahead to mark the route. The Dani who went with me picked some fern fronds. Without regard to the approaching rain, he stacked them up in a tiny pile. Busily he wiped his hand over the bird of paradise feather stuck in his nose. Then secretively he took a little split stick out of his shoulder net and stuck it between his big flat feet, slung a bamboo string around it and began to pull the ends faster and faster.

It was the fire-saw. He repeated these sawing movements several times, collecting and blowing gently on the fine shavings which fell away. All of a sudden blue smoke rose from his hand. Carefully he shoved the embers under the ferns, arched his palms around his mouth, shut his eyes and began to blow steadily, without drawing breath. Moments later a thick cloud of smoke welled up, which showed the following porter column the way.

In the evening we sat hungrily by the fire. At the edge of the village of Ilaga our hunger was so great that we gobbled down the first potatoes raw. The local Dani wanted to know whether we had visited women on Ndugundugu. For what else would we have undertaken all that trouble?

12

OVER THE MOUNTAIN

1971

MORE THAN A YEAR AFTER THE tragedy on Nanga Parbat and shortly before the outbreak of the Indo-Pakistani war, I undertook an expedition to the Diamir valley to look for my brother and to see the people who had helped me again. On the return journey from New Guinea I met and fell in love with Uschi Demeter. We flew together to Rawalpindi and then to Gilgit. Then we drove by jeep through the Indus valley to Gonar. With four local porters we began our march.

For a day we hiked through the hot, desert-like Bunar valley, crossed the roaring, ice-cold Bunar river, and the first evening we reached Diamirai, at the entrance of the Diamir valley. Diamirai was a tiny village, clinging like a nest to a rugged slope. With its autumnal-leaved apricot trees and the ripe cornfields it looked like a golden oasis in the desert of stone. From here the peasants had carried me in July 1970, on a home-made stretcher, to the Indus valley.

After the inhabitants recognised me, they greeted me touchingly. Why had I had to go over the mountain and not around it in order to get from one valley to the other, they wanted to know. That was the question which had occupied them for a year.

We sat on one of the hard planks which served as a bed. In front of us was the empty goat shed which they had offered us as night quarters. Dark-clothed men squatted in a semi-circle before us, offering eggs, milk and chapatis for sale and placing the occasional log in the fire that flickered between three stones on the earth floor. Out of the half-dark appeared a solitary woman who had been collecting wood far up in the mountains. Covered to the wrists in dirty tatters, bare feet wrapped in hides, dull ornaments in her hair, she stood before us for only a moment, then she tottered on like a spectre of past beauty.

155

In 1971 I returned to the Diamir valley with Uschi Demeter who became my wife. Uschi came on various expeditions with me, but in the end my single-minded obsession with the mountains was too much for our marriage.

The Diamir valley was everything but charming: a steep, hardly accessible gorge. Across rock slabs and drops led a path, which without mountaineering experience would have been impassable; a path up to Nanga Parbat. Below us raged the rushing river. If two lads had not helped me in 1970 I would be lying there somewhere.

Now and then we passed dark figures armed to the teeth, covered in handwoven blankets, the rolled-edge Hunza cap pulled down over their eyes. They were the peasants from the higher-lying farms going hunting or down into the valley to make purchases. We greeted them and some smiled kindly. A few recognised me again. Greetings! At once there sprang up a lively conversation in sign language and broken Urdu. I had to show my amputated toes. The peasants contemplated me with shaking heads.

The way was long and strenuous. Yet in its fierce beauty never boring. Although I knew it, I had many details wrong in my memory. Now and then we came up against Thuja trees with bizarre forms, genuine natural bonsais.

Late afternoon we reached Djel, a terraced village with grazing cows, multi-coloured goats and children playing in the fields. The women fled to their huts when they saw us coming. But when they saw Uschi they took her by the hand and led her to a hut. They touched her, gazed at her in wonder and laughed eventually. Then they brought us sour milk. A few began to stroke Uschi, feeling her hair, examining her white hands. She did not protest until one of them wanted to undress her.

One of the women invited us to inspect her home. The houses were miserable, made of stones and pieces of rock, the crevices caulked with mud and dung. Big branches and planks formed the support for the flat roof which was covered with compressed soil and made a terrace.

The interior consisted of a single, windowless room, the lack of a chimney made up for by a small hole in the roof. When I had accustomed myself to the gloom, I discerned the sparse furnishing. A plank covered with strips of hide served as bed for the whole family. For the housewife there was a tiny stool by the fireplace. The rest of the family sat on the floor, on old blankets, hides or other rags. In a corner stood a box with stores for the winter. That was all.

Now we had to visit the other women. As shelter for the night the people offered us a hut in which stores were kept. All the houses looked alike. In the night we were woken by the incessant pattering of rats.

For breakfast the women brought us sour milk, chapatis and eggs. During the whole expedition we lived mainly on the local foods which we exchanged with the local people for rupees or items of clothing. We got corn cobs, eggs, hens, chapatis, goats' milk, some pieces of mutton and a sort of green vegetable that looked like leek and tasted like spinach. They plaited it and then cooked it.

The inhabitants of the Diamir valley did not wash and wore the same clothing year in, year out, day and night. Face and hands, like garments, were covered with a patina of soot and fat. Yet they were handsome, thin and fine-limbed. Everywhere we were received with friendliness. Everywhere we were surrounded by the sick who hoped for medical aid from us. Mostly they were suffering from inflammation of the eyes and Uschi tended them as best she could.

On the fourth day the steep valley came to an end. We climbed on, crossing the scree-covered dead glacier, passing abandoned pastures and dried-up watercourses. Across a wide, scrub-covered plateau we approached the foot of Nanga Parbat and near a big boulder we pitched our tent. Then we discharged the porters and set up house.

We had reached a height of 4220 metres. Speechlessly, Uschi contemplated Nanga Parbat. The gigantic walls with the shimmering blue icefalls and the abruptly rising Mazeno crest threw long shadows. I thought of Günther, who had stood with me on the summit.

We stayed four days. To start with Uschi could not sleep. The constant thundering of the ice avalanches terrified her. I lay awake for a long time. In my thoughts I saw Günther before me and, like a film, the events of the previous summer unrolled before my eyes. The past would not let me sleep.

The weather stayed good. On the western horizon I could recognise the summits of the Hindu Kush. I set myself to search for my brother, leaving at dawn. By full moon I returned, tired and depressed. I had found nothing. How many ice avalanches had meanwhile fallen down to the foot of the face?

On the way back it snowed. The second night we spent in a stable in Ser where we cooked a fat hen. Half the village came to visit. Everybody sat round the fire and we sang until late into the night—alternately in German and in Urdu. The porters danced. Next day it snowed in Ser too. All of a sudden the mood had become wintry. We trudged on. On the way we met peasants who were fetching brushwood in big bundles or going hunting. That afternoon we reached Diamirai. I was at peace with myself. It was too late to reproach myself that Günther and I had gone over the mountain. I must live with this fact.

At the bridge in Bunar we took our leave of the porters. We had decided this time not to fly to Rawalpindi: we wanted to hitch-hike through the Indus valley. A multi-coloured Pakistani lorry gave us a lift. On the roof sat armed soldiers, behind squatted peasants with their belongings, food for the journey and hens, tied by the feet.

The Indus valley impressed by its barrenness, by its desolate, rocky slopes. The predominant colour was beige. Now and then a green patch emerged, a few farms, a few cornfields. The journey lasted three days in which we travelled on one of the roads hewn out of the rocks. It was rubbishy and washed out like a stream-bed. It was Ramadan, so during the day nothing was eaten.

At night we slept in small roadside 'hotels' which consisted of three loose walls joined together with a temporary roof and open to the street. At the back stood an open, walled hearth. By the flickering light, tea and rice and chicken were prepared there in the evening. One ate with one's fingers, all from the same plate. When we had accustomed ourselves to that it tasted excellent. We met no Europeans on this journey.

We came to Swat. The scenery became more friendly. Pine forests stood above a fertile plain. In Megora we bought fresh fruit. Across Malakand, Mardan and Nowshera we travelled in cram-full buses to Rawalpindi.

In the Hotel Flesmens the porter did not recognise us again. Then we looked at ourselves in the mirror and understood. We were sunburned, dust-encrusted, pig-dirty and flea-bitten. However, when an hour later, bathed and combed, we appeared for dinner, he winked at us archly. In the candle-light mountaineers looked like people too.

13

ASCENT OF MOUNT KENYA

1972

FOR EXPERIENCED CLIMBERS Mount Kenya is the most interesting mountain in East Africa. At 5198 metres it is one of the highest peaks on the Dark Continent. Of course Kilimanjaro is 700 metres higher but substantially easier to climb. Shortly after Christmas 1971 five of us set off there. It was a six-hour slog through swamp to Mackinder Camp. Suddenly one of the Masai porters brought me a bunch of pink everlasting-flowers. 'Because today the sun is not shining!' he said. That was our greeting to base camp.

Mackinder Camp lay at about 4200 metres: a small tented town at the foot of Mount Kenya. A world full of contrasts lay around us. On blue flowers lay icy dew. Senecios grew exuberantly at the edge of the glacier. Iridescent birds flitted over iced-up watercourses. Heat and frost awakened this apparently dead world into blossoming life. At the same time it meant the slow decay of the bizarre rocks. As I lay in the sun on the shore of an exotic lake, far above me I heard ice and rocks plunging into the abyss.

Less than a kilometre from camp, Mount Kenya soared up. Long ice cascades hung between the buttresses of dark primary rock. An impressive peak. From camp I could recognise distinctly the two main summits of the mountain: Batian on the left, Nelion on the right, named after two chiefs of the Masai. To the right of the principal massif stood the bold form of Point John.

The first few days we hiked a lot to acclimatise. Then we climbed Point Lenana, close to 5000 metres high and east of the main crest. Alone and without a rope I climbed the South Ridge of Point John.

Gradually we were getting to know the area. Three times I set off to climb the ice couloir which begins between the two summits and falls steeply for 500 metres. A fascinating first ascent. It seemed to me to be too dangerous.

I did not have the courage to burn all my bridges and climb up it. Not at night, not first thing in the morning and not during the day.

Not until the fifth day of our stay did we start our climb to the top. I wanted to do it without a bivouac. We climbed up to Top Hut, erected our tent and spent the night in it. At five o'clock I looked out of my tent. Hoar-frost lay on all the stones, it was still dark and the wind tore at the tent walls. The start of the climb lay at the other end of the glacier and we hurried in single file on a drifted track to the foot of the face. In the half-darkness we stumbled over scree and bits of rock to the edge of the glacier. After half an hour we had reached the cirque. In the first light of morning we climbed amongst rocks to get on to the face. The rock was steep. It reminded me in its structure of the granite of the western Alps. The face was free of snow and we left our crampons in our rucksacks.

Via gullies and ledges we reached the lower end of the Mackinder Chimney, the first crux of the route. Loose blocks were jammed in the slightly overhanging crack. This peak had been climbed for the first time in 1899. With respect I thought of Mr Mackinder, later Sir Halford Mackinder, who had been the first to reach this summit with guides from the Aosta valley, and after whom this chimney was named. We decided on a variation which led, right of the chimney, to a platform above. Here too one had to climb over an overhang and the two girls I was leading felt that a Grade IV climb in the Dolomites was rather different from the same grade at a height of 5000 metres.

The sun had warmed the face. Over stepped rocks we reached a gap on the ridge. In all the gullies and on the slabs lay polished ice. I fixed a rope handrail which allowed my climbing partners to make a quick crossing.

Steep and serried the face built up above us. Its small holds demanded neat climbing. This was Uschi's biggest climb. Here, just below the summit, she must not be allowed to fall. We were completely dependent on ourselves. Help could have been expected in two or three days at the earliest. Lowering an injured person was difficult.

I remembered the Innsbruck University clinic where in 1970 I had shared a room with Gerd Judmaier and listened to his account of his fall just below the summit of Batian. He broke a leg and was immobilised. His friend Bulle Oelz administered first aid, gave him all the clothing he could spare, and climbed down to the valley to fetch help. Alone he could never have rescued the injured man. At first a helicopter rescue was attempted. It crashed and the pilot was killed. Among the local climbers no one had the necessary experience to climb up with Oelz to help. It fell to a rescue team from Innsbruck to recover the injured man. For a whole week Judmaier had held out up there, tormented with pain, hunger and cold, anxious as to whether he would survive.

At such great height each step demanded more experience than in the Alps. The consequences of an error weighed doubly heavy here. Our acclimatisation was satisfactory. We reached the top at midday. The weather was better than on the previous days. After a short rest we began the descent. Down the route of ascent we abseiled, pitch by pitch. As darkness fell we crawled into our tents.

When we opened the tent next morning fresh snow was lying on the ground. So I had an excuse: the central couloir was no longer on.

14

FATEFUL HOURS ON MANASLU

1972

THE WAY TO THE SUMMIT was still not open. In the middle of the face on the 4000-metre-high southern flank of the seventh highest mountain in the world, Horst Fankhauser and I had come up against an ice labyrinth, such as I had never seen before. For a few minutes the mist parted. Below us stood an ice tower, as big as the Vajolet Towers in the Dolomites. In front of us lay an icefall with undreamed-of dimensions and above it the sinister steep summit structure of Manaslu. It was higher than the highest faces in the Alps. It would not be easy to find a way to the summit, I thought. Already below, just after the start, we had had to climb up over a vertical rock buttress, so as not to be killed by the ice avalanches which raked the face to left and right of it. So we had got into Butterfly Valley, a concealed trough which we had not been able to see from the valley.

Horst and I climbed down again to discuss the situation at base camp with Wolfi Nairz, leader of our Tyrol Himalaya Expedition. Two days later we set off again. Uncertainty must become certainty. Would it go or not?

I was no daredevil. I did not care for objectively dangerous routes. I was a mountaineer, just as I might have been a farmer or engineer. I prospected a route with my instincts, with my experience. I approached it with my abilities, with my passions, with my will-power. At that time I thought one had to plunge into and grapple with uncertainties like an adventurer, on the mountain as in many other aspects of life. Uncertainty was the mainspring for my activities. I would have been incapable of staking my all for an expedition if I had been sure beforehand of success. After Nanga Parbat, the South face of Manaslu (8156 metres) was my goal.

We had all fetched, carried and worked hard to place a route up that difficult face. On 20 April, Camp 3 was set up above the South-West Col at a height of 6600 metres. With Sherpa support, Franz Jäger and I erected Camp 4 at 7400 metres in two stages. The ice ramp between Camp 3 and Camp 4 could be compared for length, difficulty and steepness with the Ortler North Face. The ascent to the summit was prepared down to the smallest detail and was fixed for 25 April. All the expedition members were distributed between Camp 2 (5850 metres) and Camp 4 (7400 metres). A longer period of good weather gave hope of systematic progress.

In the early hours of the morning Franz Jäger and I set out for the summit. At the same time Horst Fankhauser and Andi Schlick climbed up to Camp 4. Hansjörg Hochfilzer and Hans Kofer went back to base camp for rest and recuperation. Wolfgang Nairz, Josl Knoll and our Sherpa sirdar Urkien moved up to Camp 3.

The snow conditions were good. Franz and I advanced quickly over the high plateau. It was strenuous but technically simple climbing. We climbed up an undulating snow slope. Each new swell concealed the ground beyond and, behind each ridge, we expected to see the summit. Each time, however, more snow slopes and ridges lay before us. As there were no difficulties to be overcome and the terrain was free of crevasses, we were unroped. To the north, over the mountains of Tibet, was a cloudless sky. To the south the South-West Ridge of Manaslu barred the view.

Towards ten o'clock in the morning we were standing under a steep rise when Franz decided to turn back. This decision came so suddenly that I was flabbergasted. Why turn round, the summit was reachable. But Franz considered it too far to go for the top and descend the same day. In no circumstances was he willing to bivouac. I did not want to risk a night out either but I felt myself to be in form and, although we were in the death zone, I was thinking clearly. Might I venture to make the summit bid alone? The weather appeared to be holding. Neither of us doubted for a moment that Franz could get safely back to Camp 4 by himself. He was in good condition and it was easy ground. He promised to wait for me there.

So Franz Jäger went down and I plodded upwards. For a time we could still see each other. When pausing for a breather I always glanced down at him. Then he disappeared behind a ridge. Across two steep snow slopes I reached the rocky summit ridge. Up this, traversing tower after tower, I climbed to the highest point. As the weather was changing, I stayed only a few minutes. Nevertheless, the details of the summit stamped themselves in my mind: a rock spike, some mist, a little pile of stones. That was the summit. Just below it two pitons and shreds of a tattered flag. All around, sky. To the south stood heavy, bloated clouds. They clung to the peaks until the wind hunted them on, always further northwards, nearer, away over the summit of Manaslu.

I took some photographs. Then I knocked out one of the pitons and put it in my pocket. I was not tired. The cloud bank in the south, however, and the strong wind warned me to descend. I had to reach the tent before night-fall. I picked up a handful of small stones, a present for my comrades, I thought, who were waiting for me down below.

The descent went smoothly at first and quickly. Suddenly and unexpect-edly a snowstorm got up. The descent became a race with death. The storm increased to hurricane force. With goggles on, it was impossible to see any-thing or to move. My mouth and eyes iced up. The situation seemed hope-less. I could not find Camp 4. Only when I kept coming back to the same smooth-swept ice slope, did I realise that I had gone round in circles. I did not know where I was. I had been going for hours already; but I didn't know where.

Now and then in the lulls in the storm I thought I could hear Franz's voice. It must be coming from the tent. He would direct me, I thought. I called his name. Then I waited for an answer. It never came. I was too tired to stand and there was no sense in moving. I thought then I would die. I sat in the snow. The storm tore it away under me. I was so tired that I had given up hoping. Why should I look for the tent? Snow and blood stuck to my cheeks and nose. From my beard hung centimetres-long icicles. I pulled some of them off so that I could breathe. I opened my split lips and dreamed of a swig of hot tea. Night came on. I noticed the thick mist; it was mixed with snow and stood like a cage around me.

When the storm left off a bit, I rolled on my side, then I propped a fist in the snow and stood up. I went on but with no idea where; not until my next rest stop did I have a brainwave. The wind is coming from the south, I thought; weather changes on Manaslu always came from the south. That had struck me during the expedition. So if I went against the wind, I thought, I must come to the edge of the South Face. Naturally I knew that in this snowstorm

I would never have been able to descend the South Face, not that I wanted to. Our tent stood there on the plateau, a little above the exit from the South Face. Left and right of the tent were rocks, the only ones on the broad slope. If I find them, I thought, the tent must lie in between. Against the storm and directly into the wind, therefore, I must go. To this thought I owe my life today. I walked with my back to the storm, stooping until I came to the drop of the South Face. I found the rocks. Twice I went along the stretch between them. Nothing. Three times. Nothing. At the fourth attempt I found the tent and cried with joy.

I did not recognise Horst Fankhauser at once. Franz was not there, only Horst and Andi. How was that possible?

Horst left the tent at once to look for Franz. He climbed up the plateau where he too heard Franz calling. After a short time he returned to the tent, then set off afresh with Andi in the direction of the shouts for help. The hurricane intensified, minute by minute and the calls for help lost themselves in the wind. In the extreme weather conditions and with the onset of darkness, Horst and Andi were unable to find their way back to the tent and had to dig a snow hole.

In the meantime at Camp 4 I went outside from time to time to give Horst, Franz and Andi some orientation by shouts and light signals. But I signalled in vain.

In the morning Horst came back and told me what had happened. After repeated urging by Andi Schlick, he had agreed to quit the snow hole to look for the tent. After a short time Horst had realised the hopelessness of this undertaking and dug another snow hole in which the pair took shelter. Horst massaged Andi. Suddenly Andi left the snow hole, saying he wanted to look at the weather. He did not come back. Horst searched a long time for him but found no trace. Completely despairing, Horst had crawled back into the snow hole to wait for dawn, when he could orientate himself and burrow his way back to the tent which was completely drifted in.

Together we took up the search for Franz Jäger and Andi Schlick again. But we had to accept that Franz and Andi had not survived this night of storm at 7500 metres and thirty degrees of frost.

The weather worsened again. Support from Camp 3 was unthinkable because of avalanche danger. Horst and I must cope with the descent alone. Exhausted and downcast we reached Camp 3. Josl Knoll looked after us there.

In Camp 2 the expedition doctor, Bulle Oelz, tended our frostbite, giving us injections at once. The weather failed to improve and the avalanche danger between Camp 3 and Camp 4 intensified. Another search for our dead comrades was out of the question. The expedition was abandoned and gradually we all descended to base camp. Sadly we left our two companions behind in Manaslu's ice.

15

THE SOUTH FACE OF ACONCAGUA

1973–74

IN THE SUMMER OF 1972, a few weeks after my return from Manaslu, I led a group to Noshaq in the Hindu Kush. Uschi and I had recently married and she came with me to base camp. So our honeymoon was a guided tour and at the same time a progress through a fascinating country, Afghanistan. Uschi ascended her first six-thousander and climbed all the summits around base camp.

Back home the following year we started on the renovation of the old parsonage on the hill in St Magdalena. This house had been up for auction and was knocked down to me. Although I gave up much freedom with the purchase of this old house of wood and stone, I have never regretted the decision. In all my wanderings it became the one constant factor. Between South Tyrol and Nepal, between Vienna and Hamburg I have seen many handsome places, but nowhere is so important to me as Villnöss and the Dolomites. Whenever I returned to Magdalena, and walked slowly down from the house, past the church, along the sunken way to the neighbouring farms, hearing the hens cackling, there was no man or woman working in the fields whom I did not know.

The summer I rebuilt our house I was confined to such trips as lay in the immediate vicinity. I could not make a trip to Asia. With Jochen Gruber, a young mountain farm lad from the Sarntal, I managed two first ascents in the Dolomites. He was installing heating and water in the old parsonage and sometimes we went climbing in the afternoon.

After the first ascent of the South-West Buttress of the Marmolada, I was in the mood again for rock-climbing. But it no longer satisfied me. The handicap of my amputated toes was less serious than the knowledge that there were other, bigger mountains. Not even a first ascent of the North-West

I set up home in 1973 in the old parsonage (extreme left) on the hill in St Magdalena. I have travelled the world, but no place is so important to me as the Dolomites.

Face of Pelmo was wholly to my taste. I wanted to return where I could use all my abilities: the Himalaya.

Apart from my activity as a home-owner I had no commitments. With my renunciation of a middle-class profession, I inevitably posed myself the question, how, where and when I earned my livelihood and financed my expeditions. Anyone who climbs with enthusiasm and dreams of the Himalaya must become sad or furious when he sees someone else travel a dozen times where he would like to just once in his life.

I had written some books and was also successful as a lecturer. I had started up a climbing school and I tested items of equipment. So with a few months' systematic 'work' in the year was able to finance the other months 'on the road'.

My successes bred envy and to begin with I reacted aggressively to expedition leaders who did not select me, to climbing partners who slandered me and 'friends' who wanted to finish me off. I discovered an instinct which perhaps had been there from the start: mistrust of all and sundry. Easy my life at that time was not, but in life, as on a mountain, there must be difficulties.

On my expeditions I had experienced, at first unconsciously perhaps, that our daily way of life is not a matter of course. It represents only one option among many. I had won self-confidence, also learned to do without the comfortable achievements of our technical age. If it had to be, I could live like Stone Age man. Above all, however, I had learned to distinguish what was important in the world and what was not. The important was often a handful of water, sometimes a protected bivouac site, a book, a conversation.

THE HIGHEST FACE IN THE New World was our next goal. My proposal to set off for the South Face of Aconcagua with a South Tyrol group was taken up with great enthusiasm by Jörgl Mayer and Jochen Gruber. We decided to make a first ascent of the South Buttress or the Direttissima on this huge face. Konrad Renzler, with whom I had made many first ascents, said he would take part, so did Ernst Pertl, a reliable cameraman from Bolzano. Bulle Oelz, with whom I had climbed on Manaslu, was to be both expedition doctor, and climbing member. Along with the party were Bulle's wife Ruth, and my wife Uschi.

After three days' journey and delays with our mules, we trickled late in the evening into base camp which lay in a small hollow. After unloading the mules and drinking a hefty swig of whisky with the *arrieros*, the mules trotted back to the valley that same night.

We needed two weeks to acclimatise, to prepare the route as far as the headwall. Then came setbacks. Jochen fell ill and was taken to base camp by Bulle. Konrad did not feel up to the summit wall. It was 28 January. Next day the decision must be made. Our hopes of getting to the top had dwindled minute by minute in the last twenty-four hours. I decided to venture an ascent with Jörgl.

However, first, we had to climb down the South Face again. Bulle had removed part of the ropes on an ice bulge in order to be able to belay Jochen on the transport down. We had, thus, to retrieve the ropes which we needed for belaying, in order to be able to descend the face with Konrad.

Jörgl and I set out in the early hours of the morning, over snow slopes and ice walls, up to a rock band in the headwall which had puzzled us so much on the reconnaissances. As Jörgl had broken trail on the flat section, I took over the lead on the friable and awkwardly stratified headwall. We pro-

Dr Oswald 'Bulle' Oelz on the South Face of Aconcagua, the highest summit in the Americas. I first met him when my toes were amputated in 1970 and we became partners in several expeditions through the 'eighties.

gressed only slowly, belaying each other. The height made itself felt.

At the end of the rock barrier at 6400 metres, I considered our situation. Jörgl was too slow. I ought to climb on alone to the summit, I thought. As a roped pair, we had not the slightest chance, for we had needed more than four hours for the first 400 metres. The summit was still 600 metres above us. The calculation was simple and seemed to add up. In his exhausted state, Jörgl agreed and promised to wait for me on a rock ledge. Jörgl put in a piton and belayed himself. He retained the rope. I climbed away. If I was to keep my promise to be back in four to five hours I had to climb fast. I had to put at least 200 metres per hour behind me. I knew that I could do it. I had often climbed as fast at such height. What, however, if insuperable difficulties arose?

I climbed straight up a steep ice slope. On top of a thin, hollow ice crust lay new snow. Above me was a bulge. I could not see Guanaco Ridge, so called because of the mummified carcase of a guanaco which lies there. Keeping an eye on watch and altimeter I climbed upwards. I had found my rhythm. I was making more than 200 metres height per hour now. The higher I got, the more paces I could make without having to rest on my ice axe.

The storm struck me so keenly in the face as I stretched my head up over Guanaco Ridge that I ducked down again at once. The roaring above me grew louder than breakers on the seashore. I climbed back over rotten rock and took a stance on a narrow ledge on the South Face. Here it was almost windless. Shreds of mist flew away over the knife edge.

In the lee of the last rock step, I took off my rucksack, pulled out my over-trousers and a second anorak, and put both on. Then I put a storm hood over my fur hat. I swapped my sunglasses for some ski goggles. Lastly I put on my down gloves. 'Viento Blanco', I said half aloud, thinking of the cold wind which stiffens everything to ice. I had feared this wind more than all other difficulties on this 3000-metre-high South Face. But now, a few metres below the summit, I did not want to give up. On the ridge the cold and storm ate into my clothing but now I could bear it. Initially I staggered under the force of the wind. When I recovered my balance, I began to climb as fast as I could up over a big block and cowered down in its lee. I was about halfway between the saddle and the main summit. The pointed South Summit lay below me, as did also the South Face. I struggled across Guanaco Ridge towards the summit.

It was not quite three o'clock; I must hurry. I climbed higher. Again I took bearings on a big block on the ridge. Suddenly I noticed a man below me to the left. He was climbing down a broad gully full of large stones. He was alone and obviously had come from the summit. With two ski sticks he fumbled his way down amongst the stones. Infinitely slowly. For a few moments I doubted whether it was a person. Enveloped in a red anorak, he looked like an alien being.

The tiny figure stirred itself however. At first it prodded at the loose ground below it with the left ski stick, then placed it, slowly lifted the right stick and repeated the same performance. Just as a four-legged creature steps between stones. Only when the second stick had found a hold did the figure bend forward, upper body propped on both ski sticks. The creature then took a few small steps. Its knees seemed to buckle, its boots barely cleared the rocks.

A bit below this figure must be the Canaletta, that narrowing on the

*The South Face of Aconcagua. On the left is the South Summit, on the right
the main peak, from which our route runs diagonally downwards to the left (centre
top of picture).*

ordinary route which must be climbed if one wants to reach the summit from
the north. Much further below I thought I could see tents. How small they
were. Yellow and red dots on a gigantic brown scree slope. Would the descending climber ever reach them? My head was clear and yet suddenly I was
seized with a feeling of being abandoned.

This man was nothing to do with me. He was not part of our expedition.
I did not know him. Nevertheless I was pleased to see another human being
in this life-threatening environment. I tried to call to him. Evidently he did
not hear me. Unflustered he climbed down, propped on his ski sticks. He
made me think of an amputee forcing himself to walk on crutches. Once
more I called to him but there was no reaction.

Climbing from block to block, I had left the ridge and was labouring up
a gully. About twenty metres below fluttered some shreds of material. They
hung from the corpse of a dead climber who lay there on his face among the
stones, as if he had collapsed and had not found the strength to prepare for

death. Now he seemed to be part of the stones, a red mound amongst the rocks. I saw how he had climbed down from the summit, lost his balance, fell heavily and did not get up again. He moved no more, only the storm tore at his clothes. Perhaps he had been a good mountaineer, perhaps he had wanted only to sit down. At such heights a stumble could mean death.

I did not allow myself to sit down, I had to go on. Suddenly a white cross emerged in front of me. It was about a metre high, made of aluminium and twisted by the wind. I was on the top.

To the north and west the surrounding peaks were clear. Far below, glaciers, here and there rocks. To the south, thick banners of mist hung on the ridge. After I had taken a few photographs, I pulled out a little casket from under an aluminium cover. I burrowed under all sorts of slips of paper and little flags which had been left there by my predecessors. After reading some of the names, I wrote with clammy fingers on the inside of an opened film carton: '1st Direct Ascent of Aconcagua South Face. South Tyrol Andes Expedition 1974. 23.1.1974.' Underneath I put my name, and left all as I had found it.

It was half past three in the afternoon, high time to be going down. Once more I turned and looked back at the summit, at the few smooth, grey-brown stones piled up there. I heard the wind round my head. The scree crunched under my feet and I was swallowed up by the mist on Guanaco Ridge. Along it I scrambled as far as the exit from the South Face and then down the steep slope. I had trouble finding my upwards track. The ice was blank in the upper part and my crampons had to be carefully placed, step by step, hour after hour. Jörgl was just as glad as I when we met up in the late afternoon.

It was snowing now. Every ten minutes, far above us, fresh snow slid away, flowing in small avalanches down gullies and chimneys. As we abseiled down the lower part of the headwall, small snow dust avalanches poured over us, taking our breath away. Konrad received us with hot tea at the bivouac site. Next day we were able to celebrate success all together in base camp.

16

TURNED BACK ON MAKALU

1974

FULL OF EXPECTATION WE HAD ascended the Barun valley to Makalu (8481 metres) which we wanted to climb by its unconquered South Face. I considered it to be the most beautifully shaped face on the fifth highest mountain in the world. A year before a Yugoslavian expedition had failed there. We were a group of friends, the survivors of the tragic Manaslu expedition, plus a few young climbers like Albert Precht.

In less than three weeks we passed the 7000-metre mark. The transport of loads between the first three high camps was complete. We were confident. Above Camp 3 the face became steep, the rocks were iced up and we made slow, very slow, progress. To start with two hundred, one hundred, then only fifty metres per day. But still it went. The weather turned stormy, it snowed every day. We hoped for better weather and at the first fine weather signs we climbed up to Camp 3.

Next day we set off early. Gerhard Markl stayed on the narrow ledge between the two tents. The air was cold, the sky a deep, dark blue. To the east white clouds like cotton swabs lay in the valleys. To the south and west countless peaks were flooded with red, gold, yellow and blue light. I saw these tender colours as a sign of good weather.

It was nine o'clock on 4 May 1974 as I clambered clumsily out of the tent. I pulled on my gloves as Uschi looked for my crampons under the fine drift snow. The noise in the Sherpas' tent revealed that the tea would soon be hot. This small platform at 6900 metres above sea-level, which Josl Knoll, Horst Bergmann and some Sherpas had hacked out of the fifty-degree ice two weeks ago, was audacious. The two Whillans Boxes were so positioned on the slope that the regular small avalanches poured over the tops of the tents. The space between the tents, a good two square metres to begin with, had shrunk to a narrow corridor. Each night blown snow filled the gaps between the boxes, so that entrances and footpaths had to be shovelled clear each morning.

The small white clouds which suddenly emerged from behind Makalu's East Ridge drove us to haste. By midday it would be snowing. On the platform in front of the tent we took care to secure ourselves to a handrail.

Gerhard looked around and saw the clouds and mist on the summit of Baruntse. His expression was deliberately imperturbable as he fiddled about with his crampon bindings.

Slowly I began the ascent to the fixed ropes, placing my feet where I supposed there were footholds under the fluffy snow. Tiny powder snow avalanches came down and dissolved, far below, into clouds of dust. The face, interspersed with rock, was awfully steep and, although it was not disjointed, without the fixed ropes which we had attached in the previous weeks, we would not have got far. At an interval of about fifty metres we climbed up the ropes and, for the time being, ignored the difficulties which would begin where the ropes ceased.

The screech of crampons on the steep gneiss slabs was unpleasant. In these conditions we shan't get any further with the rope-fixing, I thought. Dispassionately, I climbed on. We had put out 500 metres of rope. We rested often, gazing enquiringly at the snowed-up terrain ahead, communicating by a nod of the head only, hands firmly clamped to the fixed ropes.

The figure below me was Gerhard, masked except for a slit of face. He breathed audibly. In his movements lay strength.

When I reached the highest point of the rope, I belayed and divided up pitons, karabiners and ice hammer on my climbing harness. Heli Hagner had been this far ten days before. When Gerhard arrived, he looked at me enquiringly. I looked at the mist playing about us, then the face above us. An undefined uneasiness filled us both. Tension, anxiety and doubt.

'Are you going on?' asked Gerhard. He had not wanted to say it so discouragingly.

'I'll try it at least.'

Gerhard looked at me, then took the rope in his hands, to belay me. I cleared each foothold of new snow. Often I gripped handholds I could not see. When I had done the first thirty metres I fixed the rope to a piton. Gerhard followed. Above us hung a white cord, which we had to reach. It originated from the Yugoslavian expedition which had attacked this slope in vain eighteen months before. The Balkan climbers had found a dry wall in the 1972 post-monsoon period, but strong storms had forced the abandonment of the expedition.

The rope, some seven millimetres thick, hung like a lifeline on the snowy face. It looked rotten, much more rotten than the rest of the rope which we had come across further down. Nevertheless, belayed to the last piton, I pulled with all my might on this rope.

We were standing on a ledge, a narrow snow-covered rock sill. Above it the face built up more smoothly still. There were only two ways of getting out of this spot, one to the right over snowed-up steps, the other directly up over a wall with small holds. Fifty metres above there appeared to be a ledge.

I tried it on the right but did not get far. I traversed riskily to the left and climbed a crack, pushing my fists into it through the snow. Inside I jammed it, just as I had had to struggle in the Alps on winter ascents or after sudden changes in the weather.

Meanwhile the mists had become thicker. I could recognise Gerhard only by his outline. It was snowing. 'There's no point,' shouted Gerhard as I once again looked in vain for a way forward.

'A bit more!' I did not consider how my hesitation must be frightening him. 'You're mad!' he shouted up.

Standing on a snow ledge, I was able to knock in a reliable piton. Then I traversed to the right. In the course of the next hour I managed to climb over a rock step, yet it brought us barely twenty metres nearer to the summit. I drove in two pitons, belayed myself and leaned back as far as possible. In front of me a vertical desert of snowed-up granite. Impossible to get up there! At this point negative thoughts got the upper hand for the first time. Retreat! No, not yet. Later that day we got to the upper end of the next snow-field which gave us fresh hope.

For the fourth high camp we had discovered a makeshift place. During the descent we pictured the route to Camp 5, which at 7500 metres would be the last one we could protect.

But our last attempt on the South Face failed. It had snowed again in the night and we decided to abandon the expedition. It was still snowing a week later. I slept a lot, read, dreamed day-dreams, or sat in the smoky kitchen and watched Sona, our Sherpa cook, grilling pork on thin bamboo sticks. We had slaughtered the sow intended for the feast after the summit. It was to taste good anyway. Above the hearth, the tarpaulin kitchen roof was black. The stones between which the fire had burned continuously for seven weeks were white inside. Everything was covered with a layer of fatty soot. I had a feeling of well-being.

For the porters and Sherpas an expedition meant hard work. They would have been pleased with a success, but without this they went home just as cheerfully. We sahibs felt otherwise. Afterwards I could find no explanation for our failure. I had put my all into it. Why had we been so slow above Camp 3? Certainly, in the moment of decision to give up, no one had believed in a possible success. The South Face of Makalu was impossible, given the circumstances. And yet we sought for an explanation, perhaps even for an excuse. What was there to excuse? That it snowed every other day? That the storm would have swept us off the ridges, had there been no fixed ropes? And above all: that the team had anticipated failure gradually, without confessing it? The failure of the Makalu expedition was also the failure of a team too obsessed with thoughts of success, a team of men who were unable to develop their potential on the icy armour of this face.

17

TEN HOURS ON THE EIGERWAND

1974

WE HAD TALKED ABOUT IT—for eight years. Since the days together on the Walker Spur, it had been on the table: the Eigerwand. It surfaced in letters which we exchanged, in telephone conversations or chance meetings. Time and again, the Eiger North Face.

The first attempt was to end before the beginning of the journey. '*Eugen schläft* [Eugen asleep]—don't come. Peter', read a telegram which the Italian postman brought me. A remarkable communication from the otherwise so business-like Peter Habeler, I thought. After some reflection it dawned on me that the text should have read '*Eiger schlecht* [Eiger bad]—don't come'. That had been in the middle of the sixties.

Our second attempt was also frustrated by peculiar telegram interpretations. This time the blame lay not with the Italian post office, rather with us. Airily I instructed Peter: 'Meet Grindelwald Grund Eiger' and got on the road. At the valley station of the Eiger railway at Kleine Scheidegg—which is called Grindelwald Grund—I waited a whole day in vain; yet Peter was usually so dependable. As I was to find out days later, he was wandering around Grindelwald at the same time. He found the idea of specifying the Eiger as the base (Grund) for a journey to Grindelwald highly superfluous. Of the station 'Grindelwald Grund', he had never heard.

In the summer of 1969, during which in climbing terms I was in the best form of my life, I visited Grindelwald twice, once with Erich Lackner on my way home from the international climbing meet in Chamonix, the second time alone. On the first occasion rain and snow had repulsed us, but the weather was fine on my solo trip, so I went up to Kleine Scheidegg. Fritz von

Almen advised me against a solo ascent. However, the conditions were good. So I started up the face but turned round in the night because the rope teams ahead of me kept on kicking stones down.

It was this danger of stonefall which put the Eigerwand on the back-burner and some years passed without me thinking about it until, with increasing experience, I recognised that speed decided the outcome. The dreaded stonefall started early in the afternoon when the sun shone on the summit face and the ice which cemented the loose stones melted. Moreover, as a fast rope, one could escape a sudden change in the weather, which can be very sudden on the Eiger.

Peter Habeler agreed with me and we travelled to Grindehvald three times in the summer of 1974 before all the requirements for a safe ascent were fulfilled.

But on 14 August at last everything seemed to come together. The face was still fairly wet but the weather forecast was good. Three parties were climbing on the face. They were slow, the conditions apparently bad. In the evening we talked with Martin Boysen, Dougal Haston and other mountaineers from the film team which was just then occupied in shooting the Eiger scenes for the Hollywood film *The Eiger Sanction*. Haston, the best British climber, described the conditions on the wall and recommended us to wait. Peter and I wanted to try it at least. We packed our rucksacks with climbing equipment, bivouac gear and provisions for two to three days—one never knew.

An hour later we were sitting on a grassy ridge directly under the face. It was still dark, too dark to start climbing. We could see nothing and waited for morning. The wall above us was a gigantic featureless mass. Only where snow lay on the ice-fields, could one distinguish rocks from ice. The lights of Grindelwald were easily recognisable. On the eastern horizon the day was coming up. Suddenly we thought we could see light signals in the middle of this enormous face. Yes, there really was something blinking. It must be up by the second ice-field. I counted the seconds between the individual signals. Was someone in trouble? The signals were repeated. It was the alpine distress call! Would it perhaps be better to sound the alarm? We deliberated briefly, then plodded over scree, ice and snow to the start. We were well equipped and could help if something were wrong. Our rucksack first-aid kit was well stocked. Our pitons would suffice to lower an injured person as far as the Stollenloch, I calculated, as we started up the face over a ledge to the left of the first pillar.

It was now light, five o'clock. Waterfalls gushed over us. In Hotel Kleine Scheidegg the first light had gone on. We climbed unroped. First Pillar, Shattered Pillar...

We halted first under the Difficult Crack for a short pause while we distributed karabiners, ice and rock pitons on our harnesses. We arranged slings and belay ropes and tied on the fifty-metre rope. Bivouac equipment, food and extra clothes stayed in the rucksacks.

Soon we were standing at the right-hand edge of the Hinterstoisser Traverse. Across remnants of ice and snow I climbed as far as the edge of a flight of slabs, which separated us from the First Ice-Field. The rocks above us were smooth and water-worn but not quite vertical. Beneath us the wall fell away overhanging. Old, shredded remnants of rope showed us the route. Quickly I traversed left, belayed in a niche and told Peter to come on. Water ran from the roof of the recess on to my helmet, shoulders and rucksack. My whole body was damp and heavy.

Without stopping at the stance, Peter took over the lead. Then we climbed over wet rock, small ice-fields and vertical rock steps, leading alternately to-wards the lower edge of the Second Ice-Field. Somewhere up there the party whose light signals we had seen that morning must have bivouacked. A rock step still separated us from the biggest sheet of ice on the face. Were they still there? Did they need help? We would go down with them if we must. Via a vertical step we reached the lowest run-out of the Second Ice-Field, keeping to the rocks for as long as possible. These were downward-sloping but there were belay pitons.

I heard Peter speaking above me. It was the injured climbers, two Poles, who had given the distress signals in the early morning. Peter offered our help but at this moment a helicopter came chattering up and a man, secured on a cable, leaped out of the cabin and dangled in the air. For a moment the helicopter hovered some thirty metres above the distressed climbers. Stones, disturbed by the down-draught of the rotors, whistled past me. Then the helicopter soared away from the face. A single stone had been enough to unbalance it. The rescuer meanwhile had belayed himself next to the Poles and begun to splint the one who had broken his leg the day before in a fall of forty metres.

Peter and I had climbed scarcely a rope-length when the helicopter re-turned and hovered directly above the three-man group. A cable swung in the air. The Swiss rescuer fixed the injured man to it, gave a hand-signal and already the helicopter was lifting the rescued man from the face. Far out, away from all danger of stonefall, the injured man was hoisted into the machine. A few minutes later it landed at Kleine Scheidegg. Peter and I were so thrilled by the Swiss air rescue that we shouted our congratulations to the man who was waiting with the uninjured Pole for the third flight.

On this enormous sweep of wall, 1000 metres above the cirque, everything was done with such precision and speed that we could only look on in amazement. With such technique one could have easily avoided many of the fatal accidents which had taken place on this face in its almost forty years of climbing history. Earlier there had been nothing like it.

We had put on our crampons again and climbed directly upwards on blank ice. At the upper edge of the Second Ice-Field we would find protection from stonefall. The ice screws held well. Nonetheless, I was glad when the helicopter had fetched the other pair, for each flight meant increased danger of stonefall.

The traverse at the upper edge of the ice-field was the most exposed to stonefall and it was necessary to be doubly cautious. We chose the stances so that they were safe from stones and climbed quickly, with ears pricked. Long icicles hung like swords of Damocles above us. Now and then stones, coming directly from the Spider, smashed into the ice below us. The temperature was below freezing down to a height of 3500 metres which was a big advantage. When the upper half of the face was in sunshine, all hell must break loose here, I thought, as Peter led the last pitches over the Flat-Iron to Death Bivouac. In the afternoon it would have been suicide to climb here.

It was still early morning, about nine o'clock, as we traversed the Third Ice-Field to the Ramp. Four Austrians, who had been on the wall for three days, were climbing above us but willingly let us through.

Via a broken crack, we tried to reach the Traverse of the Gods. We were wet, for we had encountered streams of water on the Ramp. Still, we made good progress, pitch after pitch, belaying each other and at noon we were standing in the Spider. A glance upwards at the summit wall made us think. The rocks looked black, glittering; the cracks and chimneys were filled with snow. The Exit Cracks were glazed up therefore. The maze of gullies above us looked longer than I had pictured it. I knew for sure that this summit wall was impossible to climb free when iced up. Further right hung remnants of rope from the first ascent of the Winter Direttissima. Where we were there was no clue as to the way forward. Were we too far left, or were the pitons concealed under the layer of ice?

Peter Habeler (front row extreme right) and I had climbed the North Face of the Eiger in a record ten hours. Afterwards we were photographed with Clint Eastwood who happened to be filming 'The Eiger Sanction'.

On a steeply sloping stance directly above the Spider, Peter and I deliberated. The sun was still behind the peak. Ought we to wait until the warmth of the sun had melted the thin glaze of ice from hand- and footholds? Or should we utilise the remaining hours of minimal stonefall and climb on despite the increased difficulties? We decided to carry on. We had faith in one another and the second solution seemed the safer.

The first pitches in the Exit Cracks were not steep. Peter climbed as before, as if he were going for a stroll, without a single moment of hesitation.

The next pitch, a completely iced-up crack, made me think of Hermann Buhl, who had fallen six times at the same spot. Only with difficulty could I cling to the handholds de-iced by the warmth of my fingers. My calves hurt as I stood on the same finger-broad ledge far too long. I had no hand free to knock in an intermediate piton. Several times I essayed each move and was stopped at the crucial moment by the sensation of slipping. Climbing back would have been relatively easy. The holds below me were now free of ice. Going on, however, meant the risk of falling at every unmethodical move. Peter encouraged me to try it again and again. After I had expended myself a great deal on the crux pitch, Peter led the next two. He bridged away up overhangs, found isolated rusty old pitons and assured me from above that we were on the right route again. Leading alternately we then climbed over less steep parts of the face.

I thought of my wife who was waiting for us down at Kleine Scheidegg. Was she watching now with the binoculars? 'If we reach the Summit Ice-Field by early afternoon,' I had said in the morning when I left her, 'you can run the bath.' It was just two o'clock when we saw a piece of face in sunshine. Already the first stones were falling. The chimneys and cracks became small rills. 'Run the bath,' I hummed as I belayed on the stances.

I watched as small stones were set in motion by the melt-water, how they—I would almost say playfully—hopped across the abrupt summit slope, pushing other stones along, plunging as stone avalanches into the Spider. There they rolled over the bare ice, then shot like bullets down into the Second and Third Ice-Fields.

We continued on the rope for one hundred metres, then untied and climbed the last steps of the face and the Summit Ice-Field together. Now no stone could hit us, now we needed no belays.

At three o'clock in the afternoon we sat on the top of the Eiger. The weather was good. We had been climbing just ten hours; with our timetable we had escaped the terrible stonefall of the Eigerwand.

18

HIDDEN PEAK WITH THE MINIMUM

1975

I DREAMED OF THE SOUTH-WEST FACE of Everest. This in 1975 was the desired goal amongst all the extreme high-altitude mountaineers. I had joined in and pursued the development of difficult face climbs on the eight-thousanders from the start and I knew the South-West Face of Everest was possible.

In 1970 a British expedition had succeeded in the first ascent of the South Face of Annapurna, almost 4000 metres of ascent from base camp to summit and, in part, extremely difficult climbing. An ice ridge in the middle of the face and the Rock Band, a vertical rock barrier between 7000 and 7500 metres, had been the cruxes. The Britons had set up six high camps and fixed several thousand metres of rope on the face. A new phase of mountaineering had begun: the ascent of the highest faces in the world.

The higher the team climbed the harder became the face. The atmospheric pressure dropped, the supply of oxygen decreased. The logistics—changing the leading group, supply problems, choice of safest route—became harder with each metre of ascent. Chris Bonington, leader of the expedition, solved all these questions in sovereign fashion. He was just as good an organiser as climber. Two men climbed ahead, the others carried loads. With these tactics the Britons carried the supplies up to the leading rope team in a relay from camp to camp until just below the highest point. On 27 May 1970 Dougal Haston and Don Whillans reached the summit of Annapurna I. That was some success!

Chris Bonington it was, too, who more than anyone else had his eye on the South-West Face of Everest. He had already failed on it once. He was to be able to finance a second and third expedition. I was not.

On Hidden Peak (Gasherbrum I) our route ran up the great ice slopes leftwards to the shoulder and then right, up the ridge, to the summit of the 2000-metre North-West Face.

In 1975 on Hidden Peak Peter Habeler (right) and I made the first alpine-style ascent of an 8000-metre peak without supplementary oxygen, fixed ropes or high-altitude porters.

So I looked for another goal. As I had failed twice by orthodox means on an eight-thousander face, I developed a new plan. I wanted to attempt such a wall without high-altitude porters, without a chain of fixed camps, without fixed ropes. When I set off from Skardu for the Karakoram with a dozen Balti porters, to climb the North-West Face of Hidden Peak (8068 metres), the experts gave me no chance.

It was summer 1975. A few weeks before I had failed on the South Face of Lhotse with an Italian expedition. What I now intended was not only new, it was daring. I had invited Peter Habeler along because I knew his speed and that he approved of my idea. After two weeks' march we set up our base camp at the foot of Hidden Peak. We were at a height of 5000 metres.

We planned our ascent in detail. The art consisted of doing away with superfluities. Any muddle in the preparation could have led to death, a pinch in a boot to frostbite. At base camp, Peter made final adjustments to his inner boots with his pocket-knife.

At the beginning of August we climbed up the Gasherbrum icefall into a big glacier basin. A singular world opened up before us, a gigantic arena of rock and ice, surrounded by six beautifully shaped peaks, of which the highest was Hidden Peak. We wanted to climb it by its hardest face, without any preparation. It seemed to be possible. After this on-the-spot inspection we returned to base camp.

On 8 August we bivouacked in the Gasherbrum basin and studied the wall with binoculars. What if we were surprised up there by a sudden change in the weather? On the morning of 9 August we set off early.

In order to save weight we had sacrificed the rope. We would not have been able to belay with it on account of the great height and rotten rocks. Each was responsible for his own climbing equipment, and for himself. Only extreme caution and instinctive climbing ability would ensure our safety.

Late in the afternoon we reached a rock outcrop at 7100 metres. We put up our tiny tent and bivouacked again. On the third day of climbing we reached the summit and returned to our bivouac.

Two days later we were back in base camp, having descended our route of ascent. It had taken five days in all. In five more days we were back in Skardu. I was glad to have found a style which made mountaineering exciting again. Then in the autumn, in Salzburg on a lecture tour, I read in *The Times:* 'Two British climbers scale Everest by South-West Face'. The report about Dougal Haston and Doug Scott, who had been the first in Bonington's team to reach the summit of Mount Everest, stirred my own adventurous spirit. I wanted to set off again, to Mount Everest, to Alaska and to the Sahara. Adventure remained adventure. Life was good when I had my nose ahead.

Although I already sensed it, I did not know then that my readiness to set out was also dictated by the desire to go where others did not. I made myself the proxy for all those who came to my lectures after office hours to live their unrealised dreams.

19

WALL OF THE MIDNIGHT SUN

1976

LIKE A RISEN SOUFFLÉ, a structure of ice and snow some eighty metres high stood over us. At first glance I thought it must be the summit. But then it became clear to me that it was the Kahiltna Horn, standing like a watchman at the fringe of the summit slopes of Mount McKinley, at the upper edge of the South-West Face.

My friend Bulle Oelz was climbing a bit behind me. We were unroped. We had left our last camp on the West Buttress in the early morning and had needed almost ten hours for this 1800-metre slope. The oxygen-starved air was icy cold and the sun had lost all strength. It was eleven o'clock at night. The sun stood very low in the sky, the last of the light hung blue on the peaks of the surrounding five-thousanders. The western cliffs of Mount Hunter, which soared up to the right above the Cassin Rib, reflected a tinge of warmth.

Long as fingers, the icicles hung from Bulle's beard. Clouds of breath hung between us when we spoke: 'Go on.' It was like a command. Earlier we had been able to put in longer rest pauses. Now each lingering could be deadly. The few seconds which I had needed to tighten the zip-fastener on my over-trousers had been enough to render my fingertips white and without feeling. If I stood longer than five minutes the cold crept through my leggings, my treble gloves and my socks to my amputated toes. For that reason we kept our arms and legs on the move while resting. I could feel my fingers individually inside their thick down mittens, so the blood was circulating. Our noses looked bluish-white. We rubbed them mutually, there was life in them. But the danger of freezing was enormous. At 40°C below and at 6000 metres above sea-level caution was required. Not for nothing is Mount

McKinley known as the coldest mountain on earth. Many had paid for their success with amputations.

It was still an hour to midnight. Would it get still colder? Evening flowed slowly into morning. The two horns above us, floodlit by the tender, transparent light of the midnight sun, seemed at first glance to stand on another mountain. The valleys and hollows between the peaks were filled with shadows of milky blue.

Broad slopes lay before us, running in several waves up to the summit. On the hard firn snow we made good progress. Here and there was a bamboo pole, isolated or half cracked by wind; signs of people. But we were alone; the Americans who had waved to us from their camp on the ordinary route were forgotten. In the north-west the sun moved slowly on. It glided over the cloud cover on the horizon which resembled a distant mountain crest. The mountain tops gleamed now against the light like reddish-violet glass. Could we ever reach them? Time and dimensions were lost. Quite slowly the slope below us turned lilac and the north peak lost itself in the dark blue of night. Above the wall of cloud in the west appeared a dirty red streak into which the sun disappeared; less a sunset than a smouldering. With the extinction of the last warm light we felt ourselves lost, immersed in an ice-rigid, dead world. Automatically we went faster. The ground was easy. The delicate edges of the wind tracery stood out, the grain of the snow microscopically exact in the blue light.

I stayed on the summit only a few minutes, feeling like a stranger who had landed on an icy star in a strange polar night. After less than an hour the sun rose again, its light now white and cold and as if emerging from the ice-sea.

Retracing our route, we descended. On the south side of Mount McKinley the moon stood like a hole in the mauve sky. Small and cold. With our faces to the wall we climbed down the seemingly endless slope. Then below us, to the left and right of the concave face, the vertical granite buttresses emerged again on which we had orientated ourselves on the way up. The face constricted to a narrow neck. Through it we climbed down on front points, always lower. We abseiled over the bergschrund and skied down to our tent at the upper end of Windy Corner as sunlight touched the summit of Mount Foraker.

After a rest day we travelled partly on skis, partly on our tiny transport sledge, which we had dragged behind us like dogs, down to the south-east

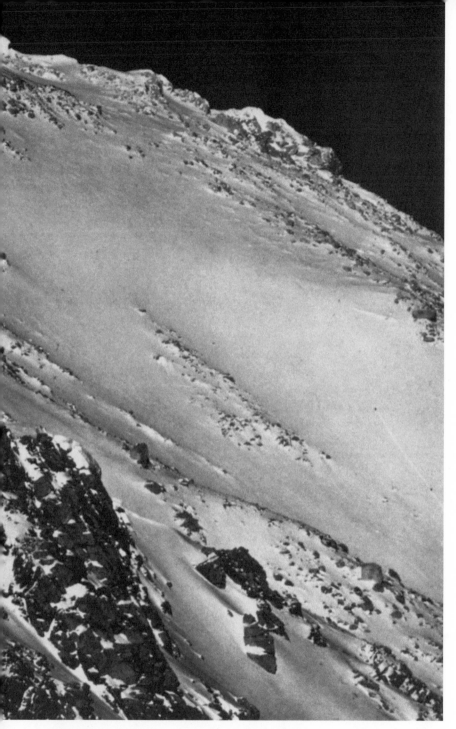

Bulle Oelz and I are two black specks, centre right, on a new route on Mount McKinley's Wall of the Midnight Sun in 1976.

Kahiltna Glacier. We needed less than four hours for this stretch. That same afternoon the famous glacier pilot Cliff Huston took us to Talkeetna in his battered Cessna. Over immense glacier streams, past gigantic granite walls—what challenges for the future!—and over the bare tundra of the north we floated back to our world.

My rendezvous with Bulle Oelz had lasted all of ten days. We had made an appointment in Talkeetna for Mount McKinley. I was on a return flight from Japan to Europe, he had applied for a few days' leave. Bulle now returned to his post at the Vanderbilt University in Nashville, Tennessee. I resumed my homeward journey.

20

RETREAT ON DHAULAGIRI

1977

ALL AT ONCE THE SUMMIT OF DHAULAGIRI no longer belonged; not to my dreams, not to this expedition, not to this adventure. I tried to envisage the best course of action while, solely not to discourage the others, I went on acting as if the summit were still possible. In this way I encouraged myself too. When I sat down to eat with the others, I talked of a last chance; as if there really were one.

Already on the march in up the narrow gorge of the Thulo Khola, I had had doubts about our chances and as we talked now in base camp of the dangers of the return march through this icy gorge, we did it to distract us from the face.

Five years before I had discovered this South Face as an idea or a possibility, just as artists suddenly discover a motif. Two years passed before I received a permit from the Nepal government. One thousand dollars I had paid for it and now we were faced with retreat. For a whole year I had planned and organised. For six months each of us had trained: Peter Habeler, Otti Wiedmann, Michael Covington and I, with steep cross-country races, weight training and in low pressure chambers. We had been on the go for four weeks but all the fears, doubt and dangers which we daily endured were to be in vain.

Peter was the first to embrace thoughts of turning round, writing in his diary: 'I am no longer willing to stake my life for a mountain. More than ever I enjoy my home, my wife who has shown unbelievably great understanding right up to the time I left. Sure, it would have been lovely to go home with a summit victory, however it seems to me more important to land at Munich in one piece.'

What disgrace, thought Otti, the youngest in the team, as our failure dawned on him for the first time. How shall I be able to explain it to my friends?

On the first reconnaissance Peter and Otti had survived an avalanche. An enormous sérac broke off from the face. Otti cried; 'Avalanche!' and ran off thirty metres, then threw himself under a rock. He believed his last hour had come. Peter lay down flat and breathed through his pullover. Scarcely twenty seconds passed then it went dark. The fine snow dust completely covered the two of them. Strong suction followed the pressure wave, then the nightmare was over but the shock remained, buried deep in their sub-conscious.

Meanwhile three weeks had gone by, three weeks in which we had searched the face hands-breadth by hands-breadth for a responsible route. We did not find it. Now Peter and I were sitting in our first high camp, 5350 metres above sea-level, at the foot of the South Buttress on which we wanted to hazard a lightning advance next morning.

The weather was good as we left the tent. The sun stood so low that our shadows swam over the wavy firn surface like a dark, extended catamaran. Only slowly did the fireball rise in the east over a bluish-violet silhouette which was the Annapurna group. Peter climbed behind me, in the same rhythm, pace for pace, without catching me up or holding me back, without saying a thing. The wall above us appeared so near in the first light of morning that we could recognise each wrinkle and crevasse. And still there were 3000 metres and an eternity to the summit. Had the climb succeeded, it would have been the most difficult ascent in the world to date.

We stopped together and craned our necks far back. My courage deserted me. It was not the feeling that this face was not meant for me that tormented me, it was the self-reproach of having underestimated the difficulties and dangers. Had I foreseen what importance this wall would have in climbing histories? Perhaps so. The Dhaulagiri face was the focal point of our vanities.

Far above the bergschrund we roped up. The wind got up and I exchanged my sunglasses for storm goggles. Peter's smile at my first steps gave me courage. I was thankful to him for each word. As I looked for a way up the rotten, icy rock on the steep wall, I looked to him for a justification for this madness. On the stance I looked around me, as if that alone would conjure up an easier possibility, a concealed ramp, a crack maybe.

Over the vertical rocks to the right of us fine driven snow was trickling. Was it ready to avalanche over there? At last Peter stood next to me. Apparently lost in thought, without anxiety, he took all the pitons, karabiners and slings and climbed a steep slanting couloir up to the right. He climbed around a brown-red rock tower on which we could have erected a bivouac in emergency. This shaky, cupboard-sized rock form was sturdily comforting in this vertically soaring ice desert. I made a note of the spot.

Peter climbed to the right above me. No, he did not climb, he clung to the wall. The smallest snow slide would have torn him away with it. Somewhere a stone fell. Why didn't he dodge? The smallest noises and movements gave me the jitters and I cowered against the face as avalanches thundered to our right. I flinched at each stone Peter dislodged.

It turned windy and fresh, as it had each morning when thick banks of mist blotted out the sky. On the edge of the South-East Ridge dark cumulus clouds towered upwards. Here and there they spilled over and menaced the basin under the South Face of Dhaulagiri like a storm tide. Our hopes of a first fine weather day were gone, yet we carried on. Perhaps the sky would clear for this despairing attempt or the way to the summit become visible.

At the upper end of the diagonal ice ramp, which made up the crux in the middle part of the buttress, Peter and I found a narrow sill. We twisted in two ice screws and tied on. Secured in this manner we could rest a little. From the projecting crag above us there trickled down a moving curtain of fine snow. The slightly overhanging rocks protected us, however, from the avalanches and stonefall to which we had been involuntarily exposed on the lower part of the face. While we were still looking for a weak spot on this bulwark of rock and ice, some pieces of ice bounced over the edge of the crag above us and whirred into space a few metres away from us. Far below on the flat broken rock they disintegrated into a thousand glittering splinters.

The stance was so narrow that we got in each other's way with every movement. The back points of our crampons stuck out over the edge of the ice. It was now so warm that we were breathing hard. When the sun broke through the moving mist, the brilliance flooded our surroundings and our eyes hurt behind our sunglasses. The depth of view was breathtaking.

As the cloud curtain tore apart we could see as far as the hills over Pokhara. The dark jungle seemed to steam. Like atomic mushrooms, cloud formations soared up above the lowlands. We stood between heaven and earth, on a foot-wide ledge at a height of more than 6000 metres. I seemed detached, no more a part of the world and yet I was full of the dull feeling of fear.

I glanced at Peter. Did he want to go on? No. His strained, disturbed face said it all. He too had doubts. Had we gone too far? Was a retreat across this exposed face still possible? We still had to ascend a spur if we wanted to know whether this route went any further or not.

Once more I adjusted the binding on my crampons. Routinely I reached for the pitons and ice screws which hung in orderly bundles on my harness, as always, when I was doing extreme climbing. Then I untied myself from the stance pitons. Belayed by Peter I climbed up the open face. It was snowing lightly and the grains bounced like tiny balls across the grey rock wall. I clenched my teeth, concentrated absolutely on climbing neatly. I had to put these few metres to the big ice shield behind me without falling, for I knew that any fall on this poor rock would be deadly, even if Peter could absorb it. Deadly because at this height and with this superhuman exertion one would not have been able to help the other. To free myself from a hanging position would have been out of the question.

Without interruption, snow trickled from above over the steep steps we had to climb, snow which, little by little, smoothed out each unevenness, snow which gradually took all feeling from my hands. To discuss the despairing situation with Peter would have been only a waste of breath. I knew that he was doing all he could to hold me in case of emergency. Every fibre in my body was tense. As I made the final moves and stamped out a stance above, I hardly dared to breathe. Saved! I was standing under an apparently endless ice slope.

Quickly Peter followed. First his helmet appeared below me, then his axe. When he reached me, he prepared to go past and climb on. The worst was over for today. Perhaps the route would still go. It does, I thought, as I watched his crisp climbing movements. Then suddenly everything was all over. Peter could not have missed the noise. It enveloped us absolutely. He took a few more paces, then pressed his body against the face as if he wanted to hide himself in it. Although I could no longer see, I knew what was happening. A fresh snow avalanche was flushing over us. It tugged at the rope, at the rucksack. It enveloped me. I felt the pressure increase on my hands with which I grasped my rammed-in axe. It threatened to hurl me from the face.

As the last snow slides between us vanished into the void, we looked around, away over the blue-green ice slope. Fear. Minds a blank. The avalanche had left the slope far behind. It was late morning. Without a word we

Aerial view of the South Face of Dhaulagiri. We wanted to climb the blunt buttress left of the central gully.

began the retreat, as quickly as possible, away from this face. There was no going on. We had no heart for it. Right now we wanted only to survive.

After a short abseil section, a second snow slide came down. Nothing of our ambition remained, only shame of death and of being dead.

The avalanches had become a nightmare which prevented all reason, living barricades which blocked the way to the summit. My hopes frequently turned to my wife, to the return march. My thoughts raced ahead of me. Failure was the only sense lacking in my consciousness and this even though I knew that we would climb no more on the face. At the foot of the face I felt as if I were freed from something. Only gradually did it become clear to me that it was a farewell for ever. A departure not only from the face, but from the hopes which had borne me up for years.

We roped down for hours, following the line of ascent. All the pitons were tricky, the rope wet and heavy. There was no going back on the face. We trudged across softened snow back to the first high camp.

The tents were empty, the Sherpas not yet arrived from base camp. I occupied myself by rereading my last letter from Uschi. Peter made a new diary entry. In thought, he was with his wife, as I with mine. 'She certainly doesn't have it easy with me and I hope that she won't run away from me one day.'

In the night the doubts came again. The final decision to give up had been unbearable. To carry on, however, was as crazy as giving up, only more dangerous. I found myself reliving the hours of storm on Manaslu. Why did I recollect that? Then I had slashed my windproof so as not to slide if I fell. I would not have survived such a hopeless situation again! Insight grew. We were not meant to continue! 'I think about us a lot and embrace you with all my heart.' Those were the last lines of the last letter which I had received from my wife. I too had thought about us a lot. Often I considered how I might have obliterated this Dhaulagiri and all the other eight-thousanders from my life. For ever.

These eight-thousanders were my goal, the focal point of my vanities. Why did I not throw them overboard?

For the time being I did not know what I would do next. I could only contemplate marching on for ever: open to any opportunity, free for every eventuality, tomorrow and in the days to come. There was nothing that was predestined.

On the approach march everything had had its order, an appointed sequence, now on the return march there was no system any more. I let myself drift. I did not want to go back to Europe yet. Perhaps my wife was not there. I should stay in this country, I thought, always amongst this scenery, lingering by the stream, never following a goal because each goal was a blind alley.

After two days' march I noticed that I had become completely relaxed. Now I walked alone for preference, so that no one could observe my musings. No one saw me present Uschi with a giant rhododendron bush which bloomed at the roadside. I sensed a pulsating world and listened to the water, to the wind in the leaves, to the feeling of life.

Two weeks later I landed at München-Riem. I did not expect my friends to gather at the airport to congratulate me on surviving. I expected only my wife. She was there, to say adieu to me. For ever! I took note of it. At this moment I remembered nothing. Perhaps it was impossible for a woman to live with a madman like me. Perhaps, in my absence, she had followed her own dreams. I had always held the view that everyone should live a full life. At first I was calm, then I grasped that a piece of my life was over. Another piece had happened in my absence. Marriage was perhaps not the best way of living together; at least, not when more time was spent in the Himalaya than at home. In the moment of my first despair I yearned to be back at the turning point of Dhaulagiri. There I would have liked to live a part of my life again in a different way.

21

THE BREACH WALL ON KILIMANJARO

1978

IN SPRING 1978 I TRAVELLED WITH a few friends to Kilimanjaro in East Africa. It was to be no more than a repeat and acclimatisation climb. This volcanic massif, which the local peoples had once upon a time regarded as an enchanted or holy mountain, was a favourite goal of ambitious mountain trekkers. Four of us set off with light luggage for, by the ordinary route, the highest peak in Africa (5895 metres) is easy to climb and for me it was excellent acclimatisation training for Mount Everest which I was planning to attempt with Peter Habeler, without oxygen.

I did 'sprints' at heights between 4000 and 6000 metres. On the way back I climbed Mawenzi, Kilimanjaro's lower and more difficult peak, with Konrad Renzler. The vegetation—giant heather, rose wood, hypericums up to eight metres high—had impressed me more than anything else.

When we met Odd Eliassen in the Marangu Hotel after the descent, we learned the details of an accident on the Breach Wall. 'Have you heard about Taylor and Barber?' Odd asked me.

'Yes,' I said, 'they attempted Breach Wall and had to give up. You did a first-class rescue job. Hearty congratulations!'

'Had to give up is rich.' Odd reported on the attempt by the two Americans. 'Taylor fell on the Icicle and sustained an open fracture of the ankle. Barber lugged him for two days across the second ice-field and brought him out. Two days for 200 metres! Then he packed Taylor in his sleeping-bag and left him so that he could fetch help. After three days he got to us. Totally exhausted. Then we went up, not expecting to find Taylor alive; but he was. He was snowed in, only his head was free. He had lived on snow and nothing else but he was all right.

'What I wanted to say,' continued Odd, not without grinning, 'Doug Scott failed, Taylor and Barber failed. Now it's your turn, Reinhold.'

'No,' I said. The idea did not interest me. 'Odd, you know I'm here to acclimatise myself. That's all.'

But my ambition was goaded. Taylor and Barber rated as two of the best climbers in the world. Deep down I began to consider at least an attempt on the Breach Wall.

I put up a token objection. 'I haven't got the right gear, Odd.' That was a laughable speech. Odd had all that I needed. The deciding factor was my conviction that I was in tip-top form. Only self-confidence and impudence were lacking. Konrad Renzler, my friend from the South Tyrol, wanted to come too; he was always ready for a dare. Eliassen placed some ropes, helmets, ice axes and ice screws at our disposal. Next day Konrad and I set off.

At midnight, arms crossed behind my head, I lay in my warm sleeping-bag and stared at the roof of our tent. Outside it had become quiet. Only isolated stones still clicked like marbles on the ice-field that must be somewhere above us.

'What do you think?' asked Konrad. 'Ought we to leave it alone?' We had been up here for six hours, on Kilimanjaro, somewhere beneath the Breach Wall; 4600 metres up. For six hours we had thought about it. Was the risk too great? Where was the boundary between calculated danger and recklessness? Why had all the others before us failed? Above all, was this wall actually climbable? We did not want to decide until first light.

Until now we had only heard of this wall, never seen it. When we had arrived here about seven o'clock the evening before—after two days' ascent through plain and jungle—dark clouds had obscured the view. We did not even know if we were in the right spot; but even if I had not believed the assurances of our two African porters, I knew we were near the wall. The thunder obliquely above us was irrefutable proof.

We had been warned but what we heard was worse than we had expected. The wall gurgled, rattled, clattered, snorted unceasingly. The face spewed out avalanches of debris. Like a runny nose, it snotted torrents of water. This was the most living face I had ever come across. I had studied a photograph: a lower ice-field that began at about 4600 metres; ice hose; second ice-field. Above that the frozen waterfall, an ice plug more than eighty metres high. Finally the exit to the Diamond Ice-Field and the summit at 5895 metres. However, a photograph didn't show you the noise.

I gathered that Doug Scott, a brilliant British climber, had failed when debris and ice damaged his rope on the first ice-field of the Breach. The drama of the two Americans Rob Taylor and Henry Barber occupied me more.

It was five o'clock in the morning when I stuck my head out of the tent. It was dark but it was completely quiet. Konrad and I looked around. We nodded. The decision was made. Five thirty. In the pale moonlight the Breach Wall emerged above us to the left; I recognised the lower ice-field. Far above was the icicle, the one thing that probably would give us a great deal of trouble. We packed our rucksacks.

The most important thing was speed. We had to reach the Icicle before the sun did. It was now -10°C but on Kilimanjaro it got warm quickly and warmth meant stonefall and water. If we were to be fast, we had to travel light. 'We must do the face in one day,' I said to Konrad. 'To bivouac is senseless.' We left everything in our bivouac tent for the porters to bring back to camp. Around ten kilos lighter, we set off for the foot of the face.

Six o'clock, bright daylight. We climbed in the direction of the first ice-field. A mirror-smooth expanse lay before us, at an angle of fifty degrees and more. The ice shimmered glassily. Dotted about lay pieces of stone the size of a child's head that had fallen from the Diamond Glacier.

We decided to climb the French way, the safest on ice and the fastest. With this method you have a pick in each hand to dig into the ice. Then you crampon up with your feet. The first hundred metres we did fast. I went ahead. A rope-length behind me came Konrad.

The fact that Odd had given us the best gear paid off. The axe was—in contrast to the conventional implement—open and hollow at the pick; more of a tube than a point. That was an immense advantage as a blow did not break the ice, yet the tube dug in deep. Similarly the pitons, to which we belayed ourselves, were specially designed, the lower part consisting of a thread which could be turned in the ice without splitting it.

Nine o'clock. We had the first ice-field behind us. No problem. Had Scott already had to give up at this point? 'If it was here his rope was damaged,' analysed Konrad, 'then he was too late in the day, started at the wrong time.'

Above us lay an ice hose, the connection with the second ice-field. We perceived the great danger in this part of the wall. In this sort of bowl debris which came down from the Diamond Glacier collected. But it was still cold, the wall was asleep. The rocks were the second danger in the hose. They were friable and bigger or smaller bits fell on us continually. Nevertheless, I managed to find a 'clean' route and a rock overhang protected us from avalanches of debris.

Eleven o'clock. It had got warmer. 'We must speed up!' I called to Konrad. 'We must reach the Icicle by twelve o'clock.'

The ice hose went smoothly. The second ice-field resembled the first, only the ice was lightly covered in snow, therefore softer. As I gazed upwards I could see the first rays of sun striking the Diamond Glacier. The first pieces of stone and ice came down.

Half past twelve. For half an hour we had been sitting at the foot of the Icicle. We paused to eat a bit of dried fruit. 'Now we have only the technical difficulties in front of us,' I comforted Konrad. We were protected as if under a roof. From above the water ran down in streams. Pieces of ice and debris whistled past us.

Now came the critical point of the ascent: the Icicle, a frozen waterfall. Thick as a church tower and just as high. A bizarre amber-coloured structure, eighty vertical metres high. I banged my axe into the ice, which splintered. So I could forget axe and ice screws. Konrad looked at me critically. 'Once is enough for that,' I said. 'We shall have to climb the thing free.'

Konrad looked for a good place and secured himself to several pitons. I roped up and started climbing. If the ice under my feet crumbled I would fall. The first cascades were steep, the ice incalculable. With each handhold, with each foothold I was anxious. If the ice broke? Within the 'church tower', the waterfall roared.After the first pitch I was tired and rattled. I tried, when I could, to climb it like a chimney, pressing sideways with my feet, so that nothing could break away. I tried to belay myself by placing slings around the thick plug of ice. Karabiner on, rope in; that felt better.

I had to believe that the ice, together with the sling, would not break away. If I fell on the rope, it was all over. Konrad was now badly placed and the belays poor. Yet I was already sixty metres up. Safety returned as the last few metres went relatively well. I was at the top of the Icicle.

I belayed myself and Konrad followed on the fixed rope. We must not push our luck. Who knew whether the creaking ice would still hold. We were 500 metres below the summit. Now only the Diamond Ice-Field still lay above us. We did not foresee how that relatively flat glacier would give us some hard work. The ice had become soft and at each step we sank in up to our hips. Our strength ran out fast.

We saw the summit in front of us, darkness too. We hoped that the snow would freeze again to make the descent easier. Who knew what darkness would bring.

'We'll make it in time,' I said to Konrad, who was all in. We decided to carry on. I had seldom been so tired in my life. At the same time I knew that we must go on. Up there on Kibo, Kilimanjaro's higher top, we would have frozen.

Six o'clock in the evening. After twelve hours we had reached the top of Kilimanjaro at 5895 metres. The Breach Wall was below us.

The risk had been incalculable. The technical difficulties of a face, I can estimate. But how to calculate avalanches of debris flying around our ears? How was I to estimate whether the piece of ice, on which my fingers were clamped, would bear my weight?

'No,' observed Konrad, as we once more mulled over this climb. 'No, I wouldn't do that again.' Nor would I.

22

LAST TABOO: EVEREST WITHOUT OXYGEN

1978

IT WAS SPRING 1977. In Kathmandu, capital of Nepal, I boarded a small Pilatus Porter with Leo Dickinson, Eric Jones, and the Swiss pilot Emil Wick to fly in the direction of Everest. In an unpressurised cabin the others soon put on oxygen masks. We had crossed the 6000-metre barrier and were flying towards the Lhotse-Nuptse Wall, when Emil turned and saw that I had no mask on. We flew over the ridge and the South Col. We were more than 8000 metres high. I was well acclimatised from Dhaulagiri and wanted to fly as long as possible without supplementary oxygen.

Above the South Col, Emil Wick spiralled the plane higher, up over the summit of Mount Everest; we were now at 9000 metres. Fascinated, I gazed down at the highest point on earth. I had seen the flight through without an oxygen mask and I was still able to talk, to think, to sense everything. Now I was certain that I would be able to climb this peak without oxygen. Up there one did not become unconscious without oxygen apparatus, as doctors and mountaineers had prophesied. Now I knew how it would be when I had the world at my feet. But I still did not know how it would be to climb Mount Everest under my own steam. Between flying up there and climbing up there was a world of difference. I saw the north side of the mountain and admired Emil for his knowledge of the ridges and slopes.

In the 1920s and 1930s the British had tried time and again to climb Mount Everest. I could see clearly the points they had reached, and episodes from climbing history came to life. When I was back on the ground, I knew what the mountain up there looked like; but I did not know what it felt like.

The north side was the ideal side for mountaineers, for already by 1924 British climbers had reached a height of 8600 metres there with primitive

Could Everest be climbed without oxygen? I was sure it could and experimented first without an oxygen mask when I flew over the summit in an unpressurised light aircraft with climber–film-maker Eric Jones in 1977.

equipment, little experience of altitude, and without oxygen gear. There were not so many icefalls as on the southern flank. However in the seventies this northern side was barred; the Chinese who had occupied Tibet permitted no ascents.

Not only that, Mount Everest was still rated as unclimbable without supplementary oxygen, from north or south, and despite the efforts of those early British climbers who must have thought it was perhaps possible without. On 29 May 1953 Edmund Hillary and Tenzing Norgay were the first to stand on the summit of Mount Everest. After they had succeeded, using oxygen, all future climbers wanted to rely on this apparatus.

We had had to wait until 1978 for a permit. Peter and I trained in order to be fast. Speed was our life insurance. Had we needed too long for the last stretch—for the death zone—we would according to the medics probably have returned impaired. In the oxygen-starved air, they said, brain cells died. I wanted to get up Everest, to be sure, but also to get back to the valley without any mental deterioration.

Directly above base camp came the dangerous section: the Khumbu Icefall, several hundred metres high and moving ceaselessly, a few metres per day. It is a shattered glacier tongue which breaks off out of the Western Cwm, which is six kilometres long and bedded in between Nuptse and the West Shoulder of Everest. It took us ten days to find a way through the icefall. Between ice debris, crevasses and avalanche tracks we laid out a route over which we could climb up and down relatively quickly. We laboured to find as safe a way as we could past obstacles like the Big Wall, a free-standing, one-hundred-metre-long, forty-metre-high and forty-metre-thick ice wall that was slowly leaning over, day by day. We calculated that sooner or later it would obey the laws of gravity and collapse. And it did collapse. Thirteen Sherpas were underway between the first high camp and the base camp. From base camp we saw an enormous cloud of dust. Each of us knew what had happened. We grabbed our binoculars from the tents. Up there all hell was let loose, everything tumbling down. When we noticed that six of the Sherpas were descending below the falling masses of ice we breathed a sigh of relief. Where were the others? We scanned the icefall with our glasses until someone discovered them. They had just stopped as the ice had begun to explode. The Sherpas had indeed had the shock of their lives but were soon smiling again.

We had installed our first high camp at 6100 metres at the upper edge of the icefall. Above this the route went through a narrow hanging valley to Camp 2 that was to stand at 6400 metres. We continued the ascent up the Lhotse Face. It was the end of April when I erected the last high camp on the South Col, the highest pass in the world. Two Sherpas were with me. We put up a tent, in order to be able to attempt the ascent to the summit next day. Within the framework of this nine-man Austrian expedition, Peter and I had the privilege of making up the first summit team. Peter, however, had remained behind. He had not felt well and had descended to the Western Cwm. My chances of making the summit alone were slim but not entirely nil. It had been strenuous climbing up from the third camp on the Lhotse Face over the Yellow Band and the Geneva Spur. I had noticed a peculiar cloud which hung over me in rainbow colours and revolved. Did it herald bad weather? I did not want to think about bad weather. I wanted good weather signs: cumulus clouds over the foothills, rising air pressure.

Hundreds of empty oxygen bottles lay around on the South Col, and gas cartridges and tent poles. Originally I had come to the idea of climbing Everest without oxygen on sport-ethical grounds. From now on ecological grounds prevailed.

We had put up the tent and in no time the storm was upon us. The storm increased during the night to hurricane force. With windspeeds of 150 kilometres per hour it tore across the col. The temperature was -40°C. We three sat in the tent and held the canvas fast from within, all the while feeling that the wind would tear us away with it, catapult us into the next valley. We were able to hold the tent upright the first night. Luckily it did not rip until the morning. We put up a second tent, intending to bide our time until the weather improved. We could not be rescued from below. No one could climb up, the storm had blown everyone down to lower camps. Things became critical. We could no longer cook. The storm forced snow dust in through the seams of the tent and blew out the cooker. A centimetre of snow lay on our sleeping-bags. Kilometre-long snow streamers hung from the South-East Ridge. We had to wait it out for fifty hours, for two days and two nights.

We were worn out by the time the storm abated somewhat. It was up to me now to get myself and the Sherpas down to the valley. 'If I come out of it this time,' I said to myself, 'I will give up on Everest.'

As we began the descent the summit of Everest, a mighty pyramid, stood over the South Col, infinitely big, impossible and remote. Reality and my dreams no longer tallied. I wanted only to be safely back in the valley. We climbed down across the Lhotse Face. In the icefall I fell into a crevasse once. On arrival in base camp, Ang Dorje, our strongest Sherpa, Mingma and I were so worn out that we just flung ourselves into our tents. We drank and slept, slept and drank. Slowly we recovered.

When I was well rested, when I was once more capable of bundling up all my energies, and collecting my powers, I knew I was still in with a chance. With decent weather, it was perhaps still possible to succeed. I had been to 8000 metres and had withstood the storm. Why should I not survive the ascent I had dreamed of for six years? Again I believed a little that Everest was possible. Was Mount Everest created for men—or only for machine men? I was once more animated by this idea. I could not have gone home without a second attempt.

In base camp there was a primitive kitchen built from four stones, with a gas and wood fire. Sonam cooked for the whole expedition. In the evening I mostly sat with him and ate honey, milk and garlic bread. Those were my snack times.

At the beginning of May, Peter and I left base camp on our second attempt. Once more we were climbing from the bottom; up the icefall, the Western Cwm, the Lhotse Face. In Camp 1, at the upper edge of the icefall, we stopped only briefly. As we went up the Western Cwm we looked upwards in the direction of the summit. The first group from our expedition were on the way to the top. While Peter and I had been recovering in base camp, Wolfgang Nairz, the expedition leader, Robert Schauer, the cameraman Horst Bergmann and the Sherpa sirdar Ang Phu had set out, to go to the top their own way. They did not want to climb without oxygen, preferring the traditional method.

Peter and I arrived at Camp 2 and were able to watch their ascent with binoculars. At the foot of the South-West Face we waited to congratulate the first summit team. All four had been impressed by the height, by the trail breaking, by the climbing. When we wanted to know whether they considered it possible to get up without oxygen, they denied it spontaneously. 'Frankly speaking, no.' Without oxygen masks Everest was impossible.

Wolfgang Nairz had taken off his mask for a short time on the summit and had become dizzy. Robert Schauer had tried to climb without a mask and could not make any headway. This was depressing news. But I still believed that it was possible to climb Mount Everest without oxygen. I had to know what it was like! Peter also wanted to get up Everest but now the others had done it, he felt he could no longer afford to fail. He suddenly confessed, 'It is not important to me how I get up, only that I do get up.'

We debated the matter in the tent in Camp 2. What could we do? Could we go together, Peter with an oxygen mask, I without? But that would be cheating. Peter would have climbed ahead, he would have made the tracks, he would have borne the responsibility. He would be able to give me oxygen if I suddenly became ill. The uncertainty which belonged to such an adventure would be neutralised. My experiment, to experience the mountain both physically and psychologically, would not be possible. I would rather go alone. Either we both climb without using oxygen or we must split up.

Until late into the night we lay in our tent and discussed it, and decided to split up. Peter wanted to climb with a mask. I understood his point of view entirely and over the radio to base camp tried to find a climbing partner for him but the others had already paired themselves into groups of two and four. So we joined forces again after all. I was grateful to Peter. As a twosome the chances of success were far greater. The two of us could do everything together, support each other psychologically, alternate the lead. Two stood the best chance. That I knew.

When we left the tents of Camp 2 on the morning of 6 May, self-confidence returned with the physical sensation of movement. We made good progress. On the Lhotse Face some Sherpas assisted us by carrying food and tents. Leo Dickinson and Eric Jones were shooting a documentary film for a British television company. Leo Dickinson made it as high as 7200 metres, turning back at Camp 3. Eric Jones was to go with us next day to the South Col, filming as far as he could. On the summit I was to do the filming myself, with a Super-8 camera which had been prepared specially for the expedition.

We slept in Camp 3 on the Lhotse Face where we had sufficient space and could cook. The air was not so thin, yet here we would only deteriorate. Once more we checked over all our equipment, from altimeter to ice axe, from crampons to the hinges on our snow goggles.

Next day we abandoned the security of Camp 3. Higher up no one would have been able to help us. Each was responsible for himself. On the ascent to the South Col a peculiar cloud hung in the sky again. Did it mean bad weather once again? I did not want to think of bad weather. Under the summit of Lhotse we traversed the Yellow band towards the Geneva Spur. We climbed slowly, a few steps, rest. Then again a few steps. Have a breather. The view downwards was of the hanging valley of the Western Cwm. Below that some-where, out of sight, base camp. To the left, the Nuptse Ridge. Beyond that I saw the tops of Kangtega and Tamserku. Below that, somewhere in the mon-astery, sat the monks who now perhaps were meditating.

In front of us was the South Col and, above, the route to the summit, the South-East Face and the South-East Ridge. Almost 900 metres height difference.

Once arrived at the tent on the South Col, we were confident. In spite of hard trail breaking we had not exhausted ourselves. We lay in the tent, melted snow and drank: soup, coffee, tea. We had to drink a lot. Through panting we had lost a lot of liquid. When I went outside that evening and looked westwards, the sun had gone down and the horizon was sharply silhouetted against the sky. I was optimistic. Next day I looked out of the tent at five thirty and was appalled: the weather was bad, the sky cloud-covered, our chances about nil. Had we come too late? Conscious that it was our last chance, we summoned up our courage. So long as we could navigate, so long as a few blue specks were above Makalu, we could climb up a bit. We climbed a hun-dred metres, mouths open, trying to suck in air, resting after a few steps, then again a few more. If we progressed this slowly, we would run out of time. The weather worsened. We climbed up into mist. Higher up we found a better rhythm. In four hours we climbed to Camp 5, a height gain of 500 metres in four hours. On Hidden Peak, Peter and I had made 200 metres per hour in the vicinity of the summit, now it was only 100 and we were still 350 metres from the top.

We rested for half an hour, made tea, a cup each. Then we struggled on. Suddenly we were under the South Summit at 8760 metres. I was now indifferent as to how high we were, also that we were climbing without oxygen. I continued upwards because the slope still went upwards, apparently without end. Whether it was Everest or the Matterhorn would have been all the same to me. I went upwards because I had not yet come to the top. We crept on. The wind tugged at us. Ice crystals burned like needle-points in our faces. Onwards! As if I could do nothing else but climb to this summit. Once on the South Summit I could see the main summit. There was a fantastic ridge in front of us. Suddenly I knew, body and soul, that we would make it. Enormous cornices projected on the right. I could not have said how far it still was, nor could I estimate how long we would need, for I no longer had any clear scale with which to measure time and space. I knew only that we would get up to the highest point where the snow fell away.

On the South Summit we roped up, for the ridge to the main summit was exposed. Belaying each other, we climbed on. To the left the face fell away to the Western Cwm, 2500 metres below. To the east the drop was 4000 metres. Climbing was now a natural movement, instinctive, like walking. Instinctively too I filmed. Now and then I fetched the camera out of the rucksack and filmed Peter, as he followed me up the Hillary Step, as he pulled his axe out of the snow, as he made a few paces.

The cornices which stuck out on the right impressed me little. Only when the ridge fell away on all sides did I know that I was on top. The ridge no longer went upwards! Initially I sensed nothing special. No feeling of happiness. I was calm. I took the camera and filmed Peter's final steps. Only when Peter stood directly in front of me did emotion overcome us both. We crouched down and sobbed. We could not stand. We did not speak, each knew what the other was feeling. I felt the relief that this emotional outburst had given me. The exertion, the tension, the anxiety, the doubt were over for the time being. We were at the final point. The tension was released. We photographed each other. Suddenly Peter was climbing down, in headlong flight. He was afraid of staying longer. I remained and gazed around, although there was not much to see: Kangchenjunga, Lhotse and Makalu. Now

Peter Habeler and I four years on. We had proved you could climb Everest without supplementary oxygen. But our partnership was not to last.

and then a window opened on Tibet. The panorama from the top of Everest was not what I had expected, just the wind chasing the snow across the ridge the whole time and a great peace overall.

When the initial exhaustion had passed, I became absent-minded, just breathing in and out quickly, like someone who had run the race of his life and knew that now he could rest for ever.

It was time to leave the summit. Down the Hillary Step I climbed, to the South Summit. I had assumed that Peter would wait there for me but he had gone on down. I descended step by step to the South Col.

The night was bad. I could no longer see. When filming I had removed my goggles too often and got snow-blind. Where my eyes had been felt like two holes burning with sand. Only tears alleviated the pain. Peter looked after me like a small child. He made tea, prepared my bed. Next day, with Peter three paces in front of me, I could recognise him mistily as I orientated myself on him. On the fixed ropes I managed by myself. Thus we groped our way down to Camp 3, where Bulle Oelz gave me some eye drops. He did not descend with me, he was on his way to the summit himself.

When I arrived in base camp, I had the feeling that something was lacking; where earlier the dream of Everest without oxygen had been was now a hole. Luckily I still had an idea: one man and an eight-thousander. I occupied myself now more and more with the goal of conquering Nanga Parbat solo. So one dream replaced another. I hoped to be capable of finding new dreams for ever.

23

NANGA PARBAT SOLO

1978

I DRANK MY SOUP IN SMALL GULPS out of a cooking pot scarcely bigger than a cup. My throat felt as hoarse and sore as if someone had been over it with a grater. I made myself force down a piece of cold corned beef out of the tin.

That was a mistake. I had to be sick. I poked my head out of the tiny tent, in which I crouched, into the snow and spewed out half the fluid which I had laboriously consumed in the course of the morning. And without sufficient fluid in my body up here I was finished from the start. My altimeter showed somewhat more than 6000 metres above sea-level. I was on the West Face of Nanga Parbat in the Himalaya in northern Pakistan.

I fetched in my socks and double-skinned boots which I had placed in front of the tent to dry in the sun. The fireball in the west went down between mushroom-shaped piles of clouds.

At once it became cold. As long as it had been warm—in the sun even stiflingly hot—I had melted snow in a tent bag. Before the melt-water froze again in the sudden cold, I poured it carefully into the small cooking pot and balanced it on the gas flame. I must drink so that my blood did not thicken. It was Monday, 7 August 1978, the second day of my attempt to reach the 8126-metre-high summit of Nanga Parbat solo.

In the morning I had started up the almost 4000-metre-high West Face without a rope, without belays. There was no one there who could have held a rope and belayed me. With only crampons on my feet and my ice axe in my right hand, I had worked my way high up three mighty ice ramparts with fifteen kilos on my back. There was no one there who could have caught me if I had slipped.

In six hours I had climbed 1600 metres. That is why I was quivering with exhaustion and had cramp in my right forearm. I had cut steps the whole time, scratched out handholds, had pulled myself over the edges of crevasses. Thus the nausea. As it got dark and the temperature sank to -15°C, I had to keep on drinking. I must not let myself be sick again; vomit once more and I must turn back if I wanted to survive.

The madman who had tried to solo an eight-thousander before me was called Maurice Wilson. He wanted to climb Mount Everest in 1934. The following year they found his corpse at 6400 metres.

The nearest people were now 2400 metres below me in a tiny base camp. Waiting there were Ursula Grether, a twenty-seven-year-old student of medicine, and Major Mohammed Tahir, called 'Derry', my official companion, a Pakistani officer and observer. Derry, who had voluntarily put in for this job out of curiosity, possessed no sort of mountain experience, nor could Ursula help me in emergency, as I carried no kind of emergency signal with me. The nearest place with occasional connection with the outside world was called Babusar and was four days' march away. There they had a crank telephone that functioned sometimes but mostly not.

To save weight I had taken no torch with me. The gas flame was my only source of light. When I had drunk enough, I rolled over to sleep, which I did really well. At night nothing could happen to me. My mini-tent stood protected under an ice overhang. I had anchored it with a cord tied to an ice screw.

The trek to the foot of Nanga Parbat had begun in Rawalpindi on 2 July. Ursula, Derry and I represented the smallest Himalayan expedition ever, the first 450 kilometres by jeep, then eight days' march with eight porters for our equipment, which altogether weighed 150 kilos. I had brought only twenty kilos with me from Europe. We had set up base camp at over 4000 metres at the end of the valley, where the meadow ended and the scree began.

Three weeks were spent reconnoitring. Day after day if the weather was clear I scanned the Diamir Face to discover a route up which I could progress as fast and steeply as possible. I did not want just to commit suicide. On 30/31 July I climbed a neighbouring six-thousander, Ganalo Peak. It was the conclusion of my training.

On 2 August I went from base camp to the foot of the West Face and bivouacked. Next morning I had to retreat because the weather had turned nasty. Not until 6 August was I able to try again.

On Tuesday, 8 August, I awoke at five o'clock in the morning with my altimeter showing fifty metres more than the evening before. I had not floated uphill in my sleep—the barometric pressure had fallen. Not a good sign. I melted hard frozen snow, then heated the water and hung a tea-bag in it. After tea there was soup made of water and a vitamin/salt concentrate.

In the icy stillness came a noise like a mighty distant waterfall. I tore open the iced-up tent entrance and stuck my head out. Unbelievable! Below me, half the ice face must have broken away. Everything seemed to be in motion. To the left of me, ice avalanches thundered into the valley. Below me, a broad avalanche rolled like a tidal wave to the foot of the mountain. It consisted of ice over which I had climbed. It rolled over the bivouac site from which I had set out exactly twenty-four hours ago. Spellbound I watched the end which would have overtaken me had I started climbing twenty-four hours later.

I did not panic although my temples were throbbing. I simply said to myself: 'There goes your way down.'

In the cold blue shadow of the face I folded up my tent and stowed things away in my rucksack: two finger-thick sleeping mats, a down sleeping-bag, the cooking utensils, seven beer-can-sized gas cartridges. I had provisions for eight to ten days with me: two tins of corned beef, one of liver sausage, a pound box of cheese spread, two half-pound hard South Tyrol flat loaves, soups and crackers, powdered coffee already mixed with sugar and milk powder, tea-bags. Then the ice screws, camera, a titanium rock piton which I never used, lip salve, sun cream, two pairs of strong sun goggles. I could not afford to go snow-blind this time like on Everest. Also, lavatory paper but I used it only once: this morning after the avalanche discharge. I also had sticking plaster with me for slight injuries. With bad injuries it would have been all up anyway. Finally, ten sleeping pills and ten pain-killers but no kind of pep pills. I knew that I would get into such difficult situations that the temptation to gulp down these pills would have overwhelmed me. And if I took them, I was dead.

For the first one hundred metres height I needed longer than the previous day; for 500 metres, almost two hours. I had the feeling of not being able to get warmed up. The snow was uneven: now blank ice, now breakable crust, now powdery. My feet only felt safe when firm ground crunched under my crampons. To the west cirrus clouds floated in the sky and on the top of Nanga Parbat a cloud sat like a slouch hat, all colours of the rainbow. A cold wind blew in my face. I feared it meant snow.

I climbed a nearly vertical ice drop, clawing the front points of my crampons into the ice and banging my ice axe into the frozen wall above me. When it held, I pulled up my own weight plus that of the rucksack a little bit higher with my right arm.

215

Towards nine thirty the sun struck me for the first time. It shone steeply down the face above. It became warm, then hot. As through a burning glass I felt the rays, although the air remained cool. I was now at over 7000 metres and had reached flatter ground. The trapezium-shaped rocky summit stood before me, a structure as weighty as a peak in the Alps, and 2500 metres higher than the highest of them. Flatter ground, but it was more laborious, snow deeper. Often I sank in to my hips. Foot by foot I wallowed on. Five paces. Pause. My breath rattled. Five paces. Pause. Pulse rate 130, 140. And this feeling of being forsaken!

In every fibre of my body I sensed how alone I was. Nobody to take over the lead. Nobody with whom I could have exchanged a few gasped swear-words or encouragements.

At last I found a campsite on the rocks of the summit massif. I was completely dehydrated, and let myself fall on the snow. To erect the tent was more than I could manage. I lay in the snow, sucking in the thin air and holding it briefly in my lungs. The afternoon sun glowed. I must drink, melt snow. With movements that seemed very slow to me and certainly were still slower, I put up my tent. Tomorrow was the decisive day.

I slept badly and it was seven o'clock before I got out of the tent. The weather was gloomy but I could see the summit. If there had been firm snow or ice between us, I would have made the ascent in a couple of hours, three at the most. But the snow through which I wallowed was bottomless and treacherous as quicksand.

Around ten o'clock, after three hours of drudgery, it was clear to me that I was never going to reach the top like that. I knew also that I would not get down if I expended myself still more. Either turn round on the spot or . . . ?

In 1979 I returned to the harsh testing landscapes of the Karakoram to tackle K2 (above and below), the second highest but most difficult of the eight-thousanders, from the south. With only five climbing companions I repeated the original ascent route by the Abruzzi Ridge (right-hand skyline above) after abandoning a reconnaissance on the South Face (above centre) which was eventually climbed in 1986 by the Poles Jerzy Kukuczka and Tadeuz Piotrowski. Below, a camp on the South Face with Friedl Mutschlechner.

(Overleaf) Using my ice axe as a tripod, I was able to photograph myself after the first solo ascent of an 8000-meter peak, on the summit of Nanga Parbat, 9 August 1978.

Or risk the last possibility which remained to me: to climb the shortest line to the summit, over the steep rock barrier which towered up near me. I climbed carefully, coming as totally alive as on the vertical Dolomite walls. But Dolomite walls were serene climbs compared with here. Bad rock, 8000 metres high, clumsy double boots on my feet and poor vision through my glacier goggles. I balanced over hands-breadth ledges, wallowed up a snow gully. All my instincts were aroused. Inner reserves that I had thought exhausted came to my aid.

At four o'clock in the afternoon on 9 August I was on the summit, standing on top of Nanga Parbat. I saw the Silver Saddle below which the two German mountaineers Willo Welzenbach and Willy Merkl had perished, and over which Hermann Buhl had reached the summit for the first time in 1953. On the right, the Rupal valley. In between, a sky-high drop. I had been here once already, eight years ago. Then my younger brother Günther had been with me. We had hugged each other. It had been our first eight-thousander.

I felt calm, not excited as then. I screwed my camera to the head of my axe, which I had had adapted so that I could use it as a tripod. I took some pictures of myself, particularly so that people could recognise the background without any doubt. Then I fastened a metal case on my unused titanium piton and fixed it to the summit rocks. In the case I placed a parchment reproduction of the first page of the Gutenberg Bible: 'In the beginning God created . . .' A friend had given it to me. I added the date and my name on the parchment and put it back again in the case.

Often I had reflected how it would be if I were simply to remain sitting on such an eight-thousander. What was the secret sense of mountaineering? To stay up there? Not to return again to the world, which I had so laboriously left behind me?

Ama Dablam is not a high mountain but it is incomparably beautiful.

Although we climbed on 100-metre ropes and were frequently harried by stonefall, Bulle Oelz still had the nerve to take photographs.

Bulle and I saw four New Zealand climbers being avalanched on the South-West Face. It took two days to make climbing contact with the three survivors, Geoff Gabites, a badly injured Peter Hillary and Merv English who held their fall and belayed his companions.

After an hour I climbed down again, not over the rock barrier, rather around it. First along the South Ridge, then through the snow of the western basin. Downwards things went more easily through the frosty snow drifts. Still in daylight I reached the tent which I had left behind at my last campsite.

Next morning snow drifts prevailed. Thick mist. Descent was not to be thought of. I would inevitably lose my way like Franz Jäger and Andi Schlick on the descent of Manaslu. In a snowstorm it is endlessly difficult to orientate oneself without marker poles. I would bide my time. How long? I must ration food and fuel. The bad weather could last a week. I crouched in the tent. I was dehydrated and very, very tired. I became clumsy. Twice in one day I knocked over the full cooking pot, thereby burning my down sleeping-bag.

The weather that evening looked bad. It was 10 August. Still three, four days in hand before I would be too weak to descend. 'If I am not back after ten days, you can dismantle base camp and report me missing to the authorities in Islamabad,' I had said to Ursula and Derry. 'For the rest, there is nothing to do. A search would be madness.'

Half past three the following morning; the weather seemed to be improving. I was giddy but there was nothing to hold me back. At five o'clock I was out of the tent. I had decided to put all my eggs in one basket. I had to try to reach base camp in a single mighty stage: down 3000 metres in the steepest direct line. If I did not make it I would not be able to survive the coming night.

With this knowledge, I set off. It was the last powerful incentive. I descended across the slope, slipped suddenly and, only by the fastest reaction, was able to cling on. I was lucky. A ricked ankle, a broken shin-bone would have meant the end. The shock made me concentrate with all my powers.

To the right of the Mummery Rib, which was subject to stonefall, I descended 2000 metres in one go, over fifty-degree blank ice, face to the wall. No more incidents. No avalanches. Late in the morning I jumped over a dozen crevasses in the flat, lower part of the face. I felt half-dead and new-born at the same time.

From base camp, Derry had seen me for a long time. Ursula came towards me over the scree of the huge cirque. She had my trainers in her hand. That was a treat! We reached each other. I took off my club-foot boots, sick of the sight of them. With the quick eye of the doctor, Ursula diagnosed that I looked 'green', like a mummy. That is why there is no photograph of my return. To snap me in this condition, Ursula felt, would have been in poor taste.

24

THE ABRUZZI RIDGE ON K2

1979

BIVOUAC AT 7910 METRES: the storm raged around the tent in which Michl Dacher and I spent the night. At seven o'clock the wind abated. The light of the sun fell glaringly on us as we crawled out into the open in our blue down-filled suits. Like moon men we stood opposite each other. I looked at the masked Michl. His movements were slow-motion, his face small and pointed.

Resolutely I set off. A little higher up I stopped and, with a wag of the head, asked whether I should wait. No, that was not necessary, Michl followed. Like two dachshunds in deep snow we wallowed up the slope. For a time we were afraid the snow masses would carry us down to the Godwin Austen glacier. There was an awful lot of snow.

It was midday when we reached the big rock which lay like a foundling in the snow-field left of the great séracs. Snow, snow, snow; as far as my eyes could see. Above it the blue-black sky. The sun stood vertically behind the peak. It was icy cold. We had time still, although it was late for the summit. Our walking had become an irregular creeping. The snow slope before us expanded with every metre that we pushed upwards. This untouched emptiness took away my sense of distance. On the slope below us our track was no longer visible. Endlessly we wallowed upwards.

I was proud of each metre of headway. What we were doing was not without danger. The ground was in places as steep as a church roof. The face fell away vertically. We had no chance of surviving if one of us slipped.

I rested propped on my axe. Out of tiredness I crouched down without previously treading a stance in the snow. For Michl and me this was the fifth day of climbing. The Abruzzi Ridge was secured with three camps and fixed ropes as far as the Black Pyramid. We had done this preparation work so as to be able to descend more easily. Friedl Mutschlechner, Alessandro Gogna and Robert Schaurer had helped with it. For the 'Magic Line', the South-West Pillar, we were too few and the time too short. There was too much snow.

From the innards of the mountain I heard a rustling. Where was it coming from? Then the noise of crampons above me. Michl crept ahead on all fours with the motions of a swimmer. As I was cold from resting, I had to go on. Michl waited. I relieved him from trail making and in passing I saw his face. It seemed unknown to me.

The stretches we put in between one rest stop and the next became ever shorter. I did not know how long they were. When I was moving I could not count the paces and while resting my mind was a blank. When I rested I lay, when I went on I moved like an animal.

It didn't have much to do with mountaineering, it was only about seeing it through, a torment beyond pain and exhaustion. Perhaps we went on only because each hoped that the other would give up first. The partnership became a grim wrestling with each other, that drove us on further. And Michl, the tough forty-five-year-old, was as stubborn as I when it came to giving up first.

On the summit pyramid the snow gradually diminished. The ridge before me ran crescent-shaped and leftwards, rising slightly, endlessly far. I could not estimate its length. Would my strength carry me that far? I made better progress now. The snow was hard in places, although I was not conscious of it.

Suddenly I was standing in the sun. At the same time I knew we were on the summit. We were there! We were up!

'We've done it!' I shouted to Michl. I wanted to shake his hand, although he was still ten paces away from me. I waited. Then we stood there together. We could not believe it. We were astonished and had forgotten why we were here. Michl's face once more wore the expression of a young scamp, just as it had on setting out. I threw the rucksack down. We conversed without speaking.

Finally I remembered the radio. I fetched it out of my rucksack, pressed the transmitter key. 'Kappa Due calling Base Camp, Kappa Due calling Base Camp, come in please.' Reception was bad, just enough to clarify our position. When I gave Michl the radio, he squatted down. As I photographed the highest rise of the ridge, I heard him ordering flowers for his wife at home.

25

DEATH ON A HOLY MOUNTAIN

1979

THEY WERE IN THE MIDDLE OF THE WALL. The South-West Face of Ama Dablam is 1300 metres high, icy, smooth and partly vertical. Peter Hillary had set out from base camp with his three New Zealand partners shortly after we had arrived there. Even in his first Himalayan trip he wanted to accomplish something quite special. Peter's father, Edmund Hillary, had climbed Everest twenty-six years before with Sherpa Tenzing Norgay and for that he had been knighted.

I watched Peter Hillary through my binoculars. The New Zealander was climbing on a rope with his compatriot Merv English. Above them, on a rock buttress, which soared out of the middle of the face like an upthrust fist, were Ken Hyslor and Geoff Gabites. It was half past one in the afternoon.

Suddenly noise. An avalanche! The midday heat had softened the ice a few hundred metres above the four climbers. A room-sized block of ice broke away. It splintered into many pieces which spattered down the steep wall, pulling a long dust cloud behind it. It was like a nightmare, no, not a nightmare, it was shockingly real, something monstrous that played itself out before my eyes.

Ken, the youngest, threw his arms together over his head and fell backwards off the face. The force of the avalanche had blown him away. Geoff, the second on the rope, could not hold him; he fell too. Their rope became entangled with Hillary. Now the lives of the trio hung on Merv's rope.

No one could escape. Merv was standing on a narrow ledge. Peter was hit by several lumps of ice, on his legs, on his shoulder, his left arm was broken. He could not hold himself and fell. Merv caught him. Peter remained hanging on the rope.

Merv was still standing on his narrow stance. He knew that the whole group would fall off if he could hold on no longer. He bent his upper body over the one sling which he had placed round a rock spike. That was his belay. It must not be fractured by the falling ice masses.

Peter Hillary was screaming with pain, Geoff hung somewhere on the face, no sign of Ken. The rope was twisted round Merv's leg. For half an hour he remained incapable of movement. When he was able to free himself at last, he made the rope fast and climbed down to the others. The rope on which Ken's body hung was stretched. He was hanging under an overhanging rock, invisible to the others. Was he injured? If they could not pull him up he would die of suffocation; or was he long since dead?

My old friend, Bulle Oelz and I were part of an Austrian expedition to attempt Ama Dablam from the south. But we knew we must suspend our own activities and act at once. We assembled the most important items: 400 metres of rope, some tents, gas cartridges, rations, pitons. Then we climbed up until late into the night. At about 5400 metres we decided to spend the night in a wind-protected basin so as to rope on to the face next day from the side to help the New Zealanders. From base camp, however, we learned that three men had started the retreat. Therefore, the fourth must be seriously injured. I knew what it meant to abseil down this face: it was a stonefall hell, an ice funnel down which all the avalanches raged.

So we decided to descend to base camp during the night, using torches, so as to be able to start up the face from below next day. We could hardly sleep. At five in the morning we were on our feet again. On the face nothing was to be seen. It was dark. Not until half past six did we see movements. After three hours we reached Hillary's camp.

Over an ice slope we climbed upwards to the avalanche cone which towered up at the foot of the South-West Face of Ama Dablam. There we discovered the body of Ken Hyslor, a dreadful sight. We buried the dead man in a crevasse. His comrades had cut the rope on which he had hung in order to be able to save themselves.

Then we watched what the three New Zealanders were doing. They progressed slowly. It was crazy for us to climb up still further that day, with so many avalanches coming down. At the foot of the face we fixed a hundred metres of rope. Then we had to flee before the falling stones and ice.

Again a short night. I fell asleep for a few minutes at a time, but mostly lay awake. The stonefall, the three New Zealanders on the wall, the danger

Bulle Oelz and Wolfgang Nairz.

in which they were suspended, all that I saw clearly before me. In the morning we set off again. With the first of the daylight my fears declined. We took the route reconnoitred the previous day. The face still lay in shadow so the danger of stonefall was slight. We found the fixed rope, reached the open face and swiftly climbed up the funnel which presented the greatest danger. We had to reach a vertical rise under which there was shelter.

From this stance I traversed into the vertical face. Above us the New Zealand party were abseiling. I suggested they should knot their torn ropes together and abseil separately down to me. The first to come was Geoff. As I pulled him in under the rock overhang out of the ice slope, he burst into tears. He wept for Ken, his best friend, and out of relief. I belayed him as Bulle Oelz spoke to him soothingly.

Next came Peter Hillary, inching his way down, rucksack between his legs. He was gritting his teeth. It was obvious that each movement hurt, and with each movement he threatened to topple out of balance, having only his right hand as support. The left one was tied under his pullover. His face was green. Bulle took care of him.

Merv came last. He too had tears in his eyes. At twenty-five he was the oldest of the group but also the strongest and the one with the best nerves. He had constantly encouraged his two companions, for forty-five long hours. While descending he had belayed them.

Again lumps of ice rumbled into the depths. Stones as big as cabbages rattled down the face, whining through the air like shell splinters. We had to get out of this area as fast as possible. The three emaciated New Zealanders would have scarcely survived another bivouac. We let Peter Hillary down to the full extent of our rope, then we followed bit by bit, until we reached a rock ledge under overhanging rocks where we were safe for some hours from stone- and icefall. The last 200 metres of the vertical wall took an eternity and we did not get back to camp at the foot of the face until six o'clock in the evening, by which time it was already dark.

Next morning the helicopter, which our expedition leader Wolfgang Nairz had already requested, arrived. The badly injured Peter Hillary was the first to be flown to Khunde, to the Hillary Hospital, named after his father. Then followed Geoff and Merv. As for ourselves, we took down our tents. Our goal, to reach the summit of Ama Dablam from the south, was forgotten. We had lost too much time and strength. All that remained to us was a peaceful journey home on foot.

26

THE FIRST SOLO ASCENT OF MOUNT EVEREST

1980

SUDDENLY THE SNOW GAVE UNDER ME. My head lamp went out. I fell into the abyss—in slow motion, or so I experienced it—striking the ice walls once with my back, once with my chest. My sense of time was gone. Had I been falling seconds or was it already minutes? Suddenly there was ground under my feet again. Now I knew I was trapped. Perhaps for ever!

I should have taken a radio with me. Then I would have been able to call Nena whom I had left far below at five o'clock that morning in our advanced base camp at 6500 metres. Nena Holguin was an experienced mountaineer. She could have climbed up here to let a rope down to free me from this icy prison. But a radio weighed as much as three gas cartridges and fuel for my cooker seemed more important than the possibility of being able to call for help.

I fingered my head lamp and suddenly there was light. I put my head back and saw, about eight metres above me, a tree-trunk-sized hole and a few stars. The ice walls, some two metres apart, of iridescent blue-green, ran up towards each other. Then I knew I could not get out. With my torch I tried to illuminate the bottom of the crevasse but there was no end to it. The snow bridge which had broken my fall was only a square metre in area. Lucky, I thought, and noticed how my whole body was trembling. I was afraid. I wondered whether I could put on my crampons on the shaky snow support but at each movement fear of falling deeper overwhelmed me. Then I discovered a ramp which led obliquely upwards. That was the way out. In a few minutes I was again on the upper surface but still on the valley side.

Trance-like, I went back to the hole through which I had disappeared ten minutes before. The first dawn light illuminated the North Col of Mount Everest. I looked at my watch: it was shortly before seven. The fall into the crevasse had made me wide awake. I knew there was only this one spot where I could cross the crevasse which cut right across the 300-metre-high ice wall under the North Col. Four weeks before, on my first reconnaissance march to the 7000-metre-high North Col, I had discovered this snow bridge, just two metres wide. Then it had borne my weight. It had to hold up briefly now for, on my solo ascent, I had no aluminium ladders and rope with me. Two ski sticks and my light alloy ice axe were my only aids. I was careful. On the other side of the crevasse was a steep snow wall. I bent forward and inserted the ski sticks, handles foremost, high on the wall. Then I swung myself across. I knew that more than ten mountaineers had lost their lives on the slopes of the North Col.

Daylight grew. Far in the east stood the mighty massif of Kangchenjunga above a blue-grey sea of mist. It had been right to break off my attempt in July. The snow, softened by the warm monsoon, had then been bottomless and the avalanche danger great. Now, on 18 August, the snow was firmly frozen and good to walk on.

The pale dawn lay over the summit of Mount Everest. It stood so clear against the deep blue sky that I could recognise clearly the free-standing rock tower on the North-East Ridge. There George Mallory and Andrew Irvine were last seen on their bold summit push in 1924. Nobody knew whether the pair had perished during the ascent or not until the descent. Had they indeed reached the summit? Were they the first to climb the highest mountain in the world which the Tibetans call Chomolungma, 'Goddess Mother of the World'?

The British had been the first to get the idea of climbing Mount Everest. After a large-scale reconnaissance in 1921 the first assault was made a year later up the route I was now climbing. With poor equipment by today's notions, with which I would not climb the Matterhorn, Mallory and his friends Norton and Somervel1 passed the 8000-metre barrier for the first time in the history of mountaineering. And that fiery spirit George Mallory already knew then that Mount Everest had to be stormed in six days from the Rongbuk Monastery base camp (5100 metres), after thorough preparation and six weeks of acclimatisation. Two years later Mallory was dead. But the attempts on the Tibetan north side of Mount Everest went on until the Second World War, after which the Chinese closed the frontier to foreigners, achieving the first ascent via the North Col themselves in 1960, and again in 1975.

In the spring of 1980 they opened the frontier. The Japanese, with a major expedition, were the first after the Chinese to make the summit up the northern route. Shortly after them, I had reached base camp via Lhasa and Shigatse. Seven weeks had passed. On this journey I had accumulated mani-fold impressions of Tibet, of this country with its almost endless distances. The pastel colours of the chains of hills had captivated me. This was the land of which previously I had only dreamed. At the same time it had often de-pressed me. From the whitewashed mud houses with the black window aper-tures Tibetan prayer flags no longer waved, there hung only red rags. The monastery at Rongbuk, earlier inhabited by 400 monks, was empty. Plun-dered. Thousands of wall paintings peeled from the decaying walls. The roofs of the temple had fallen in. In the mountain villages I had seen poor, apa-thetic faces. Here the people did not laugh as in the mountains of Nepal.

The altimeter showed 7360 metres. It was about nine o'clock. Now I was climbing more slowly. The stretch to the North Col I had done in two hours and so was able to spare myself one bivouac. Now and then the snow was ankle deep and the snow drifts cost energy. I must not exhaust myself. Tomorrow and the day after it would become much more strenuous. The two telescopic ski sticks were a big help; with their aid I could distribute my weight on arms and legs.

The northern slope to my right was a huge expanse of snow with dark islands of rock. Clearly recognisable were avalanche tracks. For the time be-ing I stayed on the blunt North Ridge. That was the safest route. No trace of my predecessors. Everything was buried under a thick mantle of snow. Only once, at about 7500 metres, did I see a red rope in the snow anchored to a rock island. On these ropes the Japanese had descended to base camp when the weather turned bad, and up them they had been able to climb hand over hand to continue the ascent.

By these tactics I had already climbed Mount Everest in 1978 by the southern route. This time I had nobody to help me with carrying or to pre-pare my bivouac, no companions to help break trail in the deep snow and no Sherpas to tote my equipment.

Like a snail with its house on its back, I carried my tent in my rucksack. I would erect it, sleep in it and take it with me for the next night. A second tent would have been too heavy. My fifteen kilos pressed so heavily at this altitude that I stopped after a dozen paces, gasped for breath and forgot everything around me. The stretches between rest pauses became shorter. Each time it required great will-power to stand up again after a breather. Step by step I tormented myself as far as 7800 metres. I had the feeling of someone behind encouraging me.

The first campsite which I stamped out in the snow did not please me. I had to camp on rock to be able to anchor the tent well. A few metres below me I saw an ideal spot but I lacked the strength to unpack my rucksack and put up the tent. I sat there and gazed down to advanced base camp whence I had set off at five o'clock. Now it was after three o'clock in the afternoon. I recognised a tiny red patch. Nena must have placed the sleeping-bag on the roof of the tent to protect herself from the heat. Up to now the heat had been worse than the cold. At night the thermometer dropped only to -10°C in base camp; up here to -20°C. During the day the sun dehydrated me. The oxygen-starved air literally rasped my throat. I remembered that I had a tiny bottle of Japanese medicinal herb oil with me and put a couple of drops on my tongue. That gave relief for a while and opened the air passages. Apart from aspirin, this herbal remedy was the only medication I took.

Nena must be able to see me with her binoculars. I hoped she wasn't worried. Before the start I had explained to her that there should be no problems if on the first day I made more than 1200 metres height. On my solo ascent of Nanga Parbat two years before, which had given me the psychological support for this solo trip to Everest, I was actually able to climb 1600 metres the first day but then I had started from 4800 metres. There was a vast difference between climbing at 6000 and 7000 metres above sea-level. Here each manoeuvre was an effort.

My tiny tent, not two kilos in weight and so constructed that it could withstand storms up to a speed of one hundred kilometres per hour, did not require much space. It was just big enough to lie in with bent knees. I had trouble putting it up because time and again a gust of wind blew in and lifted it up. I anchored it with ski sticks, ice axe and the only rock piton I had with me. I laid a finger-thick foam mat on the floor and crawled in. For a while I just lay there and listened to the wind hurling ice crystals against the tent wall. It was coming from the north-west. That was a good sign: the weather should hold.

I ought to cook. But I was so tired by the many small preparations for the night that I could not rouse myself to it, although I had eaten nothing since morning.

I thought of Maurice Wilson, a religious fanatic, who in 1934 had attempted a solo ascent of Everest, although he had been no climber. He had been steadfastly convinced that God would lead him up Everest and had not given up after the worst of snowstorms and several falls. On his first run up to the North Col he had not been able to cover the stretch from advanced base camp to the col at 7000 metres in four days. At the end of his strength, he had crawled back to his last camp where two porters awaited him. They had known he would not make it and tried to persuade him to give up. But when he was on his legs again, the madman had climbed up once more. A year later his corpse was found at the foot of the North Col. The last lines of his diary read: 'Off again, gorgeous day'.

Was I just as mad as Wilson, obsessed by an idea which nobody understood, not even mountaineers? I had already climbed Mount Everest once. Why endure the risk, the drudgery, a second time? Yet, now I was on another mountain, even if it had the same summit.

'*Fai la cucina,*' someone near me was saying, 'Get into the kitchen,' and I thought again about cooking. I talked half aloud to myself. The strong feeling of being with an invisible companion led me to hope that the other person was doing the cooking. I asked myself how we would have space enough to sleep in this tiny tent. I wanted to divide the first piece of dried meat which I fetched out of my rucksack into two equal portions. I spoke in Italian although for me, as a South Tyroler, my mother tongue was German and for three months I had been speaking only English with my Canadian friend Nena.

The wind had become so strong that the tent fluttered and every time I opened the entrance a hands-breadth to shovel snow with the lid of my cooking pot it blew out the flame on my gas cooker. It will be a bad night, I thought.

It takes a lot of snow to melt a litre of water. At first I made tomato soup, then two pots of Tibetan salt tea which I had learned how to prepare from the nomads. A palmful of herbs to a litre of water and two pinches of salt. I had to drink a lot: four litres a day if I were not to dry out.

The cooking lasted some hours. I just lay there, held the cooking pot and pushed a piece of dried meat or Parmesan cheese in my mouth. With it I chewed hard South Tyrol *Bauernbrot*, a coarse brown bread. All these small manipulations added up to a bodily ordeal.

I lay with my clothes in my sleeping-bag and dozed. When I opened my eyes I did not know whether it was morning or evening but I did not want to look at my watch. Deep down I was anxious. It was not fear of anything in particular which seized me, it was all the experiences of my mountaineering life, the exertion of thirty years of climbing awake in me. Avalanches, states of exhaustion I had experienced, condensed now into an extensive, deep-seated anxiety. I knew what could befall me up there. I knew how great the drudgery would be under the summit. Had I not known it, how could I have brought myself later, hour after hour, step by step, to go on?

As the sun struck the tent in the morning and licked the hoar-frost from the inside wall, I packed everything again, leaving behind two tins of sardines and a gas cartridge as well as half the soup and tea. I must make do with the rest of the provisions. The weather was good, next day I had to be on the summit.

For the first fifty metres I was slow, then I found my rhythm again and made good progress. I was climbing now somewhat to the right of the North Ridge and the ground became steeper and steeper. I stuck fast in the snow and progressed dreadfully slowly until I came to a place where an avalanche had broken away. To the right on the North Face I saw my chance. The whole slope was one big avalanche track. There I would be able to move fast enough and reassured myself that after two weeks of fine weather there was no danger of avalanche, that the snow had consolidated up above. The weather would still hold for a couple of days.

So I began a long, easily rising traverse, with many pauses, but regular. What with the exertion and concentration, I had not noticed that the weather had turned bad. My surroundings were shrouded in mist. The peaks below me had flattened out and I moved with the feeling of no longer belonging to the world beneath. When I looked at the altimeter at three o'clock in the afternoon near the Norton Couloir I was disappointed. It showed only 8220 metres. I would gladly have gone on further but there was no bivouac site. Besides, I was too tired, so there I stayed.

An hour later, my tent stood on a rock outcrop. I had given up taking pictures. It took too much energy to screw the camera on the ice axe and set it, to walk away ten paces and wait for the click of the delayed action release. It was much more important that I make myself something to drink.

The snow had turned to ice at the edge of the rocks. I was sure it thawed in high summer when it was windless and misty, even on the summit of Everest. Nevertheless I must not be careless because at this height a few degrees of

Alone (centre) just above the North Col of Everest. I bivouacked at 7800 and 8200 metres and reached the summit on 20 August 1980.

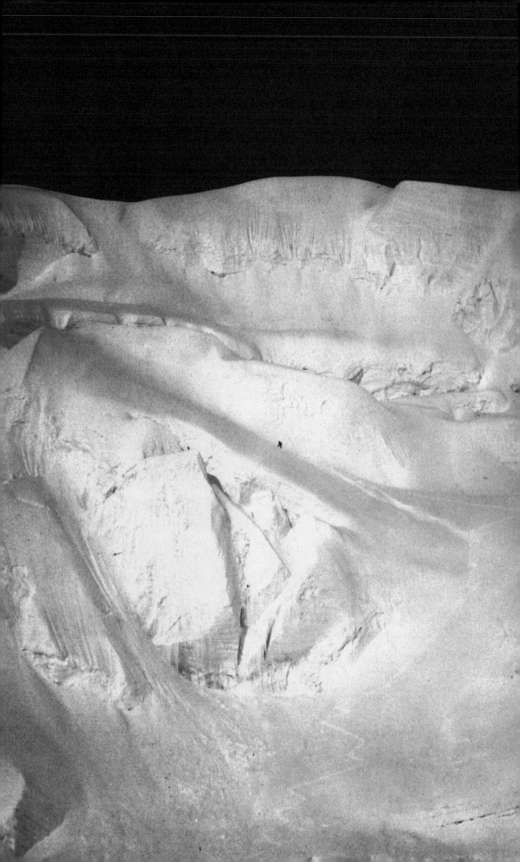

Shisha Pangma in Tibet is an easy eight-thousander but was the last to be climbed (by Chinese and Tibetans) due to its political isolation. We climbed a variant of the original North-West Face route in 1981. A year later Doug Scott, Alex MacIntyre and Roger Baxter-Jones made a new alpine-style ascent of the South Face.

A break in the middle of the sérac wall below the North Ridge of Kangchenjunga. At first we were afraid the ice would collapse, but later became quite blasé.

In 1930 G. O. Dyhrenfurth's expedition failed on the North Face of Kangchenjunga. Just over fifty years later we climbed 'his' route to the summit. That year, 1982, I climbed three eight-thousanders, Kangchenjunga, Gasherbrum II and Broad Peak.

frost could cause frostbite. What should I do in the morning if the thick mist had not dispersed? Should I wait and see? No, that was crazy. At this height one only deteriorated. The day after tomorrow I would have been so weakened that I would have been no longer capable of a summit assault. I had to either go up or go down. There was no other choice.

Twice while melting snow I took my pulse. Way over 100 beats per minute. The night lasted a long time. I kept my clumsy double-layered boots on so that they did not cool down.

The morning of 20 August I left everything behind; even my rucksack stayed in the tent, but after a short while I missed it like a true friend. It had been my conversation partner, it had encouraged me to go on when I had been completely exhausted. Lack of oxygen and the insufficient flow of blood to the brain were the cause of these irrational experiences which I had got to know on my solo ascent of Nanga Parbat. Up here, the British climber Frank Smythe had shared his biscuits with an imaginary partner in 1933.

The rucksack had been my companion but without it I got along much better. And my second friend, the ice axe, was still there.

The way up the Norton Couloir was not too difficult. A snow gully led to a steep step shot through with brightly coloured rock. In the middle there was a narrow ribbon of snow which made the ascent easier. An avalanche had gone down here not too long before, so the snow bore my weight. But then it became softer and my speed decreased. On hands and knees I climbed upwards like a four-legged creature, completely apathetic, the route never ending. By the time I was standing on a ledge below the summit the mist was so thick that I could scarcely orientate myself. A dark, vertical rock wall above me barred the way but something in me drew me to the left and I made a small detour around the obstacle.

The next three hours I lost all track of time. Every time blue sky appeared through the thick clouds I thought I saw the summit and yet I was still amazed and surprised when suddenly the aluminium tripod, the summit indicator of Everest, stood before me, barely still sticking out above the snow. The Chinese had anchored it to the highest point in 1975 in order to be able

Approaching the summit of Hidden Peak (Gasherbrum I) in a snow storm after traversing Gasherbrum II. Up above are the summit cornices.

Balti porters in the Karakoram would carry twenty kilos of expedition gear for up to twelve hours a day.

to take exact measurements but now, in the monsoon period, everything was different up here. Snow cornices, which towered up to the south, seemed to be higher than I was. I squatted down, feeling as heavy as lead. A scrap of cloth wrapped round the tripod point was frozen. I must take some pictures, I told myself, as if repeating a formula. But I could not rouse myself to it for a long time.

At the time I was not disappointed that, once again, I had no real view. For the second time I was on the highest point on earth and could see nothing. It was completely windless and the clouds welled around me, as if the earth were pulsating underneath. As yet I did not know how I had done it but I knew that I could do no more. I could only stand up to go down.

27

THE REST OF THE EIGHT-THOUSANDERS

1981–86

IT MADE NO SENSE TO CLIMB ON. For two hours I had fooled myself. The monsoon was here! Metre-high snow changed the descent route within hours to an avalanche hell. If we did not descend in time it would be too late. Navigation would become impossible as the driving snow and mist became thicker.

Friedl Mutschlechner, who was treading down the snow in front of me, was going like a bull. It had been he who had urged setting out that morning in spite of the storm. He it was who did not want to give up. He knew as well as I that this was our last chance on Shisha Pangma (8013 metres). A tiny chance. We wallowed through the knee-deep snow.

It was eight o'clock in the morning when we found a tiny tent, 7500 metres above sea-level and two and a half kilometres above the Tibetan plateau. The tent was ripped and old. Powder snow, driven in by the wind, whirled round inside like a top. We crept in and plugged the entrance with rucksacks. Crouched together, covered all over with snow, icicles on our beards, we squatted there, defeated, despairing, tired. The storm increased. There was no doubt. This was the monsoon, the warm, damp airstream, which in summer brought the so urgently needed rain to India, Bhutan and Nepal for three months, but led in the mountains to extensive snow falls. This year the monsoon buffeted the enormous wall of the Himalayan chain two weeks earlier than usual. When Bulle Oelz came up at noon the situation was hopeless. Together we climbed down.

The stony slopes were pregnant with avalanches, the mist in the Corridor, a high valley between main and fore-summit, so thick that we first saw the tent as we stood in front of it. It was all over. Bulle, whose bivouac tent lay an hour lower, led the way down on his touring skis. 'If the weather stays like this, tomorrow we must go down as far as advanced base camp,' I said on leave-taking.

'Break off the expedition?'

'Yes! The others must be frantic with worry.' Uschi, my former wife, had accompanied me on this Tibetan journey and had been guarding base camp for some days.

It was now two years since the Chinese government had first decided to allow a few foreigners into Tibet. Lhasa, the 'Holy City', had been a disappointment. There, pedestrians no longer measured their length, praying, along the roads. Now hooting lorries hurled them to the roadside. Like the Tibetans, the trucks were on their way to the factories, in which batteries, matches, carpets, cement and shoes were produced. But people and machines marched to a different tune. Lhasa had been catapulted out of serfdom into the twentieth century but the population, although confronted with a wave of new ideas, had not forgotten their religion. The monks' state was dead. Only the people in the streets still seemed to live in another time. Their faith clung to the golden roofs of the Jokhang Temple. They prayed all the time, prayed at work on the assembly line, that the Dalai Lama might return. Faces with tears in their eyes, people full of despair and hope became to me suddenly more important than all the mountains in the world.

Like a magic mountain, the Potala had stood there in the first light of morning as we travelled westwards. This fortress of stone and thatch seemed to touch the sky with its golden pagodas. Lhasa, where once millions of Asiatic believers had made pilgrimage in months-long journeys, to grasp the last mysteries of the East, was a divided city. Here monasteries, there barracks. The magical charm of this city was concentrated in the red and white Potala, which had been built over the centuries by slaves for their god-king.

Everywhere the memory of murder and subjugation mixed with belief in the reawakening of lamaism in the streets of Lhasa. 'Superstition', the Chinese rulers called it; I called it the 'elemental force of the highlands'.

On our long journey from the capital Lhasa to base camp, time and again the bumpy jeep road had led us past the ruins of desecrated monasteries. There had been 3600 monasteries before the occupation, so it was estimated. Six of them were left. During the past two years they had been restored and cleaned up. The Chinese wanted to show the Western world how tolerant the communist government was towards minorities and their religions since the overthrow of the Gang of Four. Occasionally I did find genuine monks but many of them had perished in labour camps, while others had fled. The appearance of the gompas, the temples, had altered too. Surrounded by butter lamps and Buddhas, 650 monks still meditated in Tashilhunpo Monastery in Shigatse, a lama priest assured us. They slunk through the halls in their red cowls.

Religion and trade had determined the life of the Tibetans. But now prayer and trade was forbidden. No wonder that this people, who remained loyal to the Dalai Lama in their hearts, rose up time and again against the Chinese rulers. In vain. Only in 1980, after the Afghan crisis, were a few prohibitions relaxed and merchants were allowed to join the pilgrims drawn into the towns and villages. Yak nomads lived again on the plateau under Shisha Pangma.

The whole night the storm tugged at the tent. We did not sleep. At two o'clock in the morning Friedl urged setting out. The sky was clear. The storm would diminish. Friedl said it so convincingly that I dressed myself, although I thought it was crazy. Again we set off upwards at five o'clock, again we plodded to the foot of the North Face. Again the storm hurled ice crystals in our faces. But there were still stars in the sky. Luckily for us an avalanche had swept down the left-hand of the two gullies on the North Face. We climbed high in the gully, quitted it to the left two-thirds of the way up and reached the ridge and with it the route of the first ascent. Again mist, and the storm on the east slope was so strong that we had to cower down to rest. Friedl went on ahead. He wanted to get to the summit—in spite of the monsoon and I followed him to the summit. As we caught a glimpse of a bit of the Tibetan plateau, I remembered taking leave of my mother. 'Stay in Tibet if there is war,' she had said to me on going away, trusting more to her instinct than the world political situation.

In the autumn I went to Makalu. I wanted to climb the fifth highest mountain on earth and see again the faces of the people who give life and history to the Himalaya. Nena wanted to come with me although she was pregnant. Our child was due to be born at the beginning of November, in Starnberg near Munich. Everything had been prepared. After two days' approach march Nena hurried back to Tumlingtar, in order to fly from there to Europe via Kathmandu. Meanwhile I was at base camp and then climbed the central peak of Chamlang with Doug Scott and some Sherpas.

243

In 1981 Doug Scott and I planned to traverse Makalu from south-east to north-west, but the premature birth of my daughter Layla brought me hurriedly back to Nena in Kathmandu.

As we came back to base camp, to traverse Makalu, a letter was lying there from Nena. She had given birth prematurely in Kathmandu. A girl. She was small and very weak. I read the letter, then I packed my things. In two days and two nights I ran as far as Tumlingtar, normally a march of two weeks. Once in Kathmandu I looked for Nena in the hospital. She was no longer there, nor was she at the hotel. After two days I found her with friends. Our little girl was indeed small but lively, healthy and singularly beautiful. We named her Layla.

IN THE MIDDLE OF MARCH 1982 we set out from Kathmandu. Nena and Layla, Friedl Mutschlechner and I, and a few Sherpas. The march to

Kangchenjunga base camp was to take three weeks of heat, rain and snow.

At first we walked through tropical rainforest, then through deep, arid gorges, finally over slushy spring snow. Layla was six months old. She was to withstand the height and cold better than us. During the ten weeks of expedition she was never ill.

At Pangpema, a small, flat patch of ground at 5000 metres, on the right-hand marginal moraine of the Kangchenjunga Glacier, we installed our base camp: a kitchen, some tents for the Sherpas and the liaison officer, two tents for us.

Before Friedl Mutschlechner and I started up the North Face of Kangchenjunga, we attended a long prayer ceremonial. Our deeply religious companions supplicated the gods, threw rice in the air and murmured prayer rituals. Kangchenjunga, third highest mountain in the world at 8598 metres, is a holy mountain and the name may be translated from the Sanskrit as the 'Five Treasuries of the Great Snow', probably from the five glaciers which flow from this mountain massif—glaciers which bring water, life and wealth to the people who live down in the valleys.

We promised the Sherpas to climb to only just below the summit, so as not to disturb the throne of the gods. Three weeks we climbed on the face. We jumped over crevasses, worked our way up ice chimneys, struggled up endless snow slopes. By a partly new route we climbed the North Face, the North Ridge and the summit pyramid to a few metres below the highest point.

The descent became a race with death. A hurricane ripped our bivouac tent at 8000 metres. Cooking had become impossible and we suffered hallucinations. Friedl Mutschlechner contracted severe frostbite on his hands and feet. For him the agonising return march was the end of this trip. I stayed in Asia.

In Skardu, Nazir Sabir and Sher Khan, the two strongest mountaineers in Pakistan, had been waiting for me for days. We equipped a small column of porters and set off with 500 kilos of expedition luggage, intending to march up the dangerous Braldu Gorge and across the endless Baltoro Glacier to Gasherbrum base camp. The three of us would then climb Gasherbrum II (8035 metres) and Broad Peak (8047 metres). I had given up my idea of making two traverses after Friedl had had to drop out. However, I wanted to do the hat-trick of eight-thousanders.

At base camp there were other expedition teams and bad weather. It rained and snowed for a week. When the weather improved we packed our rucksacks for the ascent of Gasherbrum II. We were so well acclimatised that we could climb from base camp straight to the summit without risk.

Sher Khan, Nazir Sabir and I climbed the broken Gasherbrum icefall. At the foot of the South-West Ridge we erected our first bivouac tent. Snow conditions were good. The platform for the second bivouac site we dug out of the slope at a height of 6800 metres. The snow conditions deteriorated more and more the higher we went. It was a strenuous route, with snow drifts, avalanche danger, hard trail making. There were only the three of us and we carried all the equipment ourselves, gas for fuel and provisions.

On the third day we climbed up to the summit pyramid of Gasherbrum II. There we bivouacked for the third time. Next morning the storm was raging around the tent. Despite thick mist and snow drifts, we decided to risk it. Navigation was the most difficult part. We found the knife-edge summit ridge, took some photographs, stayed only a few minutes.

Just a week later we set off for the summit of Broad Peak. After the descent from Gasherbrum we had moved base camp and rested for two days. The weather was good. We climbed to the summit in three days, up the West Spur, the route which twenty-five years before Hermann Buhl, Kurt Diemberger, Markus Schmuck and Fritz Wintersteller had first climbed. We stayed up there a long time—taking photographs, gazing, enjoying it all. I had achieved my hat-trick, and was already planning my next step: the double traverse of two eight-thousanders, the two highest Gasherbrum peaks, al-pine-style and without intermediate camps.

THAT WINTER HANS KAMMERLANDER AND I were to climb Cho Oyu (8153 metres). We had placed fixed ropes up to a height of 7300 metres. We knew that 200 metres higher the face was easier, strenuous to be sure but, apart from some steep rises, quite feasible. Use of the correct tactics on such a big mountain was halfway to success. It was my plan to climb up with Hans very early from Camp 2 and to secure the difficult buttress up to 7500 metres with fixed ropes. Then we wanted to turn back to the bergschrund at 7100 metres, where the three Sherpas, Ang Dorje, Phurba and Nawang, were to establish an emergency camp for a single night. Next day, 19 December, we would place this above the vertical ice buttress and from this third camp we would reach the summit in a day and be able to return to the tent without bivouacking.

On the morning of 18 December, still in camp, Ang Dorje seemed dis-tracted. He was unwilling and ill-humoured. Was he anxious? Outside, in front of the tent, the day's activities began. For a time I said nothing. Ang

The steep rise in the summit wall of the South-East Face of Cho Oyu had to be secured in order to keep the return route open. Driven back by bad weather, we eventually climbed the mountain from the southwest.

Dorje wielded pots. He breathed heavily. Time and again hoar-frost, which stuck some centimetres thick on the inner side of the tent, fell on my face. Suddenly Ang Dorje began to tell a story. He talked spontaneously and without interruption. I understood the history only when he had finished it. In the night suddenly two naked Cho Oyu gods had stood at the tent entrance. Green from head to foot, as green as the turquoise which he wore round his neck. 'Turquoise green and stark naked they were,' repeated the Sherpa. 'Come out,' the gods had shouted. Because they were not grown-up gods, but rather small, rude youths, Ang Dorje had resisted them. He seized one of them by the arm. When he touched him, however, the two young gods dissolved into thin air and a glowing beam flashed through Ang Dorje's body. Back in his sleeping-bag, full of disquiet, he had sweated for hours.

Hans had become uncertain too. Should we give up? I was not superstitious but these faces gave me a great deal of trouble. Finally we set off. Hans and I climbed ahead. Ang Dorje, who apparently had forgotten about the turquoise gods, urged on his friends. We had a strenuous day before us. The Sherpas had to be back in the second camp before nightfall.

Hans Kammerlander, Michl Dacher and Friedl Mutschlechner. With Hans I climbed seven 8000-metre peaks.

Mount Everest stood in the east like a black triangle. A cloud banner hung on Lhotse. Everything ran according to plan. Next day, however, at the end of the ice buttress, I became uncertain. The flatter the ground became, the deeper lay the snow: crystalline driven snow, like sugar, a metre deep. As I stood there, where the last camp was planned, I knew we must enter into a deadly risk or fail. There was snow slab danger. We would have had to traverse up the avalanche-pregnant slopes diagonally, from right to left. The decision to give up was not discussed. It was definite: better a failure than a corpse.

The same evening we abseiled down. Next day we descended to base camp. We were tired, worn out by the wind, but somehow still on our feet. As if in flight we went against the storm, forwards, downwards. As I stumbled over the glittering pieces of ice of a fallen sérac, I felt the great face behind me, like a storm tide in the nape of my neck. The three Sherpas in front of me were bent double, dragging the rest of the equipment behind them in a body-length sack, diagonally to the track.

As I came behind the others, with the protecting base camp in sight, I knew that we had failed. Everything had been in vain. The year's planning, the months of preparation, the four weeks of acclimatisation, the nineteen days of climbing on the face. Only one day had separated us from the summit.

On Annapurna's unclimbed North-West Face in 1985 we employed mixed tactics: expedition-style climbing lower down and alpine-style above 6000 metres.

Just when we had wanted to climb to the top, this face spat us out.

The Sherpas were happy. With laughing, relaxed faces they told the others of this latest attempt, of vertical ice ribs and bottomless snow drifts. Long into the evening we heard a chorus-like sing-song from their kitchen. They were relieved. The gods were appeased.

A few weeks later we were back in Europe. I experienced no shock on homecoming. Life was no worse than before. With the same matter of factness with which I had previously essayed the life of the East, I threw myself into the Western version. I organised, worked, hurried. The experience I brought with me from afar, I could not utilise in Europe.

However, I was not prepared, in the long run, just to become a businessman and when in spring 1983 the permit for a Cho Oyu ascent unexpectedly came through, I set off again, this time with Hans Kammerlander and Michl Dacher. We were not in a hurry. To the music of rustling woods and trickling snow we walked to base camp. We got much further than on the first attempt, we got to the summit. This time from the south-west, and after some strenuous detours. I gazed up into the faces of my two summit companions: drawn with exertion but still proud and enthusiastic. Without this mirror I might well have broken down.

WITH THE DECISION TO COMPLETE climbs of all fourteen eight-thousanders, my life became hectic again. I was for ever organising a trip or away somewhere on one. In the spring of 1984 I failed on the North-East Ridge of Dhaulagiri. But subsequently I succeeded in traversing Gasherbrum I and II with Hans Kammerlander.

Both Gasherbrum eight-thousanders, Gasherbrum I (Hidden Peak) and Gasherbrum II, I had climbed once already. They did not belong to the four which were still missing from my 'collection'. What interested me was the question whether I could ascend two eight-thousanders one after the other without pausing in between, without descending to the valley, without preparing the route or setting up depots. We succeeded. Hans and I climbed Gasherbrum II first. We then descended over a new route towards the Gasherbrum valley and on over the North Face of Gasherbrum I. We reached the summit in a snowstorm and in a snowstorm we descended the West Ridge.

That summer I began to restore Schloss Juval, a medieval castle on a rock outcrop between the Vinschgautal (Val Venosta) and the Schnalstal. I had acquired the partial ruin in 1983. I wanted to make one part habitable, and to strengthen the northern section so that it did not decay any more. This work absorbed me just as much as mountaineering or writing. But although I wanted to complete the rebuilding and move into Juval in 1985, I could not renounce my planned journeys. In April Hans Kammerlander and I stood on the summit of Annapurna I (8091 metres). We had climbed the dangerous and extremely difficult North-West Face, a route of which I was proud. Two weeks later we went up the Kali Gandaki to climb Dhaulagiri (8167 metres). Again we were successful. And we were lucky. We were able to climb alone, relying solely on our own resources. The groups which thronged to the eight-thousanders were spread around on the other peaks.

If the 'conquest' of the big eight-thousanders, with few exceptions, had been originally achieved only with oxygen masks, it was because man wanted to have everything his own way. Equipping the big expeditions of the fifties had cost a great deal of money and they were supported by individual countries. Appropriate flags were to be planted on the summits. The climbers wanted to take no risks.

By 1985 we saw considerations of another sort. Now we had almost perfect tents, boots, clothing, cookers. We knew how we had to prepare ourselves, how one acclimatised. We knew that repeated brief stays at great height contributed to better adaptation and with that to highest performances. And as a result these highest points were losing their mystery. As I perceived it, the great peaks had 'shrunk' on account of the innumerable expeditions which operated alongside each other. On the eight-thousanders once it had been above all the seclusion which had made them so inaccessible. This had vanished. I did not lament it, rather looked for other goals.

IN THE SUMMER OF 1985 I travelled with some friends to Kailas, the holiest mountain in Tibet. There I made a circuit of the 'Throne of the Gods' and nearby Lake Manasarowar. I sensed that this form of travelling could absorb me too. On the homeward journey I learned of the death of my brother Siegfried. He had been struck by lightning on the Stabeler Tower in the Dolomites, fallen and been fatally injured. He had died in hospital without regaining consciousness.

I was aware once more how much luck I had had. How many thunderstorms had I endured on the mountains, how many snowstorms? Only a few months before on Dhaulagiri Hans and I had gone many hours through thunder and lightning without getting killed. Life in the mountains was not 'hard but fair', it was above all incalculable. It was this realisation that made my mother anxious. When I returned from Tibet, Siegfried had been buried only two weeks. She asked me to give up Himalayan mountaineering. But she understood that I still wanted to climb Makalu and Lhotse, my last two eight-thousanders. Afterwards, I promised her, I would not want to climb again on such high peaks.

This promise coincided with the realisation that I knew this small world of the highest mountains too well. I seldom now experienced the unfamiliar up there. For more than a decade I had exhausted this tension between strangeness and familiarity, which consisted of perceptions, ideas, energy. I now knew how people behaved when climbing. I had made some friends, I had been disappointed by other partners, the latter only because to begin with I would not admit that, amongst climbers, too, there are honest and dishonest, complacent and willing, envious and joyful people. We are no better examples of the human race than any others, perhaps with the only difference that in life or death situations our personal qualities emerged more vividly than those of the man in the street.

In autumn 1985 I moved into Juval. That was a feeling of bliss. I had finally enough space, much of which was not even filled. I had found this place, named the individual towers and gardens, planned each detail and carried out much restoration work myself. Here I was at home and here I would stay, perhaps my whole life.

In the winter I journeyed to Nepal again. Amongst the expedition camp hangers-on I found an Italian television crew. Hans and I failed notwithstanding. The attention of the general public was not going to seduce me into increasing my readiness to take risks. Although each public appearance took freedom away from me, I knew full well that all I had to do was sell my adventures to the media and my experience to the manufacturers, if I wanted to finance further costly expeditions.

In the summer of 1986 I marched through eastern Tibet, from Kham to Lhasa and subsequently climbed Makalu with my South Tyrol friends, Friedl Mutschlechner and Hans Kammerlander. It was my fourth go at this peak. Three weeks later Hans and I stood on the summit of Lhotse in a snowstorm!

Now I felt myself free for new activities. My climbing school in South Tyrol I handed over to the guides who had already looked after it for a long time, my sports shop in Villnöss I attempted to sell. I acquired a mountain farm on Juval which I wanted to run intensively and biologically. My worry about having no practical livelihood by the age of forty had been unfounded. I was neither entrepreneur nor bureaucrat. What absorbed me was the wilderness, shaping books and films, and travelling to the world's end.

I had once revealed to my grandfather, on my father's side, with whom I spent the summer months for three years, that I wanted to be a mountain farmer. Now I had the place for it and the enthusiasm to fashion a piece of man-made alpine pasture according to my own ideas. This farm was now as important to me as the summits. In the meantime my father had died and so he was no longer able to shake his head over his second-born, whose passion for the mountain life had developed into an obsession.

Ice climbing at around 7400 metres, followed by a long and exposed summit ridge, were part of our 1985 ascent of the extremely difficult unclimbed North-West Face of Annapurna.

Hans Kammerlander and I climbed for days through thunder and lightning on Dhaulagiri in 1985. On the way home I learnt my brother Siegfried had died falling after being struck by lightning on the Stabeler Tower in the Dolomites. Life in the mountains is incalculable.

Descent from Makalu—I made it at the third attempt and thirteen of the fourteen eight–thousanders now lay behind me.

On 16 October 1986 Hans Kammerlander and I climbed Lhotse by the normal route and I completed my fourteen eight–thousanders. But the South Face was a challenge on which I had failed in 1975 and in 1979 it cost the life of my fellow eight–thousander collector, Jerzy Kukuczka. It was eventually climbed in 1990 in a brilliant solo push by Slovenian climber Tomo Česen and a mountaineering milestone was achieved.

When I am at home I am a farmer. In 1984 I began to restore the medieval Schloss Juval and acquired a mountain farm which I run intensively and biologically. The yaks are a herd I graze on an alpine pasture near my home.

28

THE SEVEN SUMMITS

1986

MOUNTAINEERING HAS ALWAYS BEEN sustained by ambitions to be the first. In 1983 two dollar millionaires from the USA set themselves a crazy goal: they wanted to be the first to climb the highest peaks on the seven continents. And that within a year. Dick Bass possessed coal interests in Alaska and ski resorts in Utah; Frank Wells was president of Warner Brothers Studios, one of the biggest film production businesses in the world. With a million-dollar budget, the best guides and a staff of advisers got to grips with the problem.

They had an aircraft converted so that it could land in the middle of Antarctica, bought their way into a Mount Everest expedition and travelled to Australia where they climbed Mount Kosciusko, a grassy humpback which is 2228 metres high. By so doing, it was clear to me that the pair had taken the soft option on defining their continents. Australia by my reckoning is only part of that greater continent Oceania, or Australasia, as it is called in English. To this belongs also New Guinea, and the jungle-girt Carstensz Pyramid which I had climbed in 1971 but which was inaccessible in 1983 on account of a local uprising. After I had stood on the 'Roof of the World' in 1978, I too had promised myself I would in time climb all the seven highest peaks. In mountaineering terms it is not an especially difficult goal but logistically a far from simple one. The old question raised itself as to whether the highest mountain in Europe was Elbrus in the Caucasus or venerable old Mont Blanc, at 4810 metres the highest peak in the Alps. Wells and Bass commissioned a team of geographers to determine their seven summits, and

Antarctica is a mountain as big as a continent. Always under way, the world grew and vanished with each step.

257

Wolfgang Thomaseth and Bulle Oelz on the summit of Mount Vinson, the highest summit in Antarctica, the last and remotest of my Seven Summits.

climbed Elbrus in the USSR because the glaciers there discharged into Europe and so the peak belonged to Europe, although it stands on the border with Asia.

A few weeks after them in 1983 I was standing in a snowstorm on the 5633-metre Mount Elbrus which is technically easy to climb. Mont Blanc I had often climbed already and fortuitously had rambled over Kosciusko in Australia. But I had already decided that the pair did not count. Of the magical 'seven summits' I now lacked only Mount Vinson in the Antarctic.

Meanwhile my millionaire 'competitors' had failed on Mount Everest. They could not buy the highest mountain in the world. That made me feel good.

In the winter 1983/84 Wells and Bass invited me to go to Mount Vinson with them, which was very generous. At last I had my chance! I got everything ready and deposited some 25,000 dollars as my expedition contribution. But at the last moment, I received a telex putting me off. Frank Wells and Dick Bass had realised in the nick of time that I was their only competitor in this game to be the first on the seven summits.

They climbed Mount Vinson. But on Mount Everest they failed a second time. Therefore my chances were still good. Frank Wells gave up the game in 1985. Everest was too high for him. Not so Dick Bass. He climbed the highest peak in the world with oxygen apparatus and help from the Sherpas. A splendid performance at the age of fifty-four, which won my respect. The Carstensz Pyramid, however, he skipped.

In the first days of December 1986 I flew with the most experienced polar pilot, Giles Kershaw, to the Vinson massif in Antarctica in an Adventure Network machine. The weather was good. The sun never set. Only forty-eight hours after landing at the foot of the mountain I was standing with my friend Bulle Oelz and cameraman Wolfgang Thomaseth on the summit of Mount Vinson. During the ascent we had bivouacked once, and we found a ski stick on the summit. Mist lay over this endless ice desert at the South Pole. We stood above it, by the latest measurements at a height of 4897 metres. Then just as quickly we went down again. It was too cold to stand around up there. At least -50°C.

It was not only cold up there. The sea of mist and the few mountain peaks which stuck up out of it made this world seem unreal. Only because Wolfi and Bulle were there too was I able to convince myself I also was there. It was as if we were standing outside the earth, despite the contradiction of our own tracks in the snow. This continent is not made for people.

Pat Morrow, a quiet Canadian, had meanwhile climbed the forbidden Carstensz Pyramid. On Mount Everest he had not climbed without oxygen to be sure, but he had got up. In 1986 he had reached the last of the seven summits a few months before me. He is the first of the genuine 'Seven Summits Summiters'.

On the way home from Antarctica I climbed Aconcagua with Bulle Oelz and Wolfgang Thomaseth. It was the second time for me, a present for my friend for whom this peak was still lacking. Bulle had already been on Mount Everest. Now he too wants to climb them all—the seven summits which mean world wandering to a climber.

29

WHITE INFINITY

1989–90

ALONGSIDE THE ARC OF LIFE, measured between birth and death, there is a second: that between strangeness and familiarity. As long as I sensed doubt, anxiety and strangeness in the Dolomites, which had been familiar to me since my childhood, I was motivated to climb there. When I knew almost everything there I went to the Himalaya and the Andes to climb. In recent years I have felt it no longer important to be the best climber or to secure various records. Collecting experiences means more to me. This, however, becomes more difficult year by year. I had exploded some myths and it was this which was now having its revenge. Higher than Mount Everest I cannot climb and more alone than solo there is not. So I have sought a new playground.

In the summer of 1986 I crossed the eastern part of Tibet on foot, from Tarchen Gompa to Lhasa. On the way the world became ever bigger to me. The mountains on the other hand had shrunk when I climbed them. So I searched the maps for regions where there were still no roads, no telephone, no airfield and few human settlements. In 1987 and 1988 I travelled through Bhutan and Tibet, in 1989 in the Judaea desert of southern Israel, and in Patagonia. My desire to traverse whole regions on foot was so elemental that often I neither photographed nor wrote a diary. Travelling was an end in itself. Experiences which I keep to myself stay alive longer than marketed adventures. A frequently photographed scene loses in aura just as much as a frequently told adventure. What enriched me was the subjective experience of climbing, of travelling, of gazing.

I am a pedestrian and will be able to lead a long life. It is also perfectly clear to me that I shall have to climb a mountain occasionally to let off steam.

Between my wanderings and journeys I live at my castle and the mountain farm belonging to it, just as I had dreamed as a child. Since 1986 I have organised a small agricultural project in South Tyrol, based on biologically dynamic methods of cultivation. We grow vegetables and fruit; rear horses, cows, sheep, miniature goats, chickens and much besides. I aspire more and more to the self-sufficient way of life.

In this complex and played-out world, living in the mountains is like a focal point for my hopes. And so I become more and more settled. When I am at home, I am a farmer. On the road I am curious. Life can not consist only of high points. Perhaps as a wanderer, and as a mountain farmer, I am full of peace and composure because I am only travelling, going nowhere, without ambitions. When I gave up wanting to be a mountaineer more peace came into my life. As a mountaineer, I had hoped too long for the summits.

Previously I had organised the expeditions according to a definite system: they were financed in advance, carried out, and afterwards exploited. Now I reduced my business activities more and more in order to be able to arrange more interesting activities.

If I have applied myself for the past twenty years to the conservation of the wild regions of this world, it is because I liked to defend our playground and respect nature as law-maker. Today each of us can choose, from endless possibilities, where he sets his standards. One does not have to climb Mount Everest in order to know how limited are our human abilities. Adventure is also about modesty. It is important that we learn all areas which we visit as we find them. Then the next generation can find that which we have sought there: a medium. Deserts and mountains are a catalyst for our humanity. On them we can discover our human abilities and limitations. Nature, in the form of rugged scenery, is the best mirror of our souls. For that reason, too, we have a big responsibility for the wild places. I want to conserve the mountains and deserts. For each tin can, each piton, each cable railway and each route, which the curious of a later generation find will be like a scratch on this mirror, and he who looks in a scratched mirror cannot perceive himself clearly.

Unadulterated landscapes, useless as they may be superficially, permit unequivocal experiences. With these ideas I was able to stimulate, in Italy and France, the 'mountain wilderness' movement and I shall not tire of insisting that the white patches on the world map shall not acquire a colour regardless. Only as 'white wildernesses' are they a form of unlimited raw material for experiences with nature, also a scale for the character of man. I did not want to traverse the Antarctic in order to serve science or national pride. I want to find a scale for myself. I want also to set an example: the Antarctic should remain the last great unspoiled region on this earth!

ANTARCTICA IS A SINGLE MOUNTAIN; a mountain of ice. A mountain as big as a continent on which, in more than 100,000 years, layers of ice crystals have created a mass almost 4000 metres high. The technical data—minimum temperature -89°C, area (equal to the USA and Europe combined)—mean nothing. They are abstract, rationally not comprehensible. The Antarctic first comes alive for people when they cross it; as a borderless ice waste, as a silence, as a peaceful space. There everything moves slowly; even when the blizzards, often up to 200 kilometres per hour, sweep across the high plateau.

My idea of crossing the ice continent on foot goes back to an historical attempt. Back in 1914 Shackleton wanted to cross Antarctica via the South Pole, from the Filchner Ice-shelf to Ross Island. Shackleton's expedition foundered before he had started the land journey. This 'last journey on Earth' of mine, carried out in the age of the space rocket with the technique of yesterday was to be one of today's posers, for since Shackleton's 1914 attempt no one had succeeded in crossing the seventh continent on foot.

All my major mountaineering problems had been posed by nature; a difficult Dolomite face without bolts, an eight-thousander alpine-style, Everest without oxygen, the first and only double traverse of an 8000-metre peak. Now I was facing nature once more. The crossing of the Antarctic was not a mountaineering exercise. Experience on ice was the only qualification I had for the attempt. In order to be able to travel in the Antarctic I had to acquire old perceptions. I must make myself familiar with Antarctic literature. Suddenly Preuss, Cassin and Buhl were no longer my mentors, rather Nansen, Amundsen and Shackleton. I wanted to travel using Scott's tactics, but without repeating his mistakes.

I found simply being under way, that was soon to become a way of life, exciting. On a mountain there is above and below, on K2 you are in base camp or on the summit, in the Antarctic you are under way. Always under way. When the division of time falls away, because above and below, day and night, spring and autumn are suspended, one passes into eternity. Sense of time dissolves and space grows. How far I could see in good weather I do not know. I knew only that behind each horizon another arose. The world grew and vanished with each step—and we took 6000 paces in each stage of the march. Five, six, eight times a day, for ninety-two days. When climbing one concentrates on holds, cloud formations, avalanche stripes—the mind remains bound by these limits. The ice travel often carried my mind far away, so that I was not aware of the exertion of sledge hauling.

We two each pulled his own sledge, a weight of 120 reducing to 50 kilos. Each followed his own rhythm; each carried out his specific tasks. Arved Fuchs navigated. I went on ahead according to his compass directions. We were the smallest possible group and the narrowness of the tent and nature dictated to us the rules of living together, as well as the length of the route. From the edge of the continent on the Weddell Sea to New Zealand's Scott Base it was 2580 kilometres as the crow flies, for us a distance of 2800 kilometres, because we had to cover almost a thousand kilometres of *sastrugi* ridges and 200 kilometres over glaciers with crevasses and ice ruptures, which put all Himalayan ice formations in the shade.

The sledges behind us and the skis beneath us matched noises which we generated ourselves. They mixed with our breathing and pulse beats in our necks. Otherwise all was silent. That silence! At first it oppressed me. I was not accustomed to such all-embracing silence. Then a peacefulness came to it, a peace that came from my inner self. I know today that peace is only possible where the world is not parcelled out amongst people, with national territorial claims. Non-desire, or the cessation of pain, the third of the Four Noble Truths of Buddhism, is transcendental for silence, peace, infinity as I have experienced it in the Antarctic. We mountaineers first took away the mystique of the Alps, then that of the Himalaya, because we first conquered then classified their summits, faces and routes. From this also arose that destructive spirit which threatens the very roots of alpinism.

Although I am now as thrilled by the Arctic and the Antarctic as by twenty vertical Dolomite rock routes and thirty high-altitude climbs, I shall continue to climb. Only I shall seek out for myself summits on which I can be alone, to find at least a fraction of the infinity, quiet and harmony which, since my Antarctic trip, have become so important to me.

The knowledge that Tomo Česen was able to climb the South Face of Lhotse a few months later strengthened me in the conviction that the great mountain adventure will survive.

30

TOMO ČESEN AND THE SOUTH FACE OF LHOTSE

1990

IN THE HISTORY OF MOUNTAINEERING there have always been moments of crystallisation: suddenly one knew why a particular deed had become the testimony of an epoch. 1865 saw the first ascent of the Matterhorn, 1890 the first ascent of the North Face of the Kleine Zinne. That was a hundred years ago. In 1938 there was the ascent of the Eiger North Face; and in 1950 Maurice Herzog and Louis Lachenal first climbed an eight-thousander, Annapurna. In 1990 Tomo Česen climbed the South Face of Lhotse alone, reaching the summit for the first time by this route. How do I know that this last accomplishment belongs to the milestones in the development of alpinism? Because I know the South Face of Lhotse and I know Tomo Česen.

The South Face of Lhotse was a logical mountaineering problem; between 1973 and 1989 more than a dozen expeditions found it a hard nut to crack. The first were Japanese. I failed in 1975 on an Italian expedition led by Riccardo Cassin. Well organised teams, like the Yugoslavians under the leadership of Alès Kunaver, could not force a route to the summit. The legendary Frenchman, Nicolas Jaeger, went missing after an uneasy solo attempt on Lhotse Shar, and Jerzy Kukuczka, who had realised nearly all the imaginable possibilities on the eight-thousanders, was to fall to his death a few hundred metres below the summit in the autumn of 1989. Six months earlier I had led a handful of climbers from Poland, France, South Tyrol and Spain on the face with the idea that a common goal increases the chances of success, even if language and outlook are different. I was to deceive myself. We failed just because each relied on the preparatory work of the other.

Tomo Česen relied only on himself and succeeded. He ascended the South Face of Lhotse in three days of solo climbing, without preparation and without technical tricks; he climbed one of the hardest faces in the world on which all previous attempts—big expeditions with high camps, fixed ropes and porters, roped pairs, soloists—had foundered. Tomo Česen succeeded because of who he is. An independent personality who shows parallels with many pioneers, yet is incomparable. It would be as irrelevant to call Česen 'the Bonatti of the Himalaya' as to compare Machapuchare with the Matterhorn. Nevertheless it will be done.

Tomo Česen, from Kranj in Slovenia, is thirty years old and has been climbing for fifteen years. On his home mountains he can take part in climbing competitions, practise on frozen waterfalls and climb to the eighth grade. Those who had been observing him for years (North faces of the Matterhorn, Eiger and Grandes Jorasses solo in winter without helicopter support within the space of a few days; first ascent of K2 South Face to the shoulder of the Abruzzi Spur; Jannu North Face solo) knew that this man can set new standards. Even before he started on the South Face of Lhotse in 1990 I had adjudged him the first 'Snow Lion', a cash prize in recognition of the ecologically purest and most creative alpine achievement (in his case the solo ascent of Jannu North Face in 1989). The first ascent of Lhotse South Face is at the same time the logical consequence of his style and proof of his ability. The one implies the other.

After a relatively short period of acclimatisation, in which he reached a height of 7200 metres on Lhotse Shar, Česen climbed high on the lower Lhotse wall in the late afternoon of 22 April. The snow conditions were good. Mostly he held to the left of that ideal line which Alès Kunaver, after a long observation of the face in 1980, had found and secured in 1981 with a strong team, as far as the bottom of the summit buttress. Česen knew members of this failed attempt and all the details. He dedicated his route to Alès Kunaver who died in a helicopter crash (together with the Hiebelers) in 1984.

Česen climbs at night, on account of stone and avalanche danger, and he climbs fast. He stays in the steep, narrow snow and ice gully which facilitates a fast ascent. He climbs for fifteen hours, as far as 7500 metres where he rests. On 23 April, from one o'clock in the afternoon he climbs for ten hours as far as the bottom of the summit buttress, and bivouacs at 8200 metres. On 24 April he climbs slowly—the difficulties in the terrific cold and height are Grade V-VI—over the crux, a badly stratified rock pillar under which Kunaver's team failed. At 2.20 pm he reaches the summit. Storm. Mist and driving snow make him anxious. It is not the joy of being the first which drives him on, much more fear of the avalanches which thunder into the depths below him. He descends, ropes down, finds the pitons left by the Kunaver attempt of 1981. In the evening he reaches a height of 7300 metres. Mist. Wind. He bivouacs. On 25 April he is back in base camp.

Tomo Česen knows exactly what this first ascent signifies. Everyone before him failed. He knows that Renato Casarotto (lost on K2 in 1986), despite his toughness, would not have been able to climb this face; he would have been much too slow. He knows that an expedition in the classic style with high camps and fixed ropes would have had less chance of success than he, and he knows how difficult it will be for others to repeat his coup. I can only congratulate him. Here is someone who has demonstrated the power of an individual's concept of himself if it is based on experience and that background respect for nature which can develop only through constant communion with the mountains.

Tomo Česen expresses himself through his deeds. If he says little it has to do with disquiet and uncertainty. But it is not self-doubt which bothers him, rather doubt as to how far outsiders understand him, can follow him, let him be Tomo Česen. He knows what he wants; he knows where he is going (both on the mountain itself and with the sponsors) and he has remained, after the South Face of Lhotse, as he was before. But he has opened our eyes.

Tomo Česen could have felt out his way and prepared beforehand with climbing partners, like Walter Bonatti in 1955 on the Dru Pillar and 1965 on the Matterhorn North Face. That he did not shows that he has developed mountaineering renunciation to a hitherto uncharted level: the highest mountains of the world via their hardest faces without preparation, without technical tricks, without drugs, solo. Tomo Česen has applied the classic style of soloing eight-thousanders to the South Face of Lhotse with the consequence that he is both sportingly and ecologically beyond reproach. Whoever repeats Tomo Česen's route on the Lhotse Face will find the same sort of problems as he did. Česen's ascent of the face has not changed it: all start from scratch.

Although he claims to have felt nothing on the summit—no joy, no sorrow, no consciousness of 'I must take pictures'—he is still a mountaineering genius. That he could evade the avalanches which threatened him during descent proves it. It is not only ability that distinguishes a genius, it is often a naïve concept of oneself which draws esteem or head shaking from onlookers, but which to the 'artist' remains incomprehensible because he can not doubt it, can not explain his act, or be amazed at himself.

No other climber is in a position to do the things which Česen's deliberation and self-confidence allow him to do. And that is what distinguishes him from all other mountaineers. Others can climb harder rock passages, perhaps a few specialists are even faster than he is, but none has his psychophysiological equilibrium and the self-confidence which comes from ability. I venture to maintain that Tomo Česen is currently the best climber in the world.

INDEX